NorthStar 4
READING & WRITING

FOURTH EDITION

Authors	ANDREW K. ENGLISH
	LAURA MONAHON ENGLISH
Series Editors	FRANCES BOYD
	CAROL NUMRICH

Dedication

To my lovely wife, Laura, without whose
support and guidance none of this would
have been possible.

Andrew K. English

NorthStar: Reading & Writing Level 4, Fourth Edition

Copyright © 2017, 2015, 2009, 2004, 1998 by Pearson Education, Inc.
All rights reserved.

Pearson Education Inc., 221 River Street, Hoboken, NJ 07030

Staff credits: The people who made up the **NorthStar: Reading & Writing Level 4, Fourth Edition** team,
representing editorial, production, design, and manufacturing, are Stephanie Bullard, Kimberly Casey,
Tracey Cataldo, Rosa Chapinal, Aerin Csigay, Mindy DePalma, Dave Dickey, Nancy Flaggman, Niki Lee,
François Leffler, Amy McCormick, Mary Perrotta Rich, Robert Ruvo, Christopher Siley, and Debbie Sistino.

Text composition: ElectraGraphics, Inc.
Editorial: Lakeview Editing Services, LLC

Library of Congress Cataloging-in-Publication Data

Haugnes, Natasha, 1965–
   Northstar 2 : Reading and writing / Authors: Natasha Haugnes, Beth Maher. — Fourth Edition.
       pages cm
   ISBN-13: 978-0-13-338216-7 (Level 2) – ISBN 978-0-13-294039-9 (Level 3) – ISBN 978-0-13-338223-5
(Level 4) – ISBN 978-0-13-338224-2 (Level 5)
1. English language—Textbooks for foreign speakers. 2. Reading comprehension—Problems,
exercises, etc. 3. Report writing—Problems, exercises, etc. I. Maher, Beth, 1965- II. Title. III.
Title: Northstar two. IV. Title: Reading and writing.
   PE1128.H394 2015
   428.2'4—dc23

                                                                                    2013050584

Printed in the United States of America

ISBN 10:   0-13-466215-6
ISBN 13: 978-0-13-466215-2

1 17

ISBN 10:   0-13-404977-2 (International Edition)
ISBN 13: 978-0-13-404977-9 (International Edition)

1 14

CONTENTS

WELCOME TO
NORTHSTAR

A BLENDED-LEARNING COURSE FOR THE 21ST CENTURY

Building on the success of previous editions, *NorthStar* continues to engage and motivate students through new and updated contemporary, authentic topics in a seamless integration of print and online content. Students will achieve their academic as well as language and personal goals in order to meet the challenges of the 21st century.

New for the FOURTH EDITION

★ Fully Blended MyEnglishLab

NorthStar aims to prepare students for academic success and digital literacy with its fully blended online lab. The innovative new MyEnglishLab: *NorthStar* gives learners immediate feedback—anytime, anywhere—as they complete auto-graded language activities online.

★ NEW and UPDATED THEMES

Current and thought-provoking topics presented in a variety of genres promote intellectual stimulation. The authentic content engages students, links them to language use outside of the classroom, and encourages personal expression and critical thinking.

★ EXPLICIT SKILL INSTRUCTION and PRACTICE

Language skills are highlighted in each unit, providing students with systematic and multiple exposures to language forms and structures in a variety of contexts. Concise presentations and targeted practice in print and online prepare students for academic success.

★ LEARNING OUTCOMES and ASSESSMENT

A variety of assessment tools, including online diagnostic, formative and summative assessments, and a flexible gradebook, aligned with clearly identified unit learning outcomes, allow teachers to individualize instruction and track student progress.

THE NORTHSTAR APPROACH TO CRITICAL THINKING

What is critical thinking?

Most textbooks include interesting questions for students to discuss and tasks for students to engage in to develop language skills. Often these questions and tasks are labeled critical thinking. Look at this question as an example:

When you buy fruits and vegetables, do you usually look for the cheapest price? Explain.

The question may inspire a lively discussion with students exploring a variety of viewpoints—but it doesn't necessarily develop critical thinking. Now look at another example:

When people in your neighborhood buy fruits and vegetables, what factors are the most important: the price, the freshness, locally grown, organic (without chemicals)? Make a prediction and explain. How can you find out if your prediction is correct? This question does develop critical thinking. It asks students to make predictions, formulate a hypothesis, and draw a conclusion—all higher-level critical thinking skills. Critical thinking, as philosophers and psychologists suggest, is a sharpening and a broadening of the mind. A critical thinker engages in true problem solving, connects information in novel ways, and challenges assumptions. A critical thinker is a skillful, responsible thinker who is open-minded and has the ability to evaluate information based on evidence. Ultimately, through this process of critical thinking, students are better able to decide what to think, what to say, or what to do.

How do we teach critical thinking?

It is not enough to teach "about" critical thinking. Teaching the theory of critical thinking will not produce critical thinkers. Additionally, it is not enough to simply expose students to good examples of critical thinking without explanation or explicit practice and hope our students will learn by imitation.

Students need to engage in specially designed exercises that aim to improve critical thinking skills. This approach practices skills both implicitly and explicitly and is embedded in thought-provoking content. Some strategies include:

- subject matter that is carefully selected and exploited so that students learn new concepts and encounter new perspectives.
- students identifying their own assumptions about the world and later challenging them.
- activities that are designed in a way that students answer questions and complete language-learning tasks that may not have black-and-white answers. (Finding THE answer is often less valuable than the process by which answers are derived.)
- activities that engage students in logical thinking, where they support their reasoning and resolve differences with their peers.

Infused throughout each unit of each book, *NorthStar* uses the principles and strategies outlined above, including:

- Make Inferences: inference comprehension questions in every unit
- Vocabulary and Comprehension: categorization activities
- Vocabulary and Synthesize: relationship analyses (analogies); comparisons (Venn diagrams)
- Synthesize: synthesis of information from two texts teaches a "multiplicity" approach rather than a "duality" approach to learning; ideas that seem to be in opposition on the surface may actually intersect and reinforce each other
- Focus on the Topic and Preview: identifying assumptions, recognizing attitudes and values, and then re-evaluating them
- Focus on Writing/Speaking: reasoning and argumentation
- Unit Project: judgment; choosing factual, unbiased information for research projects
- Focus on Writing/Speaking and Express Opinions: decision making; proposing solutions

THE NORTHSTAR UNIT

1 FOCUS ON THE TOPIC

*CT Each unit begins with a photo that draws students into the topic. Focus questions motivate students and encourage them to make personal connections. Students make inferences about and predict the content of the unit.

MyEnglishLab

CT A short self-assessment based on each unit's learning outcomes helps students check what they know and allows teachers to target instruction.

---

*indicates Critical Thinking

2 FOCUS ON READING

Two contrasting, thought-provoking readings, from a variety of authentic genres, stimulate students intellectually.

A GENIUS EXPLAINS
By Richard Johnson
The Guardian

1 Daniel Tammet is talking. As he talks, he studies my shirt and counts the stitches. Ever since the age of three, when he suffered an epileptic fit, Tammet has been obsessed with counting. Now he is 26, and a mathematical genius who can figure out cube roots quicker than a calculator and recall pi to 22,514 decimal places. He also happens to be autistic, which is why he can't drive a car, wire a plug, or tell right from left. He lives with extraordinary ability and disability.

2 Tammet is calculating 377 multiplied by 795. Actually, he isn't "calculating": there is nothing conscious about w... the answer instan... has been able to s... and textures. The... a motion, and five... I multiply numbe... The **image** starts... a third shape eme...

3 Tammet is a "**savant**," an individual with an astonishing, extraordinary mental ability. An **estimated** 10% of the autistic population—and an estimated 1% of the non-autistic population—have savant abilities, but no one knows exactly why.

4 Scans of the brains of autistic savants suggest that the right hemisphere might be **compensating** for damage in the left hemisphere. While many savants struggle with language and comprehension (skills associated primarily with the left hemisphere), they often have amazing skills in mathematics and memory (primarily right hemisphere skills). Typically, savants have a limited vocabulary, but there is nothing limited about Tammet's vocabulary.

5 Tammet is creating his own language...

10,000 HOURS TO MASTERY
by Harvey Mackay

1 For years, I have preached the importance of hard work, determination, **persistence**, and practice—make that perfect practice—as key ingredients of success. A nifty new book seems to support my theory.

2 Malcolm Gladwell has written a fascinating study, *Outliers: The Story of Success* (Little, Brown & Co.), which should make a lot of people feel much better about not achieving instant success. In fact, he says it takes about 10 years, or 10,000 hours, of practice to attain true **expertise**.

3 "The people at the very top don't just work harder or even much harder than everyone else," Gladwell writes. "They work much, much harder." Achievement, he says, is talent plus preparation. Preparation seems to play a bigger role.

4 For example, he describes the Beatles: They had been together seven years before their famous arrival in America. They spent a lot of time playing in strip clubs in Hamburg, Germany, sometimes for as long as eight hours a night. Overnight sensation? Not exactly. Estimates are the band performed 1,200 times before their big success in 1964. By comparison, most bands don't perform 1,200 times in their careers.

The Beatles

5 Neurologist Daniel Levitin has studied the formula for success extensively and shares this finding: "The **emerging** picture from such studies is that 10,000 hours of practice is required to achieve the level of mastery associated with being a world-

---

CT Students predict content, verify their predictions, and follow up with a variety of tasks that ensure comprehension.

---

4. He remembers being given a Ladybird book called *Counting* when he was four. When I looked at the numbers, I 'saw' images. It felt like a place I could go where I really belonged. *(paragraph 14)*

⟶ GO TO MyEnglishLab FOR MORE SKILL PRACTICE.

CONNECT THE READINGS

STEP 1: Organize

Reading One (R1) and Reading Two (R2) both talk about genius. A Venn diagram can show where the ideas about genius are found. Read the statements in the box. Write the number of the statement in the correct part of the diagram. Include the paragraph number where the information is found.

1. "Genius" may be the result of brain chemistry.	2. A person can be a genius and also be disabled.	3. People at the top (experts) work harder than other people.
4. Genius = talent + hard work.	5. "Genius" is being studied by scientists.	6. Expertise requires a lot of practice.
7. Special talents can also cause problems.		

"A Genius Explains" (R1)   Both   "10,000 Hours" (R2)

16   UNIT 1

CT Students are challenged to take what they have learned and organize, integrate, and synthesize the information in a meaningful way.

MyEnglishLab

Home | Help | Test student, reallylongname@emailaddress.com | Sign out

NORTHSTAR **4**   READING & WRITING

1   Unit 1

Vocabulary Practice

Match each vocabulary item with its definition. Click on the items to make a match.

Compensate	To keep facts in your memory.
Retain	The total when you add two or more numbers together.
Estimate	A genius, or very intelligent in one or more areas.
Flexible	Very worried about something, or showing you are very worried.
Predictable	Able to change easily.
Disabled	Unable to use a part of your mind/body in a way that others can.
Anxious	To judge the value or size of something.
Interaction	A picture that you have in your mind.
Image	The money or other advantages that you get from something such as insurance or the government, or as part of your job.
Benefit	
Savant	
Sum	

MyEnglishLab

Auto-graded vocabulary practice activities reinforce meaning and pronunciation.

MAKE INFERENCES

UNDERSTANDING ASSUMPTIONS

An inference is an educated guess about something that is not directly stated. In "A Genius Explains," there are quotes from Daniel Tammet and Kim Peek that show what others might assume about the two men's disabilities. What assumptions can you infer from these quotations?

Look at the example and read the explanation.

Daniel (*paragraph 6*): "I just wanted to show people that disability needn't get in the way."

People think that <u>someone with a disability cannot do as much as someone without a disability</u>.

When other people realized that Daniel had a disability, they assumed that he would have problems in other areas of his life. By showing people that he could achieve remarkable things, even though he was "technically disabled," he wanted to show that their assumptions were wrong. His disability wasn't going to hold him back.

Work with a partner. Read the following quotes from Daniel and Kim. What assumptions do the quotes show that people have made about them? Complete the sentences.

1. Daniel (*paragraph 18*): "It was also the first time I was introduced as 'Daniel' rather than 'the guy who can do weird stuff in his head.'"

   Others didn't think that Daniel was _____

   ____: "You don't have to be handicapped to be different—everybody's

   _____

   9): "It sounds silly, but numbers are my friends."

   bly think that numbers _____

   9): "It isn't only an intellectual or aloof thing that I do. I really feel
   tional attachment, a caring for numbers."

   bly assume that Daniel's relationship to numbers _____

   ): " I like to do things in my own time and in my own style, so an
   nd bureaucracy just wouldn't work."

   expect Daniel to _____

CT Step-by-step instructions and practice guide students to exercise critical thinking and to dig deeper by asking questions that move beyond the literal meaning of the text.

DISTINGUISHING VOICE IN QUOTATIONS

Distinguishing voice is an important reading skill as it can sometimes be confusing whether we are reading the author's words or someone else's words. One indication of a change in voice is quotation marks. Another indication is a change in pronouns, for example, from third person (*he, she,* or *they*) to first person (*I* or *we*). In order to fully comprehend the text, you need to notice when a shift in voice takes place to know who is speaking.

Authors often shift the voice in their writing by using quoted speech. Quotations can:

- add first-hand validity to a point the author has made.
- provide details or examples of what the author has been talking about.
- continue the story in another voice for added interest.

In paragraph 3 of Reading Two, Mackay includes two quotations from Gladwell's book. This adds validity to what Mackay says, as the words are Gladwell's. In paragraph 5, the author includes an extended quotation from Daniel Levitin. This quotation gives several details and examples of how much time it takes for true mastery to occur.

2 Read the following excerpts from Reading One. All double quotation marks have been removed. Underline the sections where the voice changes from the author's to someone else's. Add quotation marks where necessary. Then discuss the following questions with a partner:

- How do you know where the change in voice occurs?
- Who is speaking where you added quotation marks?
- Why might the author have chosen to use quotations in the examples?

1. To [Tammet], pi isn't an abstract set of digits; it's a visual story, a film projected in front of his eyes. He learnt the number forwards and backwards and, last year, spent five hours recalling it in front of an adjudicator. He wanted to prove a point. I memorised pi to 22,514 decimal places, and I am technically disabled. I just wanted to show people that disability needn't get in the way. (*paragraph 6*)

2. [Tammet] lives on the Kent coast, but never goes near the beach—there are too many pebbles to count. The thought of a mathematical problem with no solution makes him feel uncomfortable. Trips to the supermarket are always a chore. There's too much mental stimulus. I have to look at every shape and texture. Every price, and every arrangement of fruit and vegetables. So instead of thin___ week?', I'm just really uncomfortable. (*paragraph 7*)

3. Peek was shy and introspective, but he sat and held Ta___ so much—our love of key dates from history, for instan___
   ___
   ___ multaneou___
   e has read.
   ___handica___

Explicit skill presentation and practice lead to student mastery and success in an academic environment.

MyEnglishLab

Key reading skills are reinforced and practiced in new contexts. Meaningful and instant feedback provide students and teachers with essential information to monitor progress.

MyEnglishLab

1 Unit 1

Reading Skill: Distinguishing Voice In Quotations

Read the news article below about savant Stephen Wiltshire. The quotations are missing. Put the numbers corresponding to the quotations where they belong to add validity, to provide details or examples, or to continue the story in another voice for interest.

1. "I'm going to live in New York [some day]. I've designed my penthouse on Park Avenue."
2. "He is possibly the best child artist in Britain."
3. "These drawings testify to an assured draughtmanship and an ability to convey complex perspective with consummate ease. But more importantly, they reveal his mysterious creative ability to capture the sensibility of a building and that which determines its character and its voice. It is this genius which sets him apart and confers upon him the status of artist. For a child who was once locked within the prison house of his own private world, unable to speak, incapable of responding to others, this thrilling development of language, laughter and art is a miracle."
4. "I noticed early on that Stephen wasn't speaking other than random sounds. At the playground he would sit in the dirt while the other toddlers ran around."
5. "Young Stephen was an exceptional drawer even at 5 years old. He was able to accurately sketch animals, cars and architectural drawings of imaginary cityscapes."

---

3 FOCUS ON WRITING

Productive vocabulary targeted in the unit is reviewed, expanded upon, and used creatively in this section and in the final writing task. Grammar structures useful for the final writing task are presented and practiced. A concise grammar skills box serves as an excellent reference.

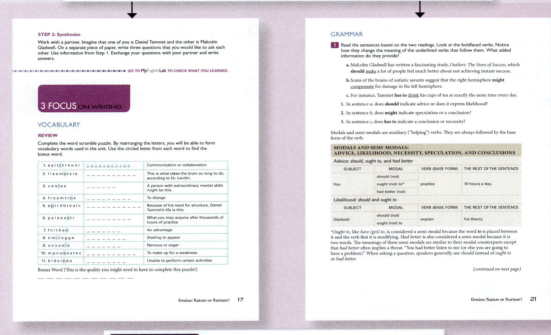

MyEnglishLab

Auto-graded vocabulary and grammar practice activities with feedback reinforce meaning, form, and function.

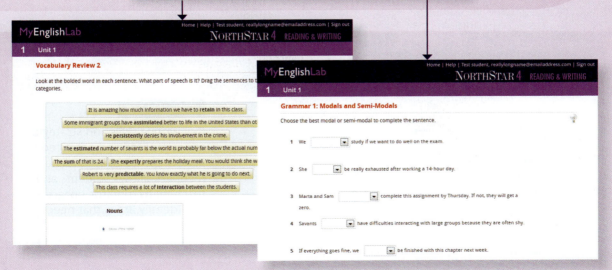

A TASK-BASED APPROACH TO PROCESS WRITING

FINAL WRITING TASK

In this unit, you read about different geniuses and how they achieved their expertise.

You are going to **write a summary paragraph about a current or past genius. Be sure to include why this person is considered a genius and how he or she achieved expertise.** Use the vocabulary and grammar from the unit.*

PREPARE TO WRITE: Group Brainstorming

Group brainstorming is a good way to get ideas for writing. In brainstorming, you think of as many ideas as you can. Don't think about whether the ideas are good or bad; just write down all ideas.

1 Work with a small group. Brainstorm a list of geniuses, past or present, that you know about. The person can be from any time period or culture. Don't stop to discuss the genius. Just concentrate on thinking of as many examples as possible.

Geniuses

1. _____   6. _____
2. _____   7. _____
3. _____   8. _____
4. _____   9. _____
5. _____   10. _____

2 Individually, choose one genius that you find interesting and want to write about. Research this person to find information about his or her life and achievements. Be sure to include why this person is considered a genius and how he or she achieved expertise. Take notes about what you find out. Make sure the notes are in your own words and not copied word-for-word.

_____

* For Alternative Writing Topics, see page 33. These topics can be used in place of the writing topic for this unit or as homework. The alternative topics relate to the theme of the unit but may not target the same grammar or rhetorical structures taught in the unit.

Genius: Nature or Nurture?   25

> **CT** A final writing task gives students an opportunity to integrate ideas, vocabulary, and grammar presented in the unit.

> **CT** Students organize their ideas for writing using a particular structural or rhetorical pattern.

1 Examine the paragraph and discuss the questions with the class.

> Autistic savants have specific abilities or skills, but they are not without certain limitations in other areas of life. An autistic savant is a person with an unusual ability, skill, or knowledge that is much more developed than that of an average person. In fact, many savants have highly developed mathematical skills. Others are able to retain large amounts of information in their memory. For example, some autistic savants can recite entire dictionaries or telephone books word for word. Still others are able to draw detailed maps of an area after flying over it once in a helicopter. Despite the fact that the autistic savant has these specific abilities or skills, he or she may have difficulties with other types of mental or physical tasks and social interactions. For instance, some savants may have trouble doing simple tasks, such as tying their shoes or driving a car. Additionally, an autistic savant may have problems talking to people or even making eye contact. So, despite their advanced skills and abilities in certain areas, savants may encounter difficulty with seemingly simple tasks.

1. What is the topic of this paragraph?
   _____

2. The first sentence is the topic sentence. What two ideas are presented in this sentence?
   _____
   _____

3. How does the content of the rest of the paragraph relate to the topic sentence?
   _____
   _____

Genius: Nature or Nurture?   27

Writing Skill: Topic Sentences and Controlling Ideas

Choose the best correction of the fragmented sentence.

1 Because many Savants have extraordinary skills.
○ Because many Savants have extraordinary skills they achieve success.
○ Because many Savants have extraordinary skills, they achieve success.
○ They achieve success because have extraordinary skills.

2 She was preparing for the exam they visited.
○ She was preparing for the exam when they visited.
○ When she was preparing for the exam they visited.
○ She was preparing for the exam and they visited.

3 The day before the big competition they practicing for five hours.
○ The day before the big competition, they practicing for five hours.
○ When the day before the big competition, they practicing for five hours.
○ The day before the big competition, they practiced for five hours.

4 After Malcom Gladwell's book was published it became a number one best seller.
○ After Malcom Gladwell's book was published, it became a number one best seller.
○ Malcom Gladwell's book was published after it became a number one best seller.
○ After, Malcom Gladwell's book was published it became a number one best seller.

> **MyEnglishLab**
> Key writing skills and strategies are reinforced and practiced in new contexts. Immediate feedback allows students and teachers to monitor progress and identify areas that need improvement.

Students continue through the writing process to learn revising techniques that help them move toward coherence and unity in their writing. Finally, students edit their work with the aid of a checklist that focuses on essential outcomes.

separated twins had developed in a remarkably similar manner. Nevertheless, the reasons for this may also have to do with environment (nurture). They may have been raised by different families, yet the environments may have been quite similar.

3. Malcolm Gladwell wrote another book, *Outliers: The Story of Success*. It was published in 2008 and was number one on the *New York Times* bestseller list for eleven straight weeks. It followed *Tipping Point*, which was published in 2000. *Tipping Point* addresses the individual's ability to change society. This non-fiction bestseller was followed by *Blink* in 2005. *Blink* is about thinking. Why are some people able to make brilliant decisions in the blink of an eye while others seem to always make the wrong decision? *Blink* also was a non-fiction bestseller.

4 Now write the first draft of your summary paragraph. Use the information from Prepare to Write and complete the organizer below to plan your paragraph (use a separate piece of paper). Make sure you have a clear topic sentence and content that supports it. The topic sentence should introduce the genius that you are going to write about and include a controlling idea. Be sure to use grammar and vocabulary from the unit.

- How long it took him or her to achieve genius
- What he or she does/did
- What is/was the result of his or her genius
- Name of Genius
- Where and when he or she lives/lived
- How he or she achieved success
- Why ... is c... a...

REVISE: Identifying and Correcting Sentence Fragments

Sentence fragments are incomplete sentences that are presented as if they were complete sentences. They are often phrases lacking either a subject or verb. Other fragments may be dependent (subordinate) clauses that are not connected to an independent clause. These fragments are usually introduced by a relative pronoun (*That, Who, Which, Whom*, etc. . . .) or a subordinating conjunction (*After, Although, Because, Since, When*, etc. . . .).

1 Work with a partner. Identify whether each item is **F** (a fragment) or **C** (a complete sentence).

_____ 1. Although autistic savants have many extraordinary skills and abilities.

_____ 2. Gladwell has written an interesting book. Which emphasizes the importance of hard work in achieving success.

_____ 3. Before Daniel received his counting book when he was four years old.

_____ 4. Before he had an epileptic seizure, there was no evidence that Daniel had extraordinary math abilities.

_____ 5. Because Dr. Levitin says that at least 10,000 hours of practice are needed to achieve success.

_____ 6. The book that Kim Peek was reading the day before he met Daniel Tammet at the library in Salt Lake City.

_____ 7. Practicing as much as ten hours a day before the math competition.

_____ 8. Einstein was voted the "Person of the 20th Century" by *Time* magazine after he received the Nobel Prize for Physics.

There are a variety of strategies for correcting sentence fragments.

- Connect the fragment to the sentence before or after it.
- Change the punctuation.
- Add a verb.
- Add more information and rewrite it as a complete sentence.
- Remove the subordinating conjunction or relative pronoun.

2 Work with a partner. Go back to Exercise 1. Using one of the strategies listed above, correct each item you identified as a sentence fragment. Use a separate piece of paper.

3 Look at the first draft of your summary paragraph. Make sure it does not include any sentence fragments.

GO TO MyEnglishLab FOR MORE SKILL PRACTICE.

EDIT: Writing the Final Draft

Go to MyEnglishLab and write the final draft of your paragraph. Carefully edit it for grammatical and mechanical errors, such as spelling, capitalization, and punctuation. Make sure you use some of the grammar and vocabulary from the unit. Use the checklist to help you write your final draft. Then submit your paragraph to your teacher.

FINAL DRAFT CHECKLIST

❑ Does the paragraph fully describe why the person is considered a genius and how he or she achieved expertise?

❑ Is there a topic sentence with a controlling idea that introduces the genius?

❑ Is the paragraph free of sentence fragments?

❑ Did you use modals and semi-modals correctly?

❑ Have you used the vocabulary from the unit?

UNIT PROJECT

Work with a partner to research an autistic savant. Take notes and write a report based on your findings. Follow these steps:

STEP 1: Choose one of these autistic savants:

Leslie Lemke, music	**Gregory Blackstock**, music, language
Henriett Seth-F, music, painting, literature	**Jedediah Buxton**, mathematical calculations
Stephen Wiltshire, accurate detailed drawings	**Ellen Bourdeaux**, music, "human clock"
Kim Peek, the real "Rain Man," calendar calculations, memory	Any other autistic savant based on your own research
Alonzo Clemons, sculptor	

STEP 2: Do research on the Internet about the person you chose. Answer the questions:

- When and where did/does the person live?
- ... al abilities?
- ... acquire these abilities?
- ... isabilities? If so, what are they?

With instant access to a wide range of online content and diagnostic tools, teachers can customize learning environments to meet the needs of every student.

USING MyEnglishLab, NORTHSTAR TEACHERS CAN:

Deliver rich online content to engage and motivate students, including:

- student audio to support listening and speaking skills.
- engaging, authentic video clips, including reports adapted from ABC, NBC, and CBS newscasts, tied to the unit themes.
- opportunities for written and recorded reactions to be submitted by students.

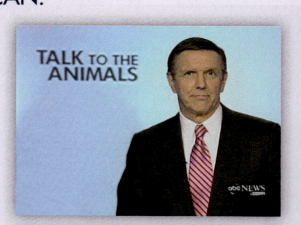

Use a powerful selection of diagnostic reports to:

- view student scores by unit, skill, and activity.
- monitor student progress on any activity or test as often as needed.
- analyze class data to determine steps for remediation and support.

Use Teacher Resource eText* to access:

- a digital copy of the student book for whole-class instruction.
- downloadable achievement and placement tests.
- printable resources including lesson planners, videoscripts, and video activities.
- classroom audio.
- unit teaching notes and answer keys.

*Teacher Resource eText is accessible through MyEnglishLab: *NorthStar*.

COMPONENTS **PRINT or eTEXT**

STUDENT BOOK and
MyEnglishLab

★ Student Book with MyEnglishLab

The two strands, Reading & Writing and Listening & Speaking, for each of the five levels, provide a fully blended approach with the seamless integration of print and online content. Students use MyEnglishLab to access additional practice online, view videos, listen to audio selections, and receive instant feedback on their work.

eTEXT and
MyEnglishLab

★ eText with MyEnglishLab

Offering maximum flexibility for different learning styles and needs, a digital version of the student book can be used on iPad® and Android® devices.

★ Instructor Access: Teacher Resource eText and MyEnglishLab (Reading & Writing 1–5)

Teacher Resource eText

Each level and strand of *NorthStar* has an accompanying Teacher Resource eText that includes: a digital student book, unit teaching notes, answer keys, downloadable achievement tests, classroom audio, lesson planners, video activities, videoscripts, and a downloadable placement test.

MyEnglishLab

Teachers assign MyEnglishLab activities to reinforce the skills students learn in class and monitor progress through an online gradebook. The automatically-graded exercises in MyEnglishLab *NorthStar* support and build on academic skills and vocabulary presented and practiced in the Student Book/eText. The teacher-graded activities include pronunciation, speaking, and writing, and are assigned by the instructor.

★ Classroom Audio CD

The Listening & Speaking audio contains the recordings and activities as well as audio for the achievement tests. The Reading & Writing strand contains the readings on audio

SCOPE AND SEQUENCE

UNIT OUTCOMES	1 PRODIGIES **GENIUS: NATURE OR NURTURE?** pages 2–33 *Reading 1: A Genius Explains* *Reading 2: 10,000 Hours to mastery*	2 OVERCOMING OBSTACLES **FACING LIFE'S OBSTACLES** pages 34–61 *Reading 1: The Education of Frank McCourt* *Reading 2: Marla Runyan*
READING	• Make and confirm predictions • Identify the main idea of each paragraph in a reading • Identify and categorize details and examples • Scan a text to locate specific information • Distinguish voice in quotations MyEnglishLab Vocabulary and Reading Skill Practice	• Make and confirm predictions • Identify the main ideas in a reading • Construct chronology from a reading • Identify different types of supporting details • Scan a text to locate specific information • Recognize the use of synonyms and antonyms to reinforce word meaning MyEnglishLab Vocabulary and Reading Skill Practice
WRITING	• Identify and write the topic sentence and controlling idea of a summary paragraph • Distinguish between sentence fragments and complete sentences • Use strategies to correct sentence fragments • Edit and revise writing for content, language, and conventions **Task:** Write a summary paragraph MyEnglishLab Writing Skill Practice and Writing Task	• Write a comparison paragraph • Identify and write topic sentences, supporting sentences, and a concluding sentence in a paragraph • Recognize inappropriate supporting ideas within a text • Edit and revise writing for content, language, and conventions **Task:** Write a biographical paragraph MyEnglishLab Writing Skill Practice and Writing Task
INFERENCE	• Infer the writer's assumptions	• Infer the meaning of idioms and expressions from context
VOCABULARY	• Infer word meaning from context • Recognize and use word forms (nouns, verbs, adjectives, and adverbs) MyEnglishLab Vocabulary Practice	• Infer word meaning from context • Identify synonyms • Classify words • Analyze relationships between words MyEnglishLab Vocabulary Practice
GRAMMAR	• Identify and categorize a range of modal and semi-modal verbs MyEnglishLab Grammar Practice	• Recognize and use gerunds and infinitives MyEnglishLab Grammar Practice
VIDEO	MyEnglishLab *Small Wonders,* ABC News, Video Activity	MyEnglishLab *A Child's Voice,* ABC News, Video Activity
ASSESSMENTS	MyEnglishLab Check What You Know, Checkpoints 1 and 2, Unit 1 Achievement Test	MyEnglishLab Check What You Know, Checkpoints 1 and 2, Unit 2 Achievement Test

3 MEDICINE
MAKING MEDICAL DECISIONS
pages 62–89

*Reading 1: Genetic Testing and Disease:
Would you want to know?*

*Reading 2: Norman Cousins's Laughter
Therapy*

4 ANIMAL INTELLIGENCE
INSTINCT OR INTELLECT?
pages 90–121

*Reading 1: Extreme Perception and
Animal Intelligence*

Reading 2: How smart are animals?

• Make and confirm predictions • Demonstrate understanding of and use a timeline to sequence events • Identify and categorize the main ideas in a reading • Identify different types of supporting details • Scan a text to locate specific information **MyEnglishLab** Vocabulary and Reading Skill Practice	• Make and confirm predictions • Identify the main ideas in a reading • Identify different types of supporting details • Scan a text to locate specific information • Recognize the role of quoted speech **MyEnglishLab** Vocabulary and Reading Skill Practice
• Organize ideas using a tree map and other organizers • Identify the introduction, body, and conclusion of an opinion essay • Identify the parts of an effective introduction • Write a comparison-and-contrast paragraph • Edit and revise writing for content, language, and conventions **Task:** Write an opinion essay **MyEnglishLab** Writing Skill Practice and Writing Task	• Organize ideas using *Wh-* questions • Summarize sources and data • Paraphrase details from text • Edit and revise writing for content, language, and conventions **Task:** Write a summary in journalistic style **MyEnglishLab** Writing Skill Practice and Writing Task
• Infer the degree of support	• Infer writer's meaning and identify hedging language
• Infer word meaning from context • Analyze relationships between words (similar and different meanings) **MyEnglishLab** Vocabulary Practice	• Infer word meaning from context • Identify synonyms • Analyze relationships between words (similar and different meanings) • Recognize Latin and Greek word roots **MyEnglishLab** Vocabulary Practice
• Recognize and use past unreal conditionals **MyEnglishLab** Grammar Practice	• Recognize and use identifying adjective clauses **MyEnglishLab** Grammar Practice
MyEnglishLab *A Sleep Clinic*, Video Activity	**MyEnglishLab** *Talk to the Animals*, ABC News, Video Activity
MyEnglishLab Check What You Know, Checkpoints 1 and 2, Unit 3 Achievement Test	**MyEnglishLab** Check What You Know, Checkpoints 1 and 2, Unit 4 Achievement Test

SCOPE AND SEQUENCE

UNIT OUTCOMES	5 LONGEVITY **TOO MUCH OF A GOOD THING?** pages 122–153 *Reading 1: Death Do Us Part* *Reading 2: Toward Immortality: The Social Burden of Longer Lives*	6 GENEROSITY **MAKING A DIFFERENCE** pages 154–187 *Reading 1: Justin Lebo* *Reading 2: Some Take the Time Gladly and Problems with Mandatory Volunteering*
READING	• Make and confirm predictions • Identify the main ideas in a reading • Identify different types of supporting details • Scan a text to locate specific information • Analyze titles and headings to improve comprehension **MyEnglishLab** Vocabulary and Reading Skill Practice	• Make and confirm predictions • Identify the main ideas in a reading • Identify different types of supporting details, examples and reasons • Scan a text to locate specific information • Recognize persuasive language **MyEnglishLab** Vocabulary and Reading Skill Practice
WRITING	• Organize ideas using a cause-and-effect diagram • Use an idea web to relate different topics to a central theme • Recognize and use figurative language to add depth to writing • Write an opinion paragraph • Edit and revise writing for content, language, and conventions **Task:** Write a descriptive essay **MyEnglishLab** Writing Skill Practice and Writing Task	• Organize ideas for an argument using a chart • Identify and organize positions, arguments, and counterarguments • Identify and write effective introductions, thesis statements, and conclusions • Write an opinion letter supported with examples from a text • Edit and revise writing for content, language, and conventions **Task:** Write a persuasive essay **MyEnglishLab** Writing Skill Practice and Writing Task
INFERENCE	• Infer characters' attitudes and feelings	• Infer the meaning of people's reactions
VOCABULARY	• Infer word meaning from context • Recognize connotations and implied meanings • Recognize and use common adjective suffixes **MyEnglishLab** Vocabulary Practice	• Infer word meaning from context • Analyze relationships between words (similar and different meanings) • Recognize and use word forms (nouns, verbs, adjectives, and adverbs) • Infer meaning of phrasal verbs **MyEnglishLab** Vocabulary Practice
GRAMMAR	• Distinguish between and use the simple past, present perfect, and present perfect continuous verb tenses **MyEnglishLab** Grammar Practice	• Recognize and use concessions to support an opinion while recognizing counterarguments **MyEnglishLab** Grammar Practice
VIDEO	**MyEnglishLab** *Living Longer*, ABC News, Video Activity	**MyEnglishLab** *Local Teen Awarded for Making Difference*, NBC News, Video Activity
ASSESSMENTS	**MyEnglishLab** Check What You Know, Checkpoints 1 and 2, Unit 5 Achievement Test	**MyEnglishLab** Check What You Know, Checkpoints 1 and 2, Unit 6 Achievement Test

7 EDUCATION
THE EMPTY CLASSROOM
pages 188–223

Reading 1: *Teaching to the World from Central New Jersey*
Reading 2: *The Fun They Had*

8 TECHNOLOGY
MANAGING YOUR SMARTPHONE
pages 224–259

Reading 1: *Addicted to Your Smartphone? Here's What to Do*
Reading 2: *Unplugging Wired Kids: A Vacation from Technology and Social Media*

• Make and confirm predictions • Identify the main ideas in a reading • Identify different types of supporting details • Scan a text to locate specific information • Follow chronological sequence of a timeline • Recognize the speaker in direct speech MyEnglishLab Vocabulary and Reading Skill Practice	• Make and confirm predictions • Identify the main ideas in a reading • Identify different types of supporting details • Scan a text to locate specific information • Identify referents for the pronoun *it* • Identify and categorize problems and solutions from a text MyEnglishLab Vocabulary and Reading Skill Practice
• Organize ideas using a chart • Recognize various types of organization in a comparison-and-contrast essay • Identify and use subordinators and transitions to introduce points of comparison or contrast • Edit and revise writing for content, language, and conventions **Task:** Write a comparison-and-contrast essay MyEnglishLab Writing Skill Practice and Writing Task	• Write summary statements • Organize ideas using a flowchart • Use subordinators, prepositional phrases, and transitions to clearly signal cause-and-effect relationships • Edit and revise writing for content, language, and conventions **Task:** Write a cause-and-effect essay MyEnglishLab Writing Skill Practice and Writing Task
• Infer the writer's degree of concern about the topic	• Infer meaning of writer's appeal to authority with experts' quotes
• Infer word meaning from context • Recognize and use word forms (nouns, verbs, adjectives, and adverbs) MyEnglishLab Vocabulary Practice	• Infer word meaning from context • Understand implied meaning and degrees of intensity MyEnglishLab Vocabulary Practice
• Distinguish between and use direct and indirect speech MyEnglishLab Grammar Practice	• Recognize and use common phrasal verbs MyEnglishLab Grammar Practice
MyEnglishLab *Homework Holiday*, ABC News, Video Activity	MyEnglishLab *Kids and Video Games*, NBC News, Video Activity
MyEnglishLab Check What You Know, Checkpoints 1 and 2, Unit 7 Achievement Test	MyEnglishLab Check What You Know, Checkpoints 1 and 2, Unit 8 Achievement Test

ACKNOWLEDGMENTS

We would like to express our gratitude to the entire *NorthStar* team of authors, editors, and assistants. Special thanks go to Carol Numrich for her vision and especially her ideas and guidance. We are, as always, honored to work with her. Thanks also to Kathleen Smith for her unending support, ideas, and attention to detail. In addition, thanks to Massimo Rubini for his timely help researching articles. Lastly, kudos to Debbie Sistino for all her hard work and support bringing this fourth edition to fruition.

—*Andrew K. English and*
Laura Monahon English

REVIEWERS

Chris Antonellis, Boston University – CELOP; Gail August, Hostos; Aegina Barnes, York College; Kim Bayer, Hunter College; Mine Bellikli, Atilim University; Allison Blechman, Embassy CES; Paul Blomquist, Kaplan; Helena Botros, FLS; James Branchick, FLS; Chris Bruffee, Embassy CES; Nese Cakli, Duzce University; María Cordani Tourinho Dantas, Colégio Rainha De Paz; Jason Davis, ASC English; Lindsay Donigan, Fullerton College; Bina Dugan, BCCC; Sibel Ece Izmir, Atilim University; Érica Ferrer, Universidad del Norte; María Irma Gallegos Peláez, Universidad del Valle de México; Jeff Gano, ASA College; Juan Garcia, FLS; María Genovev a Chávez Bazán, Universidad del Valle de México; Heidi Gramlich, The New England School of English; Phillip Grayson, Kaplan; Rebecca Gross, The New England School of English; Rick Guadiana, FLS; Sebnem Guzel, Tobb University; Esra Hatipoglu, Ufuk University; Brian Henry, FLS; Josephine Horna, BCCC; Arthur Hui, Fullerton College; Zoe Isaacson, Hunter College; Kathy Johnson, Fullerton College; Marcelo Juica, Urban College of Boston; Tom Justice, North Shore Community College; Lisa Karakas, Berkeley College; Eva Kopernacki, Embassy CES; Drew Larimore, Kaplan; Heidi Lieb, BCCC; Patricia Martins, Ibeu; Cecilia Mora Espejo, Universidad del Valle de México; Kate Nyhan, The New England School of English; Julie Oni, FLS; Willard Osman, The New England School of English; Olga Pagieva, ASA College; Manish Patel, FLS; Paige Poole, Universidad del Norte; Claudia Rebello, Ibeu; Lourdes Rey, Universidad del Norte; Michelle Reynolds, FLS International Boston Commons; Mary Ritter, NYU; Minerva Santos, Hostos; Sezer Sarioz, Saint Benoit PLS; Ebru Sinar, Tobb University; Beth Soll, NYU (Columbia); Christopher Stobart, Universidad del Norte; Guliz Uludag, Ufuk University; Debra Un, NYU; Hilal Unlusu, Saint Benoit PLS; María del Carmen Viruega Trejo, Universidad del Valle de México; Reda Vural, Atilim University; Douglas Waters, Universidad del Norte; Leyla Yucklik, Duzce University; Jorge Zepeda Porras, Universidad del Valle de México

GENIUS:
NATURE OR
Nurture?

1.   Why are some people geniuses and others are not? Does the environment a person is raised in (nurture) create a genius, or is it because the person was simply born that way (nature)? Which part do you think each of these plays in being a genius?

2.   What is one special talent or ability that you have? When did you first become aware of it? Did it come naturally, or did you have to practice a long time to perfect it? Explain. (You may instead answer these questions about someone you know who has a talent or ability.)

GO TO MyEnglishLab TO CHECK WHAT YOU KNOW.

VOCABULARY

1 Read the short piece about Daniel Tammet, who is considered by many to be a genius. Being a genius does not mean that all aspects of your life are easy or even that you are good at everything. Daniel is very good at some things but challenged by others. Pay attention to the boldfaced words. Try to understand them from the context.

Autism and autistic spectrum disorder (ASD) are names given to groups of complex developmental disorders involving the brain. Some of the symptoms of these disorders are problems with verbal and non-verbal social **interaction**, the display of repetitive behavior, and an inability to be **flexible**. Many people with ASD **compensate** for these problems and are able to be high functioning and lead "normal" lives; others are more **disabled** by the disorder.

ASD is an umbrella term that includes many subcategories. One of these subcategories is autistic **savants**. Psychologists **estimate** that 10 percent of people with ASD have some savant abilities. An autistic savant is a person with an unusual ability, skill, or knowledge that is much more developed than that of an average person. Many savants are able to **retain** large amounts of information in their memory. For example, some autistic savants can recite entire dictionaries or telephone books word for word. Others are able to draw detailed maps of an area after flying over it once in a helicopter. Although the autistic savant has these specific abilities or skills, he or she may have difficulty with other types of mental or physical tasks.

Daniel Tammet is an autistic savant. Like many people with ASD, he **benefits** from leading a **predictable** life. In other words, he has fewer problems if his life has structure and routine. If it does not, he may become **anxious**. One of Daniel's special abilities is in mathematics; he is able to almost immediately solve complex multiplication problems. When he does this, he sees each number he is multiplying as an **image**. These images transform into a third image, which is the **sum**.

Why autistic savants have these special abilities is a question that still has no definitive answer.

2 Complete the sentences with the words in the boxes.

compensate	estimate	retain

1. No one is sure of the exact number of autistic savants there are in the world, but experts _____ that there are fewer than 100.

2. Studies indicate that one hemisphere of a savant's brain may _____ for damage to the other hemisphere.

3. It is amazing how much information a small USB drive can _____.

anxious	disabled	flexible	predictable

4. Children may feel _____ about their first day in a new school because they don't know what to expect.

5. For me, it is very hard to change my plans because I am not very _____.

6. Although savants have amazing abilities and knowledge, in other areas of their lives they may appear to be _____.

7. Because I know him so well, Sam's reaction to my suggestion was very _____.

benefit	image	interaction	savant	sum

8. It is sometimes hard for people who are shy to engage in social _____, especially with people they don't know well.

9. Finding the _____ of 20 × 3 in your head is not difficult.

10. A(n) _____ can exhibit amazing mental powers and is able to memorize huge amounts of information.

11. One _____ of my new job is health insurance, and another is two weeks of paid vacation.

12. Even though Daniel had not been to Paris in many years, he still had a clear _____ in his mind of what his hotel looked like.

GO TO MyEnglishLab FOR MORE VOCABULARY PRACTICE.

You are going to read an article about Daniel Tammet, an autistic savant. Before you read, look at the statements below. Check (✓) three things about Daniel that you think you will read in the story.

_____ **1.** He can't drive a car.

_____ **2.** He has trouble remembering things.

_____ **3.** He loves going to the beach.

_____ **4.** He has lots of friends.

_____ **5.** He has invented his own language.

_____ **6.** He lives with his parents.

Now read the Daniel Tammet article.

A GENIUS EXPLAINS
By Richard Johnson
The Guardian

1   Daniel Tammet is talking. As he talks, he studies my shirt and counts the stitches. Ever since the age of three, when he suffered an epileptic fit, Tammet has been obsessed with counting. Now he is 26, and a mathematical genius who can figure out cube roots quicker than a calculator and recall pi to 22,514 decimal places. He also happens to be autistic, which is why he can't drive a car, wire a plug, or tell right from left. He lives with extraordinary ability and disability.

2   Tammet is calculating 377 multiplied by 795. Actually, he isn't "calculating": there is nothing conscious about what he is doing. He arrives at the answer instantly. Since his epileptic fit, he has been able to see numbers as shapes, colors, and textures. The number two, for instance, is a motion, and five is a clap of thunder. "When I multiply numbers together, I see two shapes. The **image** starts to change and evolve, and a third shape emerges. That's the answer. It's mental imagery. It's like maths without having to think."

3   Tammet is a "**savant**," an individual with an astonishing, extraordinary mental ability. An **estimated** 10% of the autistic population—and an estimated 1% of the non-autistic population—have savant abilities, but no one knows exactly why.

4   Scans of the brains of autistic savants suggest that the right hemisphere might be **compensating** for damage in the left hemisphere. While many savants struggle with language and comprehension (skills associated primarily with the left hemisphere), they often have amazing skills in mathematics and memory (primarily right hemisphere skills). Typically, savants have a limited vocabulary, but there is nothing limited about Tammet's vocabulary.

5   Tammet is creating his own language, strongly influenced by the vowel and image-rich languages of northern Europe. (He already speaks French, German, Spanish, Lithuanian, Icelandic, and Esperanto.) The vocabulary of his language—"Mänti," meaning a type of tree—reflects the relationships between different things. The word "ema," for instance, translates as "mother," and "ela" is what a mother creates: "life." "Päike" is "sun," and "päive" is what the

sun creates: "day." Tammet hopes to launch Mänti in academic circles later this year, his own personal exploration of the power of words and their inter-relationship.

6   Last year, Tammet broke the European record for recalling pi, the mathematical constant,[1] to the furthest decimal point. He found it easy, he says, because he didn't even have to "think." To him, pi isn't an abstract set of digits; it's a visual story, a film projected in front of his eyes. He learnt the number forwards and backwards and, last year, spent five hours recalling it in front of an adjudicator.[2] He wanted to prove a point. "I memorised pi to 22,514 decimal places, and I am technically **disabled**. I just wanted to show people that disability needn't get in the way."

7   Tammet is softly spoken, and shy about making eye contact, which makes him seem younger than he is. He lives on the Kent coast, but never goes near the beach—there are too many pebbles to count. The thought of a mathematical problem with no solution makes him feel uncomfortable. Trips to the supermarket are always a chore. "There's too much mental stimulus. I have to look at every shape and texture. Every price, and every arrangement of fruit and vegetables. So instead of thinking,'What cheese do I want this week?', I'm just really uncomfortable."

8   Tammet has never been able to work 9 to 5. It would be too difficult to fit around his daily routine. For instance, he has to drink his cups of tea at exactly the same time every day. Things have to happen in the same order: he always brushes his teeth before he has his shower. "I have tried to be more **flexible**, but I always end up feeling more uncomfortable. **Retaining** a sense of control is really important. I like to do things in my own time and in my own style, so an office with targets and bureaucracy just wouldn't work."

9   Instead, he has set up a business on his own, at home, writing e-mail courses in language learning, numeracy, and literacy for private clients. It has had the fringe **benefit** of keeping human interaction to a minimum. It also gives him time to work on the verb structures of Mänti.

10   Few people on the streets have recognised Tammet since his pi record attempt. But, when a documentary about his life is broadcast on Channel 5 later this year, all that will change. "The highlight of filming was to meet Kim Peek, the real-life character who inspired the film *Rain Man*. Before I watched *Rain Man*, I was frightened. As a nine-year-old schoolboy, you don't want people to point at the screen and say, 'That's you.' But I watched it and felt a real connection. Getting to meet the real-life Rain Man was inspirational."

11   Peek was shy and introspective, but he sat and held Tammet's hand for hours. "We shared so much—our love of key dates from history, for instance. And our love of books. As a child, I regularly took over a room in the house and started my own lending library. I would separate out fiction and non-fiction, and then alphabetise them all. I even introduced a ticketing system. I love books so much. I've read more books than anyone else I know. So I was delighted when Kim wanted to meet in a library." Peek can read two pages simultaneously, one with each eye. He can also recall, in exact detail, the 7,600 books he has read. When he is at home in Utah, he spends afternoons at the Salt Lake City public library, memorising phone books and address directories. "He is such a lovely man," says Tammet. "Kim says, 'You don't have to be handicapped to be different—everybody's different.' And he's right."

12   As a baby, he (Tammet) banged his head against the wall and cried constantly. Nobody knew what was wrong. His mother was

---

[1]**mathematical constant:** a special number that is usually a real number and is considered "significantly interesting is some way"

[2]**adjudicator:** a judge or arbitrator, especially in a dispute or competition

(continued on next page)

anxious, and would swing him to sleep in a blanket. She breastfed him for two years. The only thing the doctors could say was that perhaps he was understimulated. Then, one afternoon when he was playing with his brother in the living room, he had an epileptic fit.[3]

13 "I was given medication—round blue tablets—to control my seizures and told not to go out in direct sunlight. I had to visit the hospital every month for regular blood tests. I hated those tests, but I knew they were necessary. To make up for it, my father would always buy me a cup of squash to drink while we sat in the waiting room. It was a worrying time because my Dad's father had epilepsy and actually died of it, in the end. They were thinking, 'This is the end of Daniel's life.'"

14 He remembers being given a Ladybird book called *Counting* when he was four. "When I looked at the numbers, I 'saw' images. It felt like a place I could go where I really belonged. That was great. I went to this other country whenever I could. I would sit on the floor in my bedroom and just count. I didn't notice that time was passing. It was only when my Mum shouted up for dinner, or someone knocked at my door, that I would snap out of it."

15 One day his brother asked him a **sum**. "He asked me to multiply something in my head—like 'What is $82 \times 82 \times 82 \times 82$?' I just looked at the floor and closed my eyes. My back went very straight, and I made my hands into fists. But after five or 10 seconds, the answer just flowed out of my mouth. He asked me several others, and I got every one right. My parents didn't seem surprised. And they never put pressure on me to perform for the neighbours. They knew I was different but wanted me to have a normal life as far as possible."

16 Tammet could see the car park of his infant school from his bedroom window, which made him feel safe. "I loved assembly because we got to sing hymns. The notes formed a pattern in my head, just like the numbers did." The other children didn't know what to make of him and would tease him. The minute the bell went for playtime, he would rush off. "I went to the playground, but not to play. The place was surrounded by trees. While the other children were playing football, I would just stand and count the leaves."

17 Tammet may have been teased at school, but his teachers were always protective. "I think my parents must have had a word with them, so I was pretty much left alone." He found it hard to socialise with anyone outside the family, and, with the advent of adolesence, his shyness got worse.

18 After leaving school with three A-levels (History, French and German, all grade Bs), he decided he wanted to teach—only not the **predictable**, learn-by-rote type of teaching. For a start, he went to teach in Lithuania, and he worked as a volunteer. "It was also the first time I was introduced as 'Daniel' rather than 'the guy who can do weird stuff in his head.' It was such a pleasant relief." Later, he returned home to live with his parents and found work as a maths tutor.

19 When he isn't working, Tammet likes to hang out with his friends on the church quiz team. His knowledge of popular culture lets him down, but he's a shoo-in when it comes to the maths questions. "I do love numbers," he says. "It isn't only an intellectual or aloof thing that I do. I really feel that there is an emotional attachment, a caring for numbers. I think this is a human thing—in the same way that a poet humanises a river or a tree through metaphor, my world gives me a sense of numbers as personal. It sounds silly, but numbers are my friends."

---

[3]**epileptic fit:** (also referred to as an epileptic seizure) a brief symptom of epilepsy which may include loss of consciousness, convulsions, or losing muscle tone and slumping to the ground

MAIN IDEAS

1 Look again at your predictions from the Preview on page 6. How did they help you understand the article?

2 Many articles and textbooks contain paragraph headers. A paragraph header is like a title for the paragraph. It tells readers what they can expect to read about. Choose the best paragraph headers for each of the following sections in the article.

1. *For paragraphs 1 and 2:*

    a. Daniel Tammet—mathematical genius

    b. Daniel Tammet's abilities and disabilities

    c. Math—how he does it

2. *For paragraphs 4 and 5:*

    a. The autistic brain

    b. Mänti—Daniel's language

    c. Not the typical savant

3. *For paragraphs 7 and 8:*

    a. Everyday life can be difficult

    b. Overstimulation can be a problem

    c. Daniel's daily routine

4. *For paragraphs 10 and 11:*

    a. Kim Peek and Daniel's similarities

    b. Kim Peek and Daniel's love of books

    c. Daniel and Kim Peek connect

5. *For paragraphs 14 and 15:*

    a. Daniel starts counting

    b. Daniel's math skills emerge

    c. Numbers as images

6. *For paragraphs 16 and 17:*

    a. Daniel's love of singing

    b. Daniel's shyness

    c. Problems in school

DETAILS

Reading One gives information about Daniel's abilities and disabilities. Read the categories on the left in the chart below. Then write the details and examples from the box next to the appropriate categories. Finally, identify each detail or example as either an ability or a disability. Share your completed chart with a partner.

Daniel feels uncomfortable in the supermarket.	~~Daniel has invented his own language.~~	~~Daniel can calculate cube roots faster than a calculator.~~
Daniel can recall pi to 22,514 decimal points.	Daniel must drink his tea at exactly the same time every day.	It is hard for Daniel to socialize with anyone outside his family.
Daniel is able to read a lot of books.	Daniel has trouble making eye contact.	Daniel can multiply 377 × 795 in his head.
Daniel doesn't go to the beach because there are too many pebbles to count.	Daniel always has to brush his teeth before he showers.	The thought of a mathematical problem with no solution makes Daniel uncomfortable.
Daniel can easily remember key dates in history.	Daniel speaks seven languages.	

CATEGORY	DETAILS OR EXAMPLES	ABILITY	DISABILITY
MATH	1. Daniel can calculate cube roots faster than a calculator.	X	
	2.		
	3.		
	4.		
LANGUAGE	1. Daniel has invented his own language.	X	
	2.		
	3.		
MEMORY	1.		
	2.		
SOCIAL INTERACTION	1.		
	2.		
	3.		
NEED FOR ORDER	1.		
	2.		

MAKE INFERENCES

UNDERSTANDING ASSUMPTIONS

An inference is an educated guess about something that is not directly stated. In "A Genius Explains," there are quotes from Daniel Tammet and Kim Peek that show what others might assume about the two men's disabilities. What assumptions can you infer from these quotations?

Look at the example and read the explanation.

Daniel (*paragraph 6*): "I just wanted to show people that disability needn't get in the way."

People think that **someone with a disability cannot do as much as someone without a disability**.

When other people realized that Daniel had a disability, they assumed that he would have problems in other areas of his life. By showing people that he could achieve remarkable things, even though he was "technically disabled," he wanted to show that their assumptions were wrong. His disability wasn't going to hold him back.

Work with a partner. Read the following quotes from Daniel and Kim. What assumptions do the quotes show that people have made about them? Complete the sentences.

1. Daniel (*paragraph 18*): "It was also the first time I was introduced as 'Daniel' rather than 'the guy who can do weird stuff in his head.'"

   Others didn't think that Daniel was _____

   _____

2. Kim (*paragraph 11*): "You don't have to be handicapped to be different—everybody's different."

   Others think that _____

   _____

3. Daniel (*paragraph 19*): "It sounds silly, but numbers are my friends."

   Other people probably think that numbers _____

   _____

4. Daniel (*paragraph 19*): "It isn't only an intellectual or aloof thing that I do. I really feel that there is an emotional attachment, a caring for numbers."

   Other people probably assume that Daniel's relationship to numbers _____

   _____

5. Daniel (*paragraph 8*): " I like to do things in my own time and in my own style, so an office with targets and bureaucracy just wouldn't work."

   Other people might expect Daniel to _____

   _____

EXPRESS OPINIONS

Work in groups of three. Choose one of the questions and discuss your ideas. Then choose one person in your group to report the ideas to the class.

> **1.** Which of Daniel's abilities would be most useful to you? How would having this ability change your life?
>
> **2.** William James, the American psychologist and philosopher (1842–1910) said, "Genius means nothing more than the faculty of perceiving in an unhabitual way." How does this quotation apply to Daniel Tammet?

■■■■■■■■■■■■■■■■■■■■■■■■■■■■■ *GO TO* MyEnglishLab *TO GIVE YOUR OPINION ABOUT ANOTHER QUESTION.*

READING TWO | 10,000 HOURS TO MASTERY

READ

1 Look at the boldfaced words in the reading and think about the questions.

> **1.** Which words do you know the meanings of?
>
> **2.** Can you use any of the words or phrases in a sentence?

2 Read the article about Malcolm Gladwell's book, *Outliers: The Story of Success.* As you read, notice the boldfaced vocabulary. Try to guess the meaning of the words from the context.

10,000 HOURS TO MASTERY
by **Harvey Mackay**

1　For years, I have preached the importance of hard work, determination, **persistence**, and practice—make that perfect practice—as key ingredients of success. A nifty new book seems to support my theory.

2　Malcolm Gladwell has written a fascinating study, *Outliers: The Story of Success* (Little, Brown & Co.), which should make a lot of people feel much better about not achieving instant success. In fact, he says it takes about 10 years, or 10,000 hours, of practice to attain true **expertise**.

3　"The people at the very top don't just work harder or even much harder than everyone else," Gladwell writes. "They work much, much harder." Achievement, he says, is talent plus preparation. Preparation seems to play a bigger role.

4　For example, he describes the Beatles: They had been together seven years before their famous arrival in America. They spent a lot of time playing in strip clubs in Hamburg, Germany, sometimes for as long as eight hours a night. Overnight sensation? Not exactly. Estimates are the band performed 1,200 times before their big success in 1964. By comparison, most bands don't perform 1,200 times in their careers.

The Beatles

5　Neurologist Daniel Levitin has studied the formula for success extensively and shares this finding: "The **emerging** picture from such studies is that 10,000 hours of practice is required to achieve the level of mastery associated with being a world-class expert in anything. In study after study of composers, basketball players, fiction writers, ice skaters, concert pianists, chess players, master criminals, and what have you, the number comes up again and again. Of course, this doesn't address why some people get more out of their practice sessions than others do. But no one has yet found a case in which true world-class expertise was accomplished in less time. It seems it takes the brain this long to **assimilate** all that it needs to know to achieve true mastery."

6　Two computer giants, Bill Joy, who co-founded Sun Microsystems, and Bill Gates, co-founder of Microsoft, also were proof of the 10,000-hour theory.

7　As Gladwell puts it, "Practice isn't the thing you do once you're good. It's the thing you do that makes you good."

8　Consider these thoughts from successful folks in all walks of life:

9　• "No one can arrive from being talented alone. God gives talent; work **transforms** talent into genius."—Anna Pavlova, ballerina.

10　• "I know the price of success: dedication, hard work and an unremitting devotion to the things you want to see happen."—Frank Lloyd Wright, architect.

(continued on next page)

Genius: Nature or Nurture?　　13

11 • "The way to learn to do things is to do things. The way to learn a trade is to work at it. Success teaches how to succeed. Begin with the determination to succeed, and the work is half done already."—Mark Twain, writer and humorist.

12 Do you detect a theme here?

13 The abilities these people possessed were far-ranging, yet the formula for success was the same: hard work and lots of it. I don't know anyone who has succeeded any other way. Some people just make it look easy. Of course, you probably didn't see the first 9,999 hours of hard work. And you don't just have to work hard; you have to work smart, too.

14 **Mackay's Moral:** Some people dream about success, and others wake up and do something about it.

COMPREHENSION

Work with a partner. Complete each statement according to information in the article.

1. According to Gladwell, achievement is _____

_____.

2. The Beatles were different from most other bands because _____

_____.

3. Daniel Levitin says about success that _____

_____.

4. Levitin believes success takes so long to achieve because _____

_____.

■■ GO TO MyEnglishLab FOR MORE VOCABULARY PRACTICE.

READING SKILL

1 Go back to Reading Two. Underline the quotations. Why do you think Mackay includes these quotations?

DISTINGUISHING VOICE IN QUOTATIONS

Distinguishing voice is an important reading skill as it can sometimes be confusing whether we are reading the author's words or someone else's words. One indication of a change in voice is quotation marks. Another indication is a change in pronouns, for example, from third person (*he, she,* or *they*) to first person (*I* or *we*). In order to fully comprehend the text, you need to notice when a shift in voice takes place to know who is speaking.

Authors often shift the voice in their writing by using quoted speech. Quotations can:

- add first-hand validity to a point the author has made.
- provide details or examples of what the author has been talking about.
- continue the story in another voice for added interest.

In paragraph 3 of Reading Two, Mackay includes two quotations from Gladwell's book. This adds validity to what Mackay says, as the words are Gladwell's. In paragraph 5, the author includes an extended quotation from Daniel Levitin. This quotation gives several details and examples of how much time it takes for true mastery to occur.

2 Read the following excerpts from Reading One. All double quotation marks have been removed. Underline the sections where the voice changes from the author's to someone else's. Add quotation marks where necessary. Then discuss the following questions with a partner:

- How do you know where the change in voice occurs?
- Who is speaking where you added quotation marks?
- Why might the author have chosen to use quotations in the examples?

1. To [Tammet], pi isn't an abstract set of digits; it's a visual story, a film projected in front of his eyes. He learnt the number forwards and backwards and, last year, spent five hours recalling it in front of an adjudicator. He wanted to prove a point. I memorised pi to 22,514 decimal places, and I am technically disabled. I just wanted to show people that disability needn't get in the way. *(paragraph 6)*

2. [Tammet] lives on the Kent coast, but never goes near the beach—there are too many pebbles to count. The thought of a mathematical problem with no solution makes him feel uncomfortable. Trips to the supermarket are always a chore. There's too much mental stimulus. I have to look at every shape and texture. Every price, and every arrangement of fruit and vegetables. So instead of thinking, 'What cheese do I want this week?', I'm just really uncomfortable. *(paragraph 7)*

3. Peek was shy and introspective, but he sat and held Tammet's hand for hours. We shared so much—our love of key dates from history, for instance. And our love of books. . . . I've read more books than anyone else I know. So I was delighted when Kim wanted to meet in a library. Peek can read two pages simultaneously, one with each eye. He can also recall, in exact detail, the 7,600 books he has read. . . . 'He is such a lovely man,' says Tammet. Kim says, 'You don't have to be handicapped to be different—everybody's different.' And he's right. *(paragraph 11)*

(continued on next page)

4. He remembers being given a Ladybird book called *Counting* when he was four. When I looked at the numbers, I 'saw' images. It felt like a place I could go where I really belonged. *(paragraph 14)*

GO TO MyEnglishLab *FOR MORE SKILL PRACTICE.*

CONNECT THE READINGS

STEP 1: Organize

Reading One (R1) and Reading Two (R2) both talk about genius. A Venn diagram can show where the ideas about genius are found. Read the statements in the box. Write the number of the statement in the correct part of the diagram. Include the paragraph number where the information is found.

1. "Genius" may be the result of brain chemistry.	**2.** A person can be a genius and also be disabled.	**3.** People at the top (experts) work harder than other people.
4. Genius = talent + hard work.	**5.** "Genius" is being studied by scientists.	**6.** Expertise requires a lot of practice.
	7. Special talents can also cause problems.	

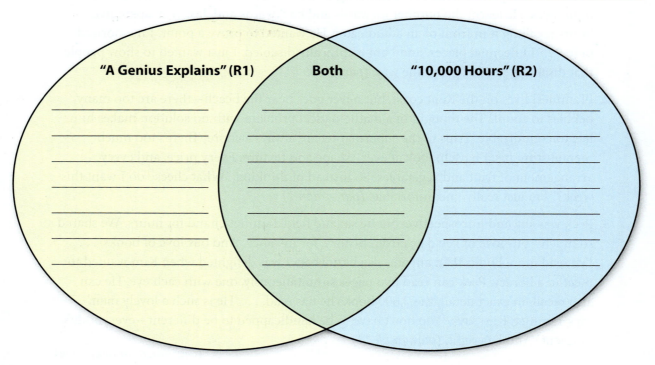

"A Genius Explains" (R1)   Both   "10,000 Hours" (R2)

STEP 2: Synthesize

Work with a partner. Imagine that one of you is Daniel Tammet and the other is Malcolm Gladwell. On a separate piece of paper, write three questions that you would like to ask each other. Use information from Step 1. Exchange your questions with your partner and write answers.

GO TO MyEnglishLab *TO CHECK WHAT YOU LEARNED.*

3 FOCUS ON WRITING

VOCABULARY

REVIEW

Complete the word scramble puzzle. By rearranging the letters, you will be able to form vocabulary words used in the unit. Use the circled letter from each word to find the bonus word.

1. e a i t c t r n o n i	<u>i n t e r a c t i o n</u>	Communication or collaboration
2. l i a a m s t s i e	_ _ _ _ _ _ _ _ _ _	This is what takes the brain so long to do, according to Dr. Levitin.
3. v a n t a s	_ _ _ _ _ _	A person with extraordinary mental skills might be this.
4. f r o a m t r n s	_ _ _ _ _ _ _ _ _	To change
5. e p i r d b t e a l c	_ _ _ _ _ _ _ _ _ _	Because of his need for structure, Daniel Tammet's life is this.
6. p e i e e x s t r	_ _ _ _ _ _ _ _ _	What you may acquire after thousands of hours of practice
7. f n i t b e e	_ _ _ _ _ _ _	An advantage
8. n m r i e g g e	_ _ _ _ _ _ _ _	Starting to appear
9. u n x a o i s	_ _ _ _ _ _ _	Nervous or eager
10. m p n o e s a t e c	_ _ _ _ _ _ _ _ _ _	To make up for a weakness
11. b l d s i e d a	_ _ _ _ _ _ _ _	Unable to perform certain activities

Bonus Word (This is the quality you might need to have to complete this puzzle!)

_ _ _ _ _ _ _ _ _ _ _ _ _

EXPAND

1 Complete the chart with the correct word forms. Use a dictionary if necessary. An **X** indicates there is no form in that category.

NOUN	VERB	ADJECTIVE	ADVERB
Prediction	(to) predict	predictable	Predictably
estimation	(to) estimate	estimated	X
sum	(to) sum	X	X
anxiety	X	anxious	anxiously
savant	X	X	X
flexibility	(to) flex	flexible	flexibly
interaction	interact	interactive	interactively
transformation	transform	1. transformed 2. transforming 3. transformable	X
retention	retain	retainable	X
benefit	(to) benefit	beneficial	X
desability	(to) disable	disabled	X
1. expertise 2. expert	X	expert	expertly
Assimilation	(to) assimilate	assimilated	X
emergence	emerge	emerging	X
persistence	persist	persistent	persistently
compensation	(to) compensate	X compensating	X

2 Complete the sentences with the words in the boxes. You may need to change the word form and/or the verb tense.

> expertise   flexible   persistence   predictable   transform

1. According to Anna Pavlova, work has the ___transformed___ effect of turning talent into genius.

2. A lack of ___flexibility___ is one of the symptoms of ASD.

3. Daniel Tammet's life is very ___predictable___; he always drinks his tea at the same time.

4. Gladwell believes that to achieve mastery you must ___persist___ in your practice and never give up.

5. Gladwell says it takes about ten years to attain true world-class ___expertise___.

anxious   compensate   emerging   estimated   interaction

6. Mathematical problems with no solution cause a feeling of ___anxious___ for Daniel Tammet.
   anxiety.

7. Scientists ___estimated___ that there are fewer than 100 autistic savants alive today.

8. Daniel Tammet's choosing to work at home instead of in an office is a type of ___compensation___ for the fact that he needs structure and has trouble with social ___interaction___.

9. The symptoms of ASD usually begin to ___emerging___ when a child is two or three years old.

CREATE

Rewrite the sentences by replacing the underlined word with the form in parentheses. Make any necessary grammatical changes.

1. Because I know Daniel Tammet well, I can <u>predict</u> how he will react in certain situations. (predictable)

   Because I know Daniel Tammet well, how he will react in certain situations is

   very predictable.

2. Many people who suffer from ASD have problems with <u>flexibility</u>. (flexible)

   - ASD

   _____

3. According to Gladwell, the <u>transformation</u> of talent into expertise requires at least 10,000 hours. (transform)

   _____

   _____

4. A lack of structure can cause <u>anxiety</u> for Daniel Tammet. (anxious)

   _____

   _____

   (continued on next page)

Genius: Nature or Nurture?   19

5. For many people with ASD, being able to <u>interact</u> socially is difficult. (interaction)

_____

_____

6. Scans of the brains of autistic savants suggest that there ~~might be~~ some <u>compensation</u> being done by the right hemisphere for damage to the left. (compensate)

Passive

Scans of the brains of autistic savants suggest that the right hemisphere ~~could~~ compensate for damage to the left.

might

7. The <u>retention</u> of large amounts of information is usually not a problem for autistic savants. (retain)

_____

_____

8. Daniel Tammet memorized pi to 22,514 decimal places to show people that, although he is technically <u>disabled</u>, it doesn't stop him from being successful. (disability)

_____

_____

■■■■■■■■■■■■■■■■■■■■■■■■■■■■■■■■■ **GO TO** MyEnglishLab **FOR MORE VOCABULARY PRACTICE.**

GRAMMAR

1 Read the sentences based on the two readings. Look at the boldfaced verbs. Notice how they change the meaning of the underlined verbs that follow them. What added information do they provide?

    a. Malcolm Gladwell has written a fascinating study, *Outliers: The Story of Success*, which **should** <u>make</u> a lot of people feel much better about not achieving instant success.

    b. Scans of the brains of autistic savants suggest that the right hemisphere **might** <u>compensate</u> for damage in the left hemisphere.

    c. For instance, Tammet **has to** <u>drink</u> his cups of tea at exactly the same time every day.

    1. In sentence *a*, does **should** indicate advice or does it express likelihood?

    2. In sentence *b*, does **might** indicate speculation or a conclusion?

    3. In sentence *c*, does **has to** indicate a conclusion or necessity?

Modals and semi-modals are auxiliary ("helping") verbs. They are always followed by the base form of the verb.

MODALS AND SEMI-MODALS: ADVICE, LIKELIHOOD, NECESSITY, SPECULATION, AND CONCLUSIONS			
Advice: *should, ought to,* and *had better*			
SUBJECT	MODAL	VERB (BASE FORM)	THE REST OF THE SENTENCE
You	should (not)	practice	10 hours a day.
	ought (not) to*		
	had better (not)		
Likelihood: *should* and *ought to*			
SUBJECT	MODAL	VERB (BASE FORM)	THE REST OF THE SENTENCE
Gladwell	should (not)	explain	his theory.
	ought (not) to		

Ought to, like *have (got) to*, is considered a semi-modal because the word *to* is placed between it and the verb that it is modifying. *Had better* is also considered a semi-modal because it is two words. The meanings of these semi-modals are similar to their modal counterparts except that *had better* often implies a threat. "You had better listen to me (or else you are going to have a problem)." When asking a question, speakers generally use *should* instead of *ought to* or *had better*.

(continued on next page)

Necessity: *must, have to,* and *have got to*

SUBJECT	MODAL	VERB (BASE FORM)	THE REST OF THE SENTENCE
Daniel's brother	must (not)	eat	at exactly the same time.
	has to		
	has got to		

Be careful. The meaning of **must not** is very different from **doesn't have to** or **hasn't got to**.

- "You **must not** drive over 50 mph" means you are not allowed to drive faster than 50 mph.

- However, "You **don't have to** drive over 50 mph," means you are not obligated to drive faster than 50 mph, but you can if you want to. It is your choice.

Modals have only one form; however, *have* in *have (got) to* changes depending on the subject.

- He **has** got to go.

- They **have** got to go.

Speculation: *may, might,* and *could*

SUBJECT	MODAL	VERB (BASE FORM)	THE REST OF THE SENTENCE
Daniel	may (not)	know	Kim Peek's sister.
	might (not)		
	could		

Conclusions: *must, have to, have got to, can not,* and *could not*

SUBJECT	MODAL	VERB (BASE FORM)	THE REST OF THE SENTENCE
Daniel's brother	must (not)	live	in a very neat house.
	has to		
	has got to		
	can not		
	could not		

Be careful.

- Both **must** and **must not** can indicate a conclusion.

- However, **have to** and **have got to** only indicate a conclusion in the affirmative; in the negative, they indicate a choice. "You don't **have to** believe Dr. Levitin."

- **Can not** and **could not** can indicate a negative conclusion based on something being impossible. "Daniel **couldn't** (or **can not**) have crashed the car because he doesn't drive."

- However, **could** in the affirmative indicates speculation or possibility. "Daniel Tammet **could** know Kim Peek's sister."

- *Can* in the affirmative indicates ability or possibility. "Daniel **can** speak seven languages."
- *May* and *might* can also be used to indicate possibility.

2 Read each sentence and decide what meaning the boldfaced modal verb expresses. Write the letter indicating its meaning.

a. Advice	b. Likelihood	c. Necessity	d. Speculation	e. Conclusion

MEANING OF MODAL OR SEMI-MODAL	
b	1. No matter how hard the mathematical problem, Daniel **ought to** be able to solve it nearly as fast as a calculator.
e	2. Daniel **could not** have met Kim's sister because she wasn't at the library when Daniel met Kim.
a	3. Daniel **shouldn't** take the job at that office. It will interfere with his routine and make him very anxious.
c	4. According to Gladwell, in order to be a world-class expert, you **have to** put in at least 10,000 hours of practice.
d	5. Daniel has started to study Swedish. Because I know he is good with languages, I think he **might** be fluent by the time I see him next if he puts his mind to it.
b	6. If you do not already have world-class expertise in some area, you **ought to** feel better after reading Gladwell's book. It takes up to ten years to reach expertise!
c	7. Daniel **must** always brush his teeth before he takes his shower.
d	8. Even though Kim Peek can read two books at the same time, one with each eye, I think he **may** really prefer to read only one at a time. I know I would.
e	9. Kim Peek **has got to** have an incredible memory. He can remember all 7,600 books that he has ever read.
a	10. You **had better not** expect to become the next Michael Jordan or Usain Bolt without putting in a lot of practice time.

3 Circle the best modal or semi-modal to complete the paragraphs.

1. Although Daniel Tammet has many abilities, he also has many disabilities. For

   example, he can't drive a car; he has never learned how. For him not to be anxious,

   his life _____ be very structured. In other words, things
   1. (could / has got to)

   _____ happen randomly. Instead, they _____
   2. (don't have to / must not)   3. (must / might)

   happen in the same order every day. In addition, he never goes to the beach because

   there are so many pebbles there, and he _____ feel he has to count
   4. (might / should)

   them. Making choices is also difficult for Daniel. That is perhaps why his parents

   think that maybe he _____ should _____ also stay out of the supermarket.
   5. (should / must)

   There are too many products for him to choose from! In terms of his abilities, Daniel

   _____ solve complex mathematical problems so fast that for most
   6. (is able to / had better)

   problems, he _____ ought to _____ be able to arrive at an answer faster than a
   7. (has got to / ought to)

   calculator. He can also retain amazing amounts of information in his memory. In fact,

   if you allow him to study a 100-digit number, he _____ should not _____ have any
   8. (should not / could not)

   trouble remembering it.

2. Malcolm Gladwell's book, *Outliers*, _____ make people who
   1. (had better / ought to)

   have not attained instant success feel better. In it, he states that if you want to reach

   true expertise, you _____ spend about 10,000 hours practicing.
   2. (might / have to)

   The ballerina, Anna Pavlova, speaking from personal experience, commented that

   no matter how talented you are, you _____ reach genius without
   3. (can't / shouldn't)

   hard work. Therefore, don't expect to become an expert at anything overnight. You

   _____ be prepared to work hard.
   4. (must / may)

■■■■■■■■■■■■■■■■ **GO TO** MyEnglishLab **FOR MORE GRAMMAR PRACTICE AND TO CHECK WHAT YOU LEARNED.**

FINAL WRITING TASK

In this unit, you read about different geniuses and how they achieved their expertise.

You are going to *write a summary paragraph about a current or past genius. Be sure to include why this person is considered a genius and how he or she achieved expertise.* Use the vocabulary and grammar from the unit.*

PREPARE TO WRITE: Group Brainstorming

Group brainstorming is a good way to get ideas for writing. In brainstorming, you think of as many ideas as you can. Don't think about whether the ideas are good or bad; just write down all ideas.

1 Work with a small group. Brainstorm a list of geniuses, past or present, that you know about. The person can be from any time period or culture. Don't stop to discuss the genius. Just concentrate on thinking of as many examples as possible.

Geniuses

1. _____   6. _____

2. _____   7. _____

3. _____   8. _____

4. _____   9. _____

5. _____   10. _____

2 Individually, choose one genius that you find interesting and want to write about. Research this person to find information about his or her life and achievements. Be sure to include why this person is considered a genius and how he or she achieved expertise. Take notes about what you find out. Make sure the notes are in your own words and not copied word-for-word.

---

* For Alternative Writing Topics, see page 33. These topics can be used in place of the writing topic for this unit or as homework. The alternative topics relate to the theme of the unit but may not target the same grammar or rhetorical structures taught in the unit.

WRITE: A Summary Paragraph

A **paragraph** is a group of sentences that are related and support a controlling idea. A **summary paragraph** identifies and extracts the main idea from a text, leaving out less important details. All summary paragraphs have a **topic sentence** with a **controlling idea**.

TOPIC SENTENCE

The **topic sentence** is an essential part of all well-written paragraphs. The topic sentence controls the content of the rest of the paragraph. This control helps the writer focus on supporting ideas in the paragraph that are directly related to the topic sentence. The first step in writing a topic sentence is to choose a topic and find a point of view or **main idea** about it.

Topics	Main Idea
Mozart	Mozart is considered a prodigy.
Autistic savants	Autistic savants have specific abilities or skills.
Malcolm Gladwell	Malcolm Gladwell has written a fascinating book.

CONTROLLING IDEA

The next step is to narrow the main idea even more by finding a **controlling idea**. The controlling idea is the idea you want to explain, illustrate, or describe in the paragraph. It makes a specific statement about a topic. The controlling ideas in the topic sentences below are underlined.

Main Idea	Main Idea + Controlling Idea = Topic Sentence
Mozart is considered a prodigy.	Mozart is considered a prodigy <u>because he was able to play the piano by age four and start composing by age six</u>.
Autistic savants have specific abilities or skills.	Although autistic savants have specific abilities or skills, <u>they may have other limitations, especially problems with social interactions</u>.
Malcolm Gladwell has written a fascinating book.	Malcolm Gladwell has written a fascinating book, <u>which emphasizes the importance of hard work</u>.

1 Examine the paragraph and discuss the questions with the class.

Autistic savants have specific abilities or skills, but they are not without certain limitations in other areas of life. An autistic savant is a person with an unusual ability, skill, or knowledge that is much more developed than that of an average person. In fact, many savants have highly developed mathematical skills. Others are able to retain large amounts of information in their memory. For example, some autistic savants can recite entire dictionaries or telephone books word for word. Still others are able to draw detailed maps of an area after flying over it once in a helicopter. Despite the fact that the autistic savant has these specific abilities or skills, he or she may have difficulties with other types of mental or physical tasks and social interactions. For instance, some savants may have trouble doing simple tasks, such as tying their shoes or driving a car. Additionally, an autistic savant may have problems talking to people or even making eye contact. So, despite their advanced skills and abilities in certain areas, savants may encounter difficulty with seemingly simple tasks.

1. What is the topic of this paragraph?

_____

2. The first sentence is the topic sentence. What two ideas are presented in this sentence?

_____

_____

3. How does the content of the rest of the paragraph relate to the topic sentence?

_____

_____

2 Each paragraph is missing a topic sentence. Circle the topic sentence that best fits the paragraph. Discuss your answers with a partner.

1. Daniel suffered an epileptic seizure when he was very young, which may be the cause of his savant abilities. Soon after, when he was four, his mother gave him a counting book, and his love of mathematics was born. From an early age, he has been able to solve complicated mathematical problems in his head. Recently, he has been able to memorize pi to 22,514 digits.

   a. Daniel Tammet is very good at math and has a great memory.

   b. Daniel Tammet is an autistic savant with exceptional memory and mathematical abilities.

   c. Daniel Tammet is an autistic savant who loves solving mathematical problems.

2. What Levitin has found is that it appears that 10,000 hours of practice are required to reach world-class expertise in any field. In fact, he has found no world-class expert who has not put in at least that many hours of preparation. He believes that this is because it takes that much time for the brain to assimilate everything necessary to reach this level of expertise.

   a. Daniel Levitin, a neurologist, has extensively studied what is needed to reach success.

   b. To reach world-class expertise requires a lot of time and practice.

   c. Daniel Levitin believes that it takes the brain a long time to assimilate the information necessary to be an expert.

3. Parents create these hothouse kids because they are attempting to create a "genius." They may begin by playing classical music for the hothouse child when he or she is still in the crib. The parents start working with their children on math and language skills at an early age, using flashcards. They also enroll their children in music and dance lessons, often as early as age three or four. In addition, they try to get their kids into the most academically challenging preschools.

   a. Hothouse kids learn math and music at an early age.

   b. Parents take a variety of approaches to ensure that their kids become geniuses and can get into the best preschools.

   c. "Hothouse kids" is a term used to define children whose parents push them to learn more quickly and earlier than a "normal" child by providing a rich educational environment.

3 Read the paragraphs. The underlined topic sentences are incomplete because they do not have a controlling idea. On a separate piece of paper, rewrite each topic sentence to include both a topic and a controlling idea.

1. <u>Wolfgang Amadeus Mozart was a genius</u>. For one thing, Mozart was a child prodigy who was playing the violin and piano by age 4 and composing by age 6. Another reason that he is considered a genius is that he was able to create over 600 compositions, including symphonies, chamber music, sonatas, and choral music in his 34-year lifetime. Additionally, he is said to have been able to compose entire symphonies in his head. He could imagine the sounds of all the different instruments without using a piano to help him compose. He was not only the best pianist of his day in Europe but also one of the top three or four violinists.

2. <u>Scientists debate the importance of nature vs. nurture</u>. In other words, the debate of nature vs. nurture asks the question: "What part does nature—the genetic information that you have inherited from your parents—play in your development? And, conversely, what part does environment— what you eat, where you went to school, how your parents raised you—play?" In an effort to understand the importance of each of these factors, studies have been done using twins who were separated at birth. While these studies are not conclusive, there were instances where the

(continued on next page)

separated twins had developed in a remarkably similar manner. Nevertheless, the reasons for this may also have to do with environment (nurture). They may have been raised by different families, yet the environments may have been quite similar.

3. Malcolm Gladwell wrote another book, *Outliers: The Story of Success*. It was published in 2008 and was number one on the *New York Times* bestseller list for eleven straight weeks. It followed *Tipping Point*, which was published in 2000. *Tipping Point* addresses the individual's ability to change society. This non-fiction bestseller was followed by *Blink* in 2005. *Blink* is about thinking. Why are some people able to make brilliant decisions in the blink of an eye while others seem to always make the wrong decision? *Blink* also was a non-fiction bestseller.

4 Now write the first draft of your summary paragraph. Use the information from Prepare to Write and complete the organizer below to plan your paragraph (use a separate piece of paper). Make sure you have a clear topic sentence and content that supports it. The topic sentence should introduce the genius that you are going to write about and include a controlling idea. Be sure to use grammar and vocabulary from the unit.

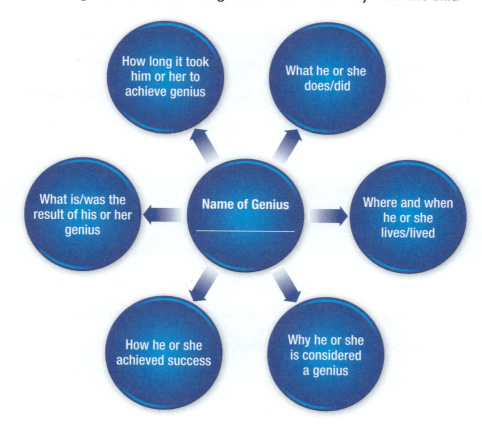

How long it took him or her to achieve genius

What he or she does/did

What is/was the result of his or her genius

Name of Genius
_____

Where and when he or she lives/lived

How he or she achieved success

Why he or she is considered a genius

REVISE: Identifying and Correcting Sentence Fragments

Sentence fragments are incomplete sentences that are presented as if they were complete sentences. They are often phrases lacking either a subject or verb. Other fragments may be dependent (subordinate) clauses that are not connected to an independent clause. These fragments are usually introduced by a relative pronoun (*That, Who, Which, Whom,* etc. . . .) or a subordinating conjunction (*After, Although, Because, Since, When,* etc. . . .).

1 Work with a partner. Identify whether each item is **F** (a fragment) or **C** (a complete sentence).

_____ **1.** Although autistic savants have many extraordinary skills and abilities.

_____ **2.** Gladwell has written an interesting book. Which emphasizes the importance of hard work in achieving success.

_____ **3.** Before Daniel received his counting book when he was four years old.

_____ **4.** Before he had an epileptic seizure, there was no evidence that Daniel had extraordinary math abilities.

_____ **5.** Because Dr. Levitin says that at least 10,000 hours of practice are needed to achieve success.

_____ **6.** The book that Kim Peek was reading the day before he met Daniel Tammet at the library in Salt Lake City.

_____ **7.** Practicing as much as ten hours a day before the math competition.

_____ **8.** Einstein was voted the "Person of the 20th Century" by *Time* magazine after he received the Nobel Prize for Physics.

There are a variety of strategies for correcting sentence fragments.

- Connect the fragment to the sentence before or after it.
- Add more information and rewrite it as a complete sentence.
- Change the punctuation.
- Remove the subordinating conjunction or relative pronoun.
- Add a verb.

2 Work with a partner. Go back to Exercise 1. Using one of the strategies listed above, correct each item you identified as a sentence fragment. Use a separate piece of paper.

3 Look at the first draft of your summary paragraph. Make sure it does not include any sentence fragments.

GO TO MyEnglishLab *FOR MORE SKILL PRACTICE.*

EDIT: Writing the Final Draft

Go to MyEnglishLab and write the final draft of your paragraph. Carefully edit it for grammatical and mechanical errors, such as spelling, capitalization, and punctuation. Make sure you use some of the grammar and vocabulary from the unit. Use the checklist to help you write your final draft. Then submit your paragraph to your teacher.

FINAL DRAFT CHECKLIST

❏ Does the paragraph fully describe why the person is considered a genius and how he or she achieved expertise?

❏ Is there a topic sentence with a controlling idea that introduces the genius?

❏ Is the paragraph free of sentence fragments?

❏ Did you use modals and semi-modals correctly?

❏ Have you used the vocabulary from the unit?

UNIT PROJECT

Work with a partner to research an autistic savant. Take notes and write a report based on your findings. Follow these steps:

STEP 1: Choose one of these autistic savants:

Leslie Lemke, music	**Gregory Blackstock**, music, language
Henriett Seth-F, music, painting, literature	**Jedediah Buxton**, mathematical calculations
Stephen Wiltshire, accurate detailed drawings	**Ellen Bourdeaux**, music, "human clock"
Kim Peek, the real "Rain Man," calendar calculations, memory	Any other autistic savant based on your own research
Alonzo Clemons, sculptor	

STEP 2: Do research on the Internet about the person you chose. Answer the questions:

- When and where did/does the person live?
- What are the person's special abilities?
- When or how did he or she acquire these abilities?
- Does the person also have disabilities? If so, what are they?

STEP 3: To proceed with your research:

1. Go to a search engine and type in the name of the savant you have chosen or key words such as "famous autistic savants" or "prodigious savant abilities."

2. Read the entries that relate to your topic.

3. Takes notes in your own words for a written report.

Be sure to check information on two or more websites.

STEP 4: Prepare a written report for the class.

ALTERNATIVE WRITING TOPICS

Write an essay about one of the topics. Use the vocabulary and grammar from the unit.

1. Kim Peek says, "You don't have to be handicapped to be different—everybody's different." What do you think he means by this? Do you agree? Explain.

2. Daniel Levitin states that it takes 10,000 hours of practice to achieve true world-class expertise. Nevertheless, many people have put in that amount of practice in their fields and still have not achieved world-class expertise. Why do you think they were not successful? What makes the experts different from the others who have also put in 10,000 hours of practice? Explain.

GO TO MyEnglishLab *TO WRITE ABOUT ONE OF THE ALTERNATIVE TOPICS, WATCH A VIDEO ABOUT CHILD PRODIGIES, AND TAKE THE UNIT 1 ACHIEVEMENT TEST.*

FACING LIFE'S Obstacles

1. There are many different kinds of obstacles: Physical and economic are two examples. What are some other examples of the kinds of obstacles that people face?

2. What are some ways that people overcome their obstacles?

3. What obstacles have you faced in your life? How have you tried to overcome them?

GO TO MyEnglishLab TO CHECK WHAT YOU KNOW.

VOCABULARY

1 Read the passage about author Frank McCourt. Try to understand the boldfaced words from the context.

Frank McCourt was born in Brooklyn, New York, in 1930. His parents, Angela and Malachy, had moved to New York from Ireland in search of a better life. Unfortunately, life was not easy in New York. His father could not earn enough money to support his family. The McCourts returned to Ireland hoping their life would improve. Again, it didn't. Life in Ireland was equally hard if not harder than in New York. Three of Frank's siblings died as babies. Eventually, his father's **abandonment** of the family forced his four sons and Angela to live a very **meager** existence.

Frank's childhood was filled with **misery**. There was never enough food. Their house was small, dirty, and very cold in the winter. When it rained, the floor would flood with water. Frank and his brothers **yearned for** a better life.

Frank did, however, have ways to escape from his **tormented** childhood. He loved to read, and because his **dilapidated** house had no electricity, he would read under the street lamp outside his home. He also had an excellent sense of humor. Humor was the McCourts' defense against their life of relentless **poverty** and **hopelessness**. Even in the worst of times, the McCourts could find something to laugh about.

In 1949, Frank returned to the United States. He was 19 years old and only had an eighth-grade education. He was full of **shame** about his past and often invented stories about his **sordid** childhood instead of telling the truth. However, Frank was never **defeated** by his obstacles; in fact, Frank eventually used his humor and his storytelling talents to overcome the challenges life had set before him.

2 Answer the questions with a partner.

1. Frank had a hard life growing up. What were some of the obstacles or challenges he had to overcome?

2. What did Frank enjoy doing as a child?

3. Why did Frank reinvent his past when he came to America?

3 Find the boldfaced words in the reading passage. Write each word next to its synonym.

1. _____misery_____ sadness
2. _____meager_____ poor, sparse *"migar"*
3. _____shame_____ embarrassment
4. _____defeated_____ beaten, overcome by
5. _____yearned for_____ strongly desired, wanted (look for).
6. _____tormented_____ painful
7. _____sordid_____ immoral, dishonest
8. _____poverty_____ having little money or few material things
9. _____abandonment_____ leaving someone behind .
10. _____hopelessness_____ being without hope
11. _____dilapidated_____ falling apart, in terrible condition

GO TO MyEnglishLab *FOR MORE VOCABULARY PRACTICE.*

Read the first two paragraphs of *The Education of Frank McCourt*. Work with a partner to answer the questions. Then read the rest of the article.

1. Where is Frank McCourt now?

2. What do you think he means by "They gave me so much more than I gave them?"

3. What do you think happened to Frank between 1949 and 1997?

THE EDUCATION OF FRANK McCOURT

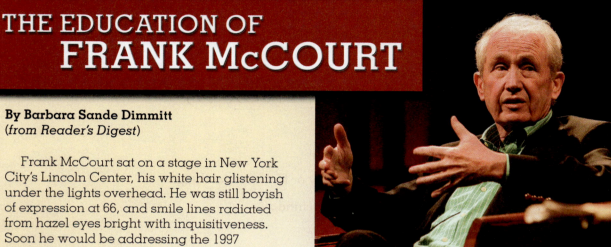

By Barbara Sande Dimmitt
(from Reader's Digest)

1   Frank McCourt sat on a stage in New York City's Lincoln Center, his white hair glistening under the lights overhead. He was still boyish of expression at 66, and smile lines radiated from hazel eyes bright with inquisitiveness. Soon he would be addressing the 1997 graduating class of Stuyvesant High School, where he had taught English for 18 years.

2   He let his mind wander as he gazed out at the great hall. *I've learned so much from kids like these,* he thought. *They gave me much more than I gave them.*

3   "Yo, Teach!" a voice boomed. Frank McCourt scanned the adolescents in his classroom. It was the fall of 1970 and his first week of teaching at Seward Park High School, which sat in the midst of **dilapidated** tenement buildings on Manhattan's Lower East Side. McCourt located the speaker and nodded. "You talk funny," the student said, "Where ya from?"

4   "Ireland," McCourt replied. With more than ten years of teaching experience under his belt, this kind of interrogation[1] no longer surprised him. But one question in particular still made him squirm[2] "Where'd you go to high school?" someone else asked.

5   *If I tell them the truth, they'll feel superior to me,* McCourt thought. *They'll throw it in my face.* Most of all, he feared an accusation he'd heard before—from himself: You come from nothing, so you are nothing.

6   But McCourt's heart whispered another possibility: Maybe these kids are **yearning for** a way of figuring out this new teacher. Am I willing to risk being humiliated in the classroom to find out?

---

[1] **interrogation:** intense questioning
[2] **squirm:** feel embarrassed or ashamed

7   "Come on, tell us! Where'd you go to high school?"

8   "I never did," McCourt replied.

9   "Did you get thrown out?"

10   *I was right*, the teacher thought. *They're curious.* McCourt explained he'd left school after the eighth grade to take a job.

11   "How'd you get to be a teacher, then?" they asked. "When I came to America," he began, "I dreamed bigger dreams. I loved reading and writing, and teaching was the most exalted profession I could imagine. I was unloading sides of beef[3] down on the docks when I decided enough was enough. By then I'd done a lot of reading on my own, so I persuaded New York University to enroll me."

12   McCourt wasn't surprised that this story fascinated his students. Theirs wasn't the kind of **poverty** McCourt had known; they had electricity and food. But he recognized the telltale signs of need in some of his students' threadbare[4] clothes and sensed the bitter **shame** and **hopelessness** he knew all too well. If recounting his own experiences would jolt these kids out of their defeatism so he could teach them something, that's what he would do.

13   A born storyteller, McCourt drew from a repertoire of accounts about his youth. His students would listen, spellbound[5] by the gritty details, drawn by something more powerful than curiosity. He'd look from face to face, recognizing a bit of himself in each sober gaze.

14   Since humor had been the McCourts' weapon against life's **miseries** in Limerick, he used it to describe those days. "Dinner usually was bread and tea," he told the students. "Mam[6] used to say, 'We've got our balanced diet: a solid and a liquid. What more could we want?'"

15   The students roared with laughter.

16   He realized that his honesty was helping forge a link with kids who normally regarded teachers as adversaries. At the same time, the more he talked about his past, the better he understood how it affected him.

17   While at college, a creative-writing professor had asked him to describe an object from his childhood. McCourt chose the decrepit bed he and his brothers had shared. He wrote of their being scratched by the stiff stuffing protruding from the mattress and of ending up jumbled together in the sagging center with fleas[7] leaping all over their bodies. The professor gave McCourt an A, and asked him to read the essay to the class.

18   "No!" McCourt said, recoiling at the thought. But for the first time, he began to see his **sordid** childhood, with all the miseries, betrayals, and longings that **tormented** him still, as a worthy topic. *Maybe that's what I was born to put on the page,*[8] he thought.

19   While teaching, McCourt wrote occasional articles for newspapers and magazines. But his major effort, a memoir of 150 pages that he churned out in 1966, remained unfinished. Now he leafed through his students' transcribed essays. They lacked polish, but somehow they worked in a way his writing didn't. *I'm trying to teach these kids to write*, he thought, *yet I haven't found the secret myself.*

20   The bell rang in the faculty lounge at Stuyvesant High School in Manhattan. When McCourt began teaching at the prestigious[9] public high school in 1972, he joked that he'd finally made it to paradise. Some 13,000 students sought admission each year, competing for approximately 700 vacancies. Part of the fun of working with these bright students was keeping them a few degrees off-balance. McCourt asked at the beginning

(continued on next page)

---

[3] **sides of beef:** very large pieces of meat

[4] **threadbare:** very thin from being used a lot

[5] **spellbound:** very interested in something you are listening to

[6] **Mam:** a word for *mother*

[7] **fleas:** tiny insects that bite

[8] **put on the page:** to write

[9] **prestigious:** admired or respected as one of the best or most important

of a creative writing class, "What did you have for dinner last night?" The students stared at him as if he'd lost his wits.

21   "Why am I asking this? Because you need to become good observers of detail if you're going to write well." As answers trickled in, McCourt countered with more questions. "Where did you eat?" "Who else was there?" "Who cleaned up afterward?"

22   Student after student revealed families fragmented by divorce and loneliness. "We always argue at the table." "We don't eat together." As he listened, McCourt mentally catalogued the differences and similarities between his early life and theirs. He began to appreciate more the companionship that enriched the **meager** meals his mother had struggled to put on the table.

23   That night McCourt lay awake in bed, harvesting the bounty of his chronic insomnia.[10] He visualized himself standing on a street in Limerick and took an imaginary walk about. He looked at shops and pubs, noting their names, and peered through their windows. He read street signs and recognized people walking past. Oblivious to time, he wandered the Limerick of his mind, collecting the details of scenery and a cast for the book that festered inside him.

24   Yet when he later picked up a notebook and tried to set down the previous night's travels, he stopped. McCourt knew that he was still holding back. Before, he had done it out of respect for his mother, who would have been mortified to see the darkest and most searing episodes of his childhood in print.[11] But she had died in 1981, and with her had died his excuse.

25   At least the bits and pieces that bubbled into his consciousness enlivened the stories he told in class. "Everyone has a story to tell," he said. "Write about what you know with conviction, from the heart. Dig deep," he urged. "Find your own voice and dance your own dance!"

26   On Fridays the students read their compositions aloud. To draw them out, McCourt would read excerpts from his duffel bag full of notebooks. "You had such an interesting childhood, Mr. McCourt," they said. "Why don't you write a book?" They threw his own words back at him: "It sounds like there's more to that story; dig deeper . . ."

27   McCourt was past 50 and painfully aware of the passage of time. But despite his growing frustration at his unfinished book, he never tired of his students' work.

28   *These young people have been giving you lessons in courage*, he thought. *When will you dare as mightily as they?*

29   It was October 1994. Frank McCourt, now retired, sat down and read his book's new opening, which he had written a few days before and still found satisfying. But many blank pages lay before him. *What if I never get it right?* he wondered grimly.

30   He stared at the logs glowing in the fireplace and could almost hear students' voices from years past, some angry, some **defeated**, others confused and seeking guidance. "It's no good, Mr. McCourt. I don't have what it takes."

31   Then Frank McCourt, author, heard the steadying tones of Frank McCourt, teacher: Of course you do. Dig deeper. Find your own voice and dance your own dance.

32   He scribbled a few lines. "I'm in a playground on Classon Avenue in Brooklyn with my brother Malachy. He's two, I'm three. We're on the seesaw." In the innocent voice of an unprotected child who could neither comprehend nor control the world around him, Frank McCourt told his tale of poverty and **abandonment**.

33   In September 1996 *Angela's Ashes* hit bookstores. Within weeks McCourt received an excited call from his agent: His book was getting warm reviews and selling at an unbelievable rate. The most surprising call came on April 7, 1997, when McCourt learned

---

[10] **insomnia:** sleeplessness

[11] **in print:** in a book, newspaper, or magazine

that *Angela's Ashes* had received America's most coveted literary award: the Pulitzer Prize.

34   McCourt laid his hands on the lectern, finishing his commencement address[12] at Lincoln Center. "Early in my teaching days, the kids asked me the meaning of a poem," he said. "I replied, 'I don't know any more than you do. I have ideas. What are your ideas?' I realized then that we're all in the same boat. What does anybody know?

35   "So when you go forth tonight, fellow students—for I'm still one of you—remember that you know nothing! Be excited that your whole life is before you for learning."

36   As he gave them a crooked smile, the students leapt to their feet, waving and whistling. *This is too much*, he thought, startled by the intensity of their response. During months of speeches and book signings, he had received many accolades.[13] But this—this left him fighting back tears. It's the culmination of everything, coming from them.

37   Their standing ovation continued long after Frank McCourt, the teacher who had learned his own lessons slowly but well, returned to his seat.

---

[12] **commencement address:** speech given at a graduation
[13] **accolades:** praise and approval for someone's work

MAIN IDEAS

1 Look again at the Preview on page 38. How did your answers to the questions help you understand the story?

2 Complete the timeline with information from Vocabulary on pages 36–37 and Reading One.

1934	Frank McCourt's family returned to Ireland.
1949	Frank McCourt returned to the United States.
1970	
1981	
1994	
1996	
1997	

DETAILS

Complete the left side of the chart using information from Main Ideas on page 41. Then complete the right side of the chart with details about why the event took place and what happened as a result. Look at Vocabulary on pages 36–37 and Reading One for the information.

1934 Event: Frank McCourt's family returned to Ireland.	The McCourts wanted a better life, so they returned to Ireland. Their life was still very hard. Three children died. The family remained very poor and very hungry.
1949 Event:	
1970 Event:	
1981 Event:	
1994 Event:	
1996 Event:	
1997 Event:	

MAKE INFERENCES

INFERRING THE MEANING OF IDIOMS AND EXPRESSIONS FROM CONTEXT

An inference is an educated guess about meaning. Readers can often infer the meaning of idioms and expressions from the context of a story. By closely reading the information in the sentence where the idiom or expression is used, as well as reading the sentences before and after that sentence, readers can often determine the meaning of an idiom or expression.

Look at the example and read the explanation.

What does the idiom in bold mean? *(paragraph 4)*

"With more than ten years of teaching experience **under his belt**, this kind of interrogation no longer surprised him."

In the sentence we read that McCourt has more than ten years of teaching experience; we also read that the students' questions do not surprise him. We can infer that McCourt's teaching experience makes him feel strong enough to face his students. We can guess that the meaning of the idiom is "already achieved or experienced."

Read the following idioms and expressions in context. Refer to the paragraphs in parentheses. Use context clues to determine meaning. Write a synonym or definition of the idiom or expression. Compare your answers with another student's and discuss context clues that helped you figure out the meaning.

1. throw it in my face *(paragraph 5)*

— Sude someone

2. forge a link *(paragraph 16)*

Make a connection

3. churned out *(paragraph 19)*

Produce massive productions

4. leafed through *(paragraph 19)*

5. lost his wits *(paragraph 20)*

6. harvesting the bounty *(paragraph 23)*

talking advantage of a situation

(continued on next page)

Facing Life's Obstacles   **43**

7. bubbled into his consciousness *(paragraph 25)*

_____

8. dig deep *(paragraph 25)*

_____

9. dance your own dance *(paragraph 25)*

be yourself.
_____

10. in the same boat *(paragraph 34)*

_____

EXPRESS OPINIONS

Discuss the questions with a partner. Then share your answers with the class.

1. Frank McCourt had many obstacles in his life. What do you think was Frank McCourt's greatest obstacle? How did he overcome it?

2. How did Frank McCourt's students give him the courage he had been lacking to overcome his obstacles?

■ **GO TO** MyEnglishLab **TO GIVE YOUR OPINION ABOUT ANOTHER QUESTION.**

READING TWO MARLA RUNYAN

READ

1 Look at the boldfaced words in the reading and think about the questions.

1. Which words do you know the meanings of?

2. Can you use any of the words or phrases in a sentence?

Marla Runyan is an accomplished athlete who is legally blind. Despite her blindness, she has excelled in many fields in addition to athletics. How has she been able to do so much? She explains it by saying, "A poor attitude can be far more disabling than blindness."

2 Read the article about Marla Runyan. As you read, notice the boldfaced vocabulary. Try to guess its meaning from the context.

MARLA RUNYAN
By Peter Rugg

1   Marla Runyan is a woman used to questions. There are the interviews about how she made history chasing an Olympic dream, runners who want to know how she trains, people looking for advice on how to overcome the obstacles in their lives. They come to her looking for answers sometimes mundane and sometimes profound. But since she was a child, there has been one question that has followed her above all others. What do you see?

2   At the age of nine, Runyan was diagnosed with Stargardt's Disease. It's a genetic condition that causes progressive vision loss, and most who suffer from it have their sight degenerate[1] to the point of legal blindness.

3   Now 44, Runyan's vision is reduced to shadows and indistinct shapes, though she retains some peripheral sight.

4   "Here's what I do see: a permanent blot in front of my eyes that almost has physical properties," she described in her autobiography, *No Finish Line: My Life As I See It*. "Imagine that someone took a flash picture, and the flash got in your eyes. For a few moments, you'd see a purplish or grey splotch. In a few minutes it would fade away, and the world around you would appear normal again. For me, it stays."

5   However, she has refused to be defined by her condition. Today she holds the Paralympic World Records in the B3 division for the 100m, 200m, 400m, 800m, 1500m, High Jump, Long Jump, and Pentathlon.

6   Her success has extended far beyond athletics. She has been a teacher, a public speaker, a coach, the race director for the Camarillo Half Marathon, a philanthropist[2] for Camp Ability, and, with the publication of her autobiography *No Finish Line: My Life as I See It*, a bestselling author.

7   This was not the life most thought Runyan would have. As a child, the specialists told her to lower her expectations. They told her she shouldn't expect to get the same grades as her fellow students because she wouldn't be able to learn the way they did. They told her that meant she likely wouldn't get into a good college.

8   While Runyan may not have been graced with perfect eyes, she was given a loving mother who instilled in her a sense of hard work, **self-reliance**, and pride.

9   "A poor attitude can be far more disabling than blindness," Runyan would later say.

10   All of the specialists were wrong. Runyan refused to give up because of her disability. In 1987, she graduated from Adolfo Camarillo High School, then went on to attend the University of San Diego to complete her Master's Degree in 1994. She studied education for deaf and blind students.

11   Still, none of it came easily.

(continued on next page)

---

[1]**degenerate:** to become worse

[2]**philanthropist:** a person who donates his or her time or money to help others

12   As an adult, Runyan admitted to struggling in the classroom because schoolwork was so **laborious** for her. However, one place she felt free was on the field. She'd always been an athletic girl, and in college she found herself drawn to the track.

13   When she was running, the divisions between herself and the students with perfect vision fell away. She felt as if she could do as well as everyone else.

14   It was a feeling she would chase the rest of her life, and following it would lead her into history.

15   In 2000, when she journeyed to Sydney, she became the first legally blind person ever to compete in the Olympic Games.

16   Then, in 2002, she finished the New York Marathon in fourth place with a time of 2 hours, 27 minutes, and ten seconds, becoming the fastest American in that year's competition and the second fastest American woman ever to cross the finish line.

17   In preparation for those games, Runyan told reporters that her biggest challenge was to keep track of the people just ahead of her as she navigated the field.

18   To compensate for her handicap, Runyan prepared for a style of racing she described as "fast and tactical—a combination of both."

19   The one thing she didn't plan for, or want, was sympathy.

20   "I don't expect any mercy, no mercy whatsoever," she said. "They're not going to say, 'Go ahead Marla.' That's not going to happen."

21   Runyan's unique story put her in the international spotlight and brought her fans across the globe.

22   Runyan explained to reporters that, though she loves knowing that she inspires people, seeing how strongly some people react to her story can be shocking.

23   In that interview, Runyan went on to recount how she received an email from a woman whose son wanted to be a skateboarder but had also been diagnosed with Stargardt's. At first the mother refused to allow him, but once she read Runyan's story, she told him "Go get the ramp."

24   As much as these stories inspire Runyan to continue her example, she admits that even reading them can be a **struggle**. Reading is extremely difficult, and she can only do so with a voice output system on her computer. The words have to be enlarged so much that sometimes only three letters at a time can fit on the screen.

25   There are moments when she simply **gives up** for the day. Even the simple act of reading an email is too much.

26   Those moments never last long.

27   "I've never known anyone to be successful if all they do is blame, if they choose to be a victim," she told reporters. "If you choose to be a victim of this or that, or of what others have done to you, or what you believe to be someone else's fault, [you're] just constantly making excuses. I think the secret to achieving something is holding yourself **accountable** for your choices, good and bad, and learning from your mistakes, and then re-grouping and moving on. It's an ongoing process."

COMPREHENSION

Two of the three choices for each question are correct. Cross out the answer that is incorrect.

wrong answer

1. What does Marla "see"?

    a. a permanent blot

    b. shadows and indistinct shapes

    c. blindness

2. How has her life defied the experts' predictions? *challenge!*

    a. She graduated from college.

    b. She struggled in the classroom.

    c. She became a bestselling author.

3. How did she feel on the field?

    a. She felt equal to everyone else.

    b. She felt free.

    c. She felt she needed sympathy.

4. What strategies have helped her to be successful?

    a. lowering her expectations

    b. having a good attitude

    c. working hard

5. How does she feel about her effect on other people?

    a. She is shocked.

    b. She is inspired.

    c. She is self-reliant.

■■■■■■■■■■■■■■■■■■■■■■■■■■■■■■■■■■ GO TO MyEnglishLab FOR MORE VOCABULARY PRACTICE.

READING SKILL

1 Go back to Reading Two and see how many synonyms and antonyms you can find.

RECOGNIZING POSITIVE REDUNDANCY

Authors often use synonyms and antonyms in their writing for positive redundancy. This use of synonyms and antonyms in a text allows readers to read ideas more than once but with different vocabulary. In this way, meaning is reinforced, but language is new. The writer's ideas stay with the reader as related vocabulary is threaded through a text.

   Look at the example and read the explanation.

Reread paragraph 4 of Reading Two, "Marla Runyan."

"Here's what I do see: a permanent **blot** in front of my eyes that almost has physical properties," she described in her autobiography, *No Finish Line: My Life As I See It*. "Imagine that someone took a flash picture, and the flash got in your eyes. For a few moments, you'd see a purplish or grey splotch. In a few minutes it would fade away, and the world around you would appear normal again. For me, it stays."

In the first sentence, Marla uses the word *blot*. What synonym for the word *blot* does she use later in the paragraph?

Answer: splotch

This synonym adds interest to her description. Instead of repeating the word *blot*, the author uses a synonym to repeat an idea, but with new language.

Noticing synonyms and antonyms will help you see where the author emphasizes important information and ideas.

2 Work with a partner to identify synonyms and antonyms for the words given. Then discuss the effect of using different language rather than repeating the same words or expressions.

1. In paragraph 3, the author mentions *shadows*. What similar expression is also used in this paragraph? _____

2. In paragraph 8, the author uses the word *graced*. What synonym is also used in this paragraph? _____

3. In paragraph 10, the author uses the phrase *give up*. What antonym is also used in this paragraph? _____

4. In paragraph 12, the author talks about *struggling*. What two-word expression with an opposite meaning is also used in this paragraph? _____

5. In paragraph 19, the author uses the word *sympathy*. What synonym is used in paragraph 20? _____

6. In paragraph 24, the author says reading can be a *struggle*. What similar phrase is also used in this paragraph? _____

7. In paragraph 27, the author talks about *blame*. What similar expression is also used in this paragraph? _____

GO TO MyEnglishLab *FOR MORE SKILL PRACTICE.*

CONNECT THE READINGS

STEP 1: Organize

Both Frank McCourt in Reading One (R1) and Marla Runyan in Reading Two (R2) faced many obstacles and challenges in their lives. These same challenges also helped them to discover and develop their talent and become successful. Complete the chart comparing Frank McCourt and Marla Runyan.

	FRANK MCCOURT (R1)	MARLA RUNYAN (R2)
1. Obstacles they faced		
2. Person or people who influenced and inspired them		
3. Personal values, traits, or characteristics that helped them face their obstacles		
4. Talent or gift that resulted from the challenges they faced		

STEP 2: Synthesize

On a separate piece of paper, write a short paragraph comparing the lives of Frank McCourt and Marla Runyan. Use the information from Step 1. Describe their obstacles and triumphs.

GO TO MyEnglishLab *TO CHECK WHAT YOU LEARNED.*

VOCABULARY

REVIEW

The chain diagram below shows the three stages of overcoming obstacles: facing an obstacle, dealing with an obstacle, and overcoming an obstacle. Write the words from the box in the correct circles. Some of the words may be put in more than one circle. Discuss your answers with a partner.

accountable	exalted	inquisitiveness	pride
confused	expectations	laborious	self-reliance
darkest	free	misery	struggle
defeated	give up	mortified	suffer
disability	hopelessness	paradise	yearning for

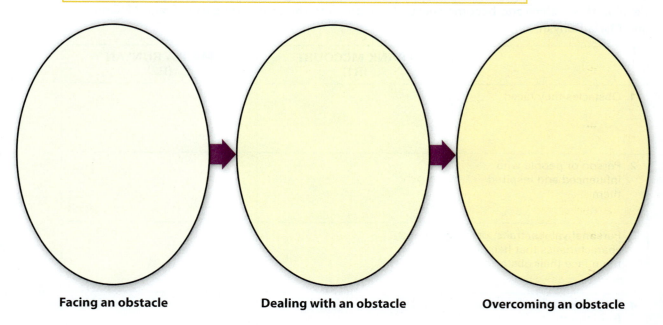

Facing an obstacle   **Dealing with an obstacle**   **Overcoming an obstacle**

EXPAND

An **analogy** is a comparison between two words that seem similar or are related in some way. In this exercise, the word pairs are either synonyms or antonyms. For example, in item 1, *struggle* is a synonym of *fight*; in the same way, *embarrassment* is a synonym of *shame*.

Work with a partner. Discuss the relationship between the words. Circle the word that best completes each analogy. Then circle *synonym* or *antonym* for each set of words. Use a dictionary if you need help.

1. struggle : fight = embarrassment : _____   *synonym*   *antonym*

   a. expectation   **b.** sadness   **c.** shame

2. confusion : understanding = hopeful : _____   *synonym*   *antonym*

   a. defeated   **b.** enlivened   **c.** liberated

3. exalted : noble = free : _____   *synonym*   *antonym*

   a. embarrassed   **b.** confused   **c.** liberated

4. poverty : wealth = misery : _____   *synonym*   *antonym*

   a. hopelessness   **b.** happiness   **c.** yearning

5. yearning : longing = self-reliance : _____   *synonym*   *antonym*

   a. inquisitiveness   **b.** independence   **c.** pride

6. laborious : difficult = falling apart : _____   *synonym*   *antonym*

   a. dilapidated   **b.** sordid   **c.** mortified

7. inquisitiveness : indifference = give up : _____   *synonym*   *antonym*

   a. struggle   **b.** continue   **c.** compensate

8. meager : plentiful = accountable : _____   *synonym*   *antonym*

   a. irresponsible   **b.** mortified   **c.** inquisitive

9. darkest : unhappiest = immoral : _____   *synonym*   *antonym*

   a. tormented   **b.** liberated   **c.** sordid

CREATE

Choose one of the situations. On a separate piece of paper, write a letter using words and phrases from Review and Expand.

1. Imagine you are the skateboarder's mother. Write a letter to Marla Runyan. Explain how she helped and inspired you and your son.

2. Imagine you are one of Frank McCourt's former students. You have just graduated from college. Write a letter to Frank McCourt. Explain how he helped and inspired you to overcome an obstacle.

■■■■■■■■■■■■■■■■■■■■■■■■■■■■■ *GO TO* MyEnglishLab *FOR MORE VOCABULARY PRACTICE.*

GRAMMAR

1 Examine the sentences and answer the questions with a partner.

   a. Teaching was the most exalted profession I could imagine.

   b. McCourt enjoyed **writing** about his childhood.

   c. McCourt had done a lot of **reading**.

   d. Marla Runyan refused **to give up** because of her disability.

   e. McCourt persuaded New York University **to enroll** him.

   f. After McCourt's mother died, he felt free **to write** his memoirs.

   g. Marla Runyan has the ability **to inspire** others with her actions.

1. In sentence *a*, what is the subject?

2. In sentence *b*, what is the object of the verb *enjoyed*?

3. In sentence *c*, what word follows the preposition *of*?

4. Look at the boldfaced words in *a, b,* and *c*. They are gerunds. How are gerunds formed?

5. In sentence *d*, the main verb is *refused*. What is the verb that follows it?

6. In sentence *e*, the main verb is *persuaded*. What is the object of the main verb? What is the verb that follows it?

7. In sentence *f*, what is the verb that follows the adjective *free*?

8. In sentence *g*, what is the verb that follows the noun *ability*?

9. Look at the boldfaced words in *d, e, f,* and *g*. They are infinitives. How are infinitives formed?

GERUNDS AND INFINITIVES	
Gerunds To form a gerund, **use the base form of the verb + -ing**.	read + ing = reading write + ing = writing* *Note that for verbs ending in a consonant and final "e," drop the "e" before adding "ing".*
1. Use the gerund as the **subject** of a sentence.	**Writing** is very important to Frank McCourt.
2. Use the gerund as the **object** of a sentence after certain verbs (such as *enjoy, acknowledge, recall*).	Frank McCourt enjoys **writing**. McCourt recalled **not wanting** to offend his mother, and that held him back.
3. Use the gerund **after a preposition** (such as *of, in, for, about*).	Frank McCourt is interested in **writing**.

Infinitives

To form an infinitive, use **to + the base form of the verb**.	to read to write

4. Use the infinitive **after certain verbs**.
 	
    a. some verbs are followed directly by an infinitive (such as *learn, decide, agree, refuse*)
 	
    b. some verbs are followed by an object + an infinitive (such as *urge, persuade*)
 	
    c. some verbs are followed by an infinitive or an object + an infinitive (such as *want, ask, need*)
	
	McCourt's students **learned to write** about their personal experiences.
	
	McCourt **urged his students to write** about their personal experiences.
	
	McCourt **wanted to write** about his personal experiences.
	McCourt **wanted them to write** their personal experiences.

5. Use the infinitive **after certain adjectives** (such as *free, able, hard*).	McCourt's students were **free to write** about whatever they wanted.
6. Use the infinitive **after certain nouns** (such as *ability, freedom*).	McCourt's students had the **freedom to write** about whatever they wanted.

2 Work with a partner. Underline the gerund or infinitive in each sentence. Write the number of the grammar rule that applies to each.

   1   **a.** <u>Doing</u> schoolwork was very laborious for Marla Runyan.

_____ **b.** Marla Runyan has the ability to run as fast as sighted competitors.

_____ **c.** McCourt acknowledged not going to high school.

_____ **d.** Marla Runyan was able to compete in the 2000 Olympics.

_____ **e.** A professor asked McCourt to describe an object from his childhood.

_____ **f.** Marla Runyan has refused to be defined by her condition.

_____ **g.** Many people don't feel free to write about their lives.

_____ **h.** Recounting his experiences inspired McCourt's students.

_____ **i.** McCourt couldn't think about writing his memoirs while his mother was alive.

_____ **j.** McCourt's students urged him to write a book.

3 Read the information about Frank McCourt and Marla Runyan. Rewrite each situation using a form of the first verb given and the gerund or infinitive form of the second verb.

1. McCourt was worried that his memoirs would embarrass his mother. After she died, he didn't have to worry about this. (feel free / write)
   After his mother died, McCourt felt free to write his memoirs.

2. Before Marla runs a marathon, she spends months preparing. It takes a long time to get ready for a 26-mile race. (need / train)
   _____

3. McCourt had no high school education, but he had read a lot. He told New York University it should admit him. (persuade / allow)
   _____

4. Marla's unique story has brought her fans from around the globe. She is happy that her story is helping others. (enjoy / inspire)
   _____

5. Frank McCourt hadn't gone to high school. He was afraid of what his students would think about him. (worry about / tell)
   _____

6. At first the boy's mother did not want him to skateboard, but after she read about Marla's story, she changed her mind. (decide / let)
   _____

7. McCourt's students didn't think they were able to write. He gave them lots of encouragement and told them "everyone has a story to tell." (urge / write)
   _____

8. Because Marla is legally blind, it is a struggle for her to read the words on a computer screen. (be hard / see)
   _____

9. McCourt remembered the town of Limerick. He could see and imagine what it was like when he was a child. (recall / live)
   _____

10. Specialists told Marla she couldn't expect to get good grades. Despite their predictions, Marla attended the University of San Diego and completed her Master's degree. (be able / graduate)
    _____

GO TO MyEnglishLab FOR MORE GRAMMAR PRACTICE AND TO CHECK WHAT YOU LEARNED.

FINAL WRITING TASK

In this unit, you read personal accounts of how people overcame obstacles.

You are going to *write a biographical paragraph about how you or someone you know overcame an obstacle*. Use the vocabulary and grammar from the unit.*

PREPARE TO WRITE: Listing

Listing is a prewriting activity in which you list information about a topic or category before you begin to write a paragraph or essay.

Look back at Connect the Readings on page 49 to complete the first column of the chart. In the second column, write three or more obstacles that you or someone you know has faced.

OBSTACLES FACED BY FRANK MCCOURT AND MARLA RUNYAN	OBSTACLES FACED BY ME OR SOMEONE I KNOW

WRITE: A Biographical Paragraph

A **paragraph** is a group of sentences that are related and that support a controlling idea. A **biographical paragraph** describes a person's life and sometimes focuses on one particular aspect. All paragraphs have three parts: the **topic sentence**, the **supporting sentences**, and the **concluding sentence**.

TOPIC SENTENCE

The **topic sentence** introduces the main idea and the controlling idea, which is your idea or opinion about the main idea. The topic sentence controls what you write in the rest of the paragraph. All the sentences in the paragraph must relate to, describe, or illustrate the controlling idea in the topic sentence.

(continued on next page)

---

* For Alternative Writing Topics, see page 61. These topics can be used in place of the writing topic for this unit or as homework. The alternative topics relate to the theme of the unit but may not target the same grammar or rhetorical structures taught in the unit.

SUPPORTING SENTENCES

The second part of the paragraph includes **supporting sentences** that give details or examples that develop your ideas about the topic. This is usually the longest part of the paragraph, since it discusses and explains the controlling idea.

CONCLUDING SENTENCE

The **concluding sentence** is the last part of the paragraph. It can do one or more of the following: summarize the paragraph, offer a solution to the problem, restate the topic sentence, or offer an opinion.

1 Read the paragraph. Then answer the questions with a partner.

Michael Jordan said, "Obstacles don't have to stop you. If you run into a wall, don't turn around and give up. Figure out how to climb it, go through it, or work around it." This attitude can be seen all around us. Many people have faced great obstacles in their lives but have found ways to overcome and actually benefit from these obstacles. For example, Greg Barton, the 1984, 1988, and 1992 U.S. Olympic medalist in kayaking, was born with a serious disability. He had club feet, his toes pointed inward, and as a result, he could not walk easily. Even after a series of operations, he still had limited mobility. Even so, Greg was never defeated. First, he taught himself to walk, and even to run. Then he competed on his high school running team. He knew, though, he would never become an Olympic runner, so he looked for other sports that he could play. Happily, he discovered kayaking, a perfect sport for him because it required minimal leg and foot muscles. Using his upper body strength, he was able to master the sport. Finally, after many years of training and perseverance, Greg made the 1984 Olympic team. He says of his accomplishments, "Each step of the road has been made easier by looking just as far as necessary—yet not beyond that." In short, even though that road was paved with obstacles, he was able to overcome them and achieve the impossible.

1. What is the topic of the paragraph? How do you know?

Overcoming obstacles.

2. What is the controlling idea?

Sentence #5 → . Make examples.

3. Underline the sentences that support the topic and controlling ideas. How do they relate to the controlling idea?

4. What is the concluding sentence? What does it do?

The last sentences.

Note: For more information on topic sentences and controlling ideas, see Unit 1.

2 Now write the first draft of your biographical paragraph. Use the information from Prepare to Write and complete the chart below to plan your paragraph. Make sure you have a topic sentence, supporting sentences, and a concluding sentence. Be sure to use grammar and vocabulary from the unit.

Topic Sentence: _at least 1 verb._

1.

Supporting Sentences:

2.

3.

4.

5.

6.

Concluding Sentence:

7.

REVISE: Choosing Appropriate Support

The **supporting sentences** in a paragraph help the reader to better understand the controlling idea. Supporting sentences provide examples, details, and facts, and must relate directly to the topic sentence.

1 Read each topic sentence. Two ideas support the topic sentence and one does not. Cross out the idea that does not support the topic sentence.

1. Ever since Greg Barton was in high school, he longed to be an Olympic champion.

   a. Greg's sports records

   b. How Greg trained for the Olympics

   c. ~~Greg's academic achievements~~

2. The achievements of people like Greg Barton and Marla Runyan have inspired many others.

   a. Explanation of how they have inspired others

   b. How many people have read about Greg Barton and Marla Runyan

   c. Greg Barton's and Marla Runyan's obstacles

3. The poverty-stricken lives of Frank McCourt's students deeply affected him.

   a. How Frank saw himself in his students

   b. How Frank taught his students to write

   c. How the students inspired Frank to write

4. Training to run a marathon is a very difficult and time-consuming process.

   a. The patience needed to run a marathon

   b. Reasons why people should run a marathon

   c. The amount of practice and time needed to run a marathon

2 Each paragraph has one supporting sentence that does not directly relate to the topic sentence. Cross out the sentence and explain why it is unrelated.

1. Helen Keller lost her sight at a very early age and, so, was very frustrated as a child. First of all, because she could neither hear nor speak, she couldn't understand what was happening around her. She felt her mother's lips moving as she spoke, but this made no sense to her. She couldn't understand what her mother was doing. ~~Her mother could hear and speak.~~ Secondly, once she learned what words were, she felt she could never communicate with them as quickly as sighted people could. As a result of all her frustration, she would often cry and scream until she was exhausted.

   Explanation: _The sentence focuses on her mother's abilities, not Helen's frustrations._

2. Succeeding in sports liberated Marla Runyan and Greg Barton. They both faced overwhelming obstacles, but sports freed them from their hardest struggles. For example, when Marla was on the field, she finally felt she could do as well as everyone else. Similarly, when Greg found the best sport for his physical limitations, he excelled. In addition, Marla has become a bestselling author. They are both great athletes who were freed from their struggles by sports.

Explanation: _____

_____

3. Some of the world's most talented and famous people have overcome some of the hardest obstacles. For example, Ludwig van Beethoven became deaf at age 46. Franklin D. Roosevelt was paralyzed by polio and was often in a wheelchair, but he was elected president of the United States four times. Finally, Steven Hawking is a world-famous scientist who is completely paralyzed and cannot speak. Furthermore, he lives in England. These people show us that we should never give up or let obstacles defeat us.

Explanation: _____

_____

3 Look at your first draft. Make sure your supporting sentences give clear examples and details that connect with and support the controlling idea.

GO TO MyEnglishLab **FOR MORE SKILL PRACTICE.**

EDIT: Writing the Final Draft

Go to MyEnglishLab and write the final draft of your paragraph. Carefully edit it for grammatical and mechanical errors, such as spelling, capitalization, and punctuation. Make sure you use some of the grammar and vocabulary from the unit. Use the checklist to help you write your final draft. Then submit your paragraph to your teacher.

FINAL DRAFT CHECKLIST

❏ Does the paragraph describe a person who was faced with challenges and overcame them?

❏ Is there a topic sentence stating the obstacle that the person overcame?

❏ Do all the supporting sentences relate directly to the topic sentence?

❏ Is there a concluding sentence that restates the main idea of the paragraph, offers an opinion, or suggests a solution?

❏ Did you use gerunds and infinitives correctly?

❏ Have you used vocabulary from the unit?

UNIT PROJECT

RESEARCH: A Famous Person Who Has Overcome an Obstacle

In this unit, you have read about two people who have overcome obstacles. Many famous people have overcome great obstacles, including emotional, physical, and political obstacles. You are going to write a biographical essay about a famous person who has overcome an obstacle. Follow these steps:

STEP 1: Choose a famous person you admire or a person from the list below who has overcome an obstacle.

<u>**Artists / Performers**</u>
Christopher Reeve
Mary Cassat
50 Cent
Vincent van Gogh
Michelangelo
Oprah Winfrey
Stevie Wonder

<u>**Writers / Scientists**</u>
Steven Hawking
Sigmund Freud
Charles Darwin
Thomas Edison
Hans Christian Andersen
Jorge Luis Borges

<u>**Sports Figures**</u>
Jackie Robinson
Magic Johnson
Natalie du Toit
Jeremy Lin
Bethany Hamilton
Tahmina Kohistani

<u>**Politicians / Leaders**</u>
The Dalai Lama
Mahatma Ghandi
John F. Kennedy
Golda Meir
Franklin D. Roosevelt
Nelson Mandela

STEP 2: Do research on the Internet about the person you chose. Check information on two or more websites.

1. If you need help getting started with Internet research, go back to Unit 1, pages 32–33.

2. Read the entries that relate to your topic.

3. Takes notes in your own words for a written report.

STEP 3: Use your notes to write a biographical essay. Be sure it includes the answers to these questions:

- When and where did/does the person live?
- What is/was the person famous for?
- What did this person achieve?
- What obstacles did this person have to overcome? How did he or she overcome them?
- What personal characteristics helped this person overcome his or her obstacles?
- What has researching this person taught you about life and overcoming obstacles?

STEP 4: Present your biography to the class by giving an oral presentation that summarizes your research.

ALTERNATIVE WRITING TOPICS

Write a paragraph about one of the topics. Use the vocabulary and grammar from the unit.

1. Read the quotation.

   "I've missed more than 9,000 shots in my career. I've lost almost 300 games. 26 times, I've been trusted to take the game winning shot and missed. I've failed over and over and over again in my life. And that is why I succeed."

   —Michael Jordan

   How does this quotation apply to a person you have read about in the unit, to another famous person, or to yourself?

2. What are two of the most important values and personal characteristics people need in order to overcome obstacles? How do people apply these values and characteristics to their lives?

■■■■■■■■■■■■■■■■■■■■■■■■■■■ *GO TO* MyEnglishLab *TO WRITE ABOUT ONE OF THE ALTERNATIVE TOPICS, WATCH A VIDEO ABOUT A GIRL WITH AUTISM, AND TAKE THE UNIT 2 ACHIEVEMENT TEST.* ■■■■■■■■■■■

MAKING MEDICAL
Decisions

1. What role can genes play in medicine?

2. Do you think medical treatment could be more effective if doctors had genetic information about their patients?

3. Genetic testing is now available very cheaply. Would you want to be tested to find out if you have the gene for a certain disease, even if there were no cure for the disease?

GO TO MyEnglishLab *TO CHECK WHAT YOU KNOW.*

2 FOCUS ON READING

READING ONE GENETIC TESTING AND DISEASE: WOULD YOU WANT TO KNOW?

VOCABULARY

1 Read the timeline about the history of medicine and medical decision-making. Try to understand the boldfaced words from the context.

PRIMITIVE TRIBAL SOCIETIES ↓	A shaman (holy person) held all the existing medical knowledge. By **interpreting** the patient's symptoms, he would decide on a treatment.
ANCIENT GREECE (5ᵀᴴ CENTURY B.C.E.) ↓	Socrates began the practice of questioning and testing beliefs to discover knowledge. This "Socratic method" had a tremendous **impact** on medical decision-making because it allowed physicians to evaluate treatment methods. As a result, treatments became more **reliable**.
4ᵀᴴ CENTURY B.C.E. ↓	Medical practice was **revolutionized** by Hippocrates, the "father of western medicine." He changed medicine in many ways. For example, he was an **advocate** for publishing medical knowledge, focusing on patient care rather than diagnosis, and demanding physicians act professionally. He also recognized that disease could be caused by the **environment**. That is, diet and living habits are **linked** to disease, and their modification can be beneficial in reducing disease.
2ᴺᴰ CENTURY C.E. ↓	The Skeptics saw the life-saving **potential** of *trial and error* as the basis of medical decision-making.
17ᵀᴴ CENTURY C.E. ↓	Rene Descartes wrote about the mind-body **interaction**, which is the basis of psychology and psychiatry today.
2003	The Human Genome Project identified all the genes in the human body. Now patients are able to make medical decisions based on their own genetic **risk factor**. However, even with the knowledge provided by human gene mapping, there is not always **consensus** about what the best treatment is for a specific patient. Different doctors may recommend different treatments. That is why in the end, patients must weigh the emotional and medical **aspects** of each option and then make their own decision.

2 Find the boldfaced words in the timeline in Exercise 1. Write each word next to its definition.

1. _____ (**n.**) something that is likely to hurt you or be dangerous

2. _impact_____ (**n.**) the effect that an event or situation has on someone or something

3. _potential_____ (**n.**) the possibility that something will develop or happen in a particular way

4. _environment_____ (**n.**) the circumstances, objects, or conditions that surround you

5. _interaction_____ (**n.**) the action or influence of people, groups, or things on one another

6. _aspects_____ (**n.**) parts or features of a situation, idea, problem, etc.

7. _Concensus_____ (**n.**) an agreement that everyone in a group reaches

8. _avocate_____ (**n.**) strong supporter of a particular way of doing things

9. _interpreting_____ (**n.**) explaining or deciding on the meaning of an event

10. _reliable_____ (**adj.**) able to be trusted; dependable

11. _linked_____ (**v.**) made a connection between two or more events, people, or ideas

12. _revolutionize____ (**v.**) to have completely changed the way people think or do things

GO TO MyEnglishLab FOR MORE VOCABULARY PRACTICE.

PREVIEW

Read the first two paragraphs of *Genetic testing and disease: Would you want to know?* Work with a partner to answer the questions. Then read the rest of the article.

1. Why do you think Kristen wants to know?

2. How can knowing if she has the gene for Huntington's disease help her live her life better?

3. What do you think Kristen's father thinks about her being tested?

Genetic testing and disease: Would you want to know?

By Janice Lloyd, USA TODAY

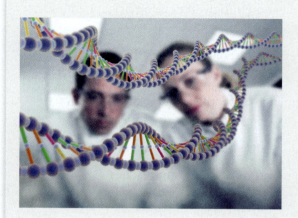

1   Kristen Powers finishes packing her lunch and opens the kitchen door to leave for high school with her brother, Nate, in tow.[1] "I drive but always let him pick the music," she says, smiling. He gives her a gentle nudge[2] and they set off to the car.

2   Nothing like having a kid brother behind you, especially when you are embarking[3] on a courageous journey. Kristen, 18, is having blood work done May 18 to find out whether she inherited the defective gene for Huntington's disease, a fatal, neurodegenerative disorder that can debilitate victims as early as their mid-30s. The siblings have a 50-50 chance of developing the rare disease, which claimed their mother's life last year at age 45.

3   Nate, 16, doesn't know whether he'll follow his sister's lead. Only people 18 or older can be tested, unless they're exhibiting symptoms, because a positive result can be shattering news. There's also no cure. Huntington's is devastating on so many levels: People lose coordination, developing wild jerky movements; they suffer behavioral changes, often becoming depressed and psychotic; and in the end, they develop dementia and require total care. One of their last images of their mother was in a wheelchair in a nursing home.

4   Nate "has been amazingly supportive of my wanting to get tested," Kristen says. "He is interested in the whole process, but he's been hesitant over the years to commit to testing, while I've known since I was 15 that I wanted to do this."

5   "Know thyself" has taken on a scientific meaning for a growing number of people who, like Kristen, want a crystal ball to look into their DNA. Ever since the Human Genome Project identified the 20,000 to 25,000 genes in 2003, researchers have continued to identify the ones that play roles in diseases, from Alzheimer's to type 2 diabetes to certain types of cancer. Though lifestyle and environment are big pieces of the puzzle, consider this: Genetic tests could become part of standard care for everyone and **revolutionize** the way medicine is practiced, proponents say.

6   Gone would be the days of waiting to develop a disease. People would know about diseases they are at risk for and could change their living habits or consider treatments.

---

[1] **in tow:** following closely behind someone or something

[2] **nudge:** push

[3] **embarking:** starting something new, difficult, or exciting

Opponents warn about the **potential** for invasion of privacy—threatening employment and insurance—and the possibility that people equipped with the knowledge of their genetic makeup might make risky and unhealthy decisions.

7   Kristen has had counseling at the University of North Carolina to prepare her for dealing with her testing news, and she copes with stress by walking with her rescue dog, Jake. "Walking is critical for me," she says. She will return to the campus at the end of May with her father, Ed Powers, to get the results.

8   "She's always wanted to take matters into her own hands," her father says. "She's constantly asking what we can do to make things better. I am her biggest backer and want to be there for her every step of the way during this."

Leaning on social media

9   Kristen leans on her kitchen table and explains in a quiet, clear voice that she is ready to handle the news and has no plans to keep it secret. "I started out trying to find answers on the Internet about Huntington's disease," she says, "but I quickly became very disappointed. There's not a good video or an **advocate** for it, like Michael J. Fox is for Parkinson's disease."

10   She has raised $17,580 on the website Indiegogo.com and hired a video crew to make a documentary about the emotional and medical **aspects** of testing on her and her family. "Social media can be a real unifier. There's not much out there yet for young people on Huntington's. I want to change that."

11   Her mother, Nicola Powers, was diagnosed in 2003 after struggling with symptoms for several years. "I remember watching her stumble and walk like a drunk person at times," Kristen says. "That was before we knew what was wrong with her. She was really struggling. It was very scary."

12   Nicola Powers didn't know the disease ran in her family. She grew apart from her biological father after her parents divorced. Once she looked into his medical history because of her symptoms, she discovered he had Huntington's.

13   Kristen doesn't want the gene to be passed on again. She says she won't have children if she tests positive: "I can be candid with potential partners and be responsible," she says.

14   Genetic counselors warn about the emotional **impact** of testing on the person and family. "Some people like to plan everything out," says Brenda Finucane, president of the National Society of Genetic Counselors. "They think the information is empowering, while some people want to see how life plays out."

15   Robert Green has found that most people will not seek out risk information about late-onset Alzheimer's disease if they're not psychologically prepared to handle it. But "it turns out many people handle this kind of information quite well," says Green, associate director for research in genetics at Brigham and Women's Hospital in Boston. "Some changed their wills,[4] and some made lifestyle changes. Taking these tests is all about actionability.[5]"

16   Timing can be tricky, though. Kristen's father and stepmother, Betsy Banks Saul, suggested she hold off until she has a support system at college. "She's a very intelligent,

---

[4] **wills:** legal documents that show whom you want to have your money and property after you die

[5] **actionability:** being able to act upon

(continued on next page)

strong young woman, and we trust her, but we wish we could be nearby to support her," Betsy says.

17   After high school graduation in June, she will attend Stanford, in California — far from her farm, family, and friends. Kristen listened to her parents' concerns and considered putting off testing, "but I am a type A person who has always craved getting information. I want to know."

Not all tests are equal

18   Her test will look for the single gene that causes Huntington's, but most diseases have a more complicated genetic profile. A growing number of tests look at multiple genes that might increase or decrease a person's risk for developing thousands of diseases. Companies market the tests for as little as $100 on the Internet and don't require a physician's signature. But those kinds of results are not always **reliable**, says Ardis Dee Hoven, former chair of the American Medical Association.

19   "In the absence of a medical professional, a patient might have difficulty **interpreting** the test and make decisions that are not healthy decisions," Hoven says. For instance, someone who tests negative for BRCA1 and BRCA2—genes that put people at a higher risk for developing certain breast and ovarian cancers—might not know there are other **risk factors**. Unless the patient has a physician guiding her, Hoven says, she might think she's home-free[6] and skip routine screening tests.

20   David Agus, author of the new book *The End of Illness*, says that's why the company he co-founded, Navigenics, requires customers to get a signature from their doctors before being tested. Navigenics also offers genetic counseling as part of the $300–$400 fee. "Genetics are a small piece of the puzzle, but they're a very important piece," says Agus, head of the Center for Applied Molecular Medicine at the University of Southern California.

21   A cancer specialist, Agus discovered he has an above-average risk for cardiovascular disease and a slightly lower-than-average risk for colon cancer. His doctor put him on a statin to help prevent heart disease, and, he says, "my kids took it upon themselves to keep me away from french fries." He also had a colonoscopy at age 43, earlier than medical standards call for, and had a polyp removed. "Could my polyp have turned into cancer? Who knows? But why should I wait for that to happen? Unless our country can focus on prevention, which testing is all about, our health care costs will be completely out of control."

22   A study of 1,200 patients that was presented in March at an American College of Cardiology meeting found that those who were told they had a gene **linked** to heart disease improved their adherence to statin therapy by 13% compared with those who had not been tested for the gene.

23   "I could see how testing could become embedded[7] in how we treat our patients," Hoven says. "It's always better to prevent disease than to treat it, and quality of life is so much better for people."

How accessibility could change

24   Since the human genome was unraveled[8] a dozen years ago, genetic testing has been

---

[6] **home-free:** safe and without problems
[7] **embedded:** put something firmly and deeply into something else
[8] **was unraveled:** something very complicated was understood or explained

cost-prohibitive for the average person. The promise was that this breakthrough would lead to a better understanding of myriad[9] diseases and, ultimately, individualized treatments. Whole genome testing studies the **interaction** of our 20,000 to 25,000 genes with one another and with a person's **environment**. The $10,000 price tag, though, is expected to drop to $1,000 within the decade. When the tests become mainstream, doctors could face a dilemma.[10]

25   A study in March reports that 10 of 16 specialists (62%) favored telling a patient he carried the gene for Huntington's if the finding was incidental to why the test was ordered. The study noted that the specialists unanimously agreed on disclosing 21 of 99 commonly ordered genetic conditions for adults, and "multiple expert panels" might be needed to agree on what to tell patients.

26   "This is one of the toughest issues facing the rollout of clinical sequencing (whole genome sequencing)," Green says. He adds that after the study, he co-chaired a forum March 28 of the American College of Medical Genetics to discuss how to form a **consensus**.

27   That's a non-issue for Kristen. She knows she will get an answer. One of her hardest decisions has been picking who will be in the room when she gets her results. She knows she wants the videographers taping. At first she didn't want her father to be there, but she relented when he asked her to reconsider.

28   "I know I can take the news," she says, "Knowledge is power. But I didn't think I could get a positive result and then watch my father cry. I've never seen him cry before."*

---

[9] **myriad:** a very large number of something

[10] **dilemma:** situation in which you have to make a choice between two or more difficult actions

*Kristin tested negative for Huntington's disease.

MAIN IDEAS

1 Look again at your answers to the questions from the Preview on page 65. How did your answers help you understand the article?

2 Reading One presents the pros and cons of genetic testing. Complete the chart with the information in the box. Then compare answers with a partner.

can choose appropriate treatment plan	There are other risk factors in addition to genes.	can change lifestyle	Positive result can lead to risky, unhealthy decisions.
can prevent diseases rather than just treat them	Positive result can be shattering for patient and family.	Patient may interpret test results incorrectly.	may threaten employment and insurance

POSITIVE	NEGATIVE

I. Can revolutionize medicine
  a.
  b. Quality of life is better.
	I. Emotional and physical impact
	  a.
	  b.

II. Information is empowering for patient.
  a.
  b.
	II. Invasion of privacy
	  a.

	III. Results are not always reliable.

	IV. Professional interpretation is not required.
	  a.
	  b.

DETAILS

Reading One mentions many people, places, and names of diseases connected with genetic testing. Match the people, places, and diseases on the left with the information on the right.

1. _____ Ardis Dee Hoven

    a. A progressive, degenerative disorder that attacks the brain's nerve cells, or neurons, resulting in loss of memory, thinking and language skills, and behavioral changes. It can be identified through genetic testing.

2. _____ Robert Green

    b. Head of the Center for Applied Molecular Medicine at the University of Southern California, author of *The End of Illness*, and co-founder of Navigenics, a genetic testing company

3. _____ Human Genome Project

    c. Location of Kristen Powers' counseling center

4. _____ Alzheimer's disease

d. An incurable fatal, neurodegenerative disorder that can debilitate victims as early as their mid-30s. It can be identified through genetic testing.

5. _____ David Agus

e. A 2003 study which identified the 20,000–25,000 genes in the human body

6. _____ BRCA1 & BRCA2

f. A well-known advocate for Parkinson's disease

7. _____ Huntington's disease

g. Website where Kristen Powers raised money to hire a video crew

8. _____ University of North Carolina

h. Former chair of the American Medical Association who warned that genetic test results are not always reliable

9. _____ Indiegogo.com

i. President of the National Society of Genetic Counselors who talks about the emotional impact of testing

10. _____ Brenda Finucane

j. Genes that indicate a high risk factor for developing certain breast and ovarian cancers

11. _____ Michael J. Fox

k. Associate director for research in genetics at Brigham and Women's Hospital. He talks about using the test results to take (positive) action.

MAKE INFERENCES

INFERRING DEGREE OF SUPPORT

When reading a text dealing with a controversial topic, it is important to be able to infer the degree of support that different people express about it. Some may be more supportive than others. Some may not be supportive at all. How do we "read between the lines" to get a sense of how supportive a person is? What language is used? How often does a statement of support occur? What reservations are expressed?

  Look at the example and read the explanation.

Reading One deals with genetic testing. This is clearly a controversial topic as evidenced by the varying viewpoints of the people mentioned in the story.

How strong is Kristen's support of genetic testing?

Very Weak	Weak	Neutral	Strong	Very Strong

In paragraph 4, she notes, "I've known since I was 15 that I wanted to do this." She adds in paragraph 17, "I am a type A person who has always craved getting information. I want to know." Finally, in paragraph 28, she states, "I know I can take the news. Knowledge is power."

From these statements, we can infer that Kristen's support of genetic testing is *Very Strong*.

Understanding the position of people mentioned in a text concerning controversial topics enables the reader to understand the text more thoroughly.

Think about the people mentioned in Reading One. Rate their support of genetic testing, based on what they say and do, by putting an **X** in the correct column. Reread the indicated paragraph(s) to support your choice. Compare your answers with a partner's.

	Paragraph(s)	Very Weak	Weak	Neutral	Strong	Very Strong
NATE, KRISTEN'S BROTHER	3					
KRISTEN'S FATHER	7, 8					
BRENDA FINUCANE	14					
ROBERT GREEN	15, 26					
BETSY BANK SAUL	16					
ARDIS DEE HOVEN	18, 19					
DAVID AGUS	20, 21					

EXPRESS OPINIONS

Discuss the questions in a small group. Then share your answers with the class.

1. If you were in Kristen's position, would you have chosen to be tested?

2. Do you think genetic testing has more potential benefits than possible problems? Explain.

3. If you had a genetic test and it indicated you were at risk for a certain disease, who would you share the information with? Would you tell your children, brothers and sisters, cousins? How would you make this decision? Explain.

GO TO MyEnglishLab TO GIVE YOUR OPINION ABOUT ANOTHER QUESTION.

READ

Norman Cousins was a well-known American writer and editor. When he was diagnosed with a serious illness, he was not content to let the doctor make all of his medical decisions. He decided to use his own type of alternative therapy. He focused on the importance of a positive attitude in healing. After writing about his successful recovery, he received mail from all over the world. Many letters came from doctors who supported his ideas.

1 Look at the boldfaced words in the reading and think about the questions.

1. Which words do you know the meanings of?

2. Can you use any of the words or phrases in a sentence?

2 Read the article about Norman Cousins. As you read, notice the boldfaced vocabulary. Try to guess its meaning from the context.

Charlie Chaplin

Norman Cousins's Laughter Therapy

1   In the summer of 1964, well-known writer and editor Norman Cousins became very ill. His body ached, and he felt constantly tired. It was difficult for him to even move around. He **consulted** his physician, who did many tests. Eventually, he was diagnosed as having ankylosing spondylitis, a very serious and destructive form of arthritis.[1] His doctor told him that he would become immobilized[2] and eventually die from the disease. He was told he had only a 1 in 500 chance of survival.

2   Despite the diagnosis,[3] Cousins was determined to overcome the disease and survive. He had always been interested in medicine and had read the work of organic chemist Hans Selye, *The Stress of Life* (1956). This book discussed the idea of how body chemistry and health can be damaged by emotional stress and negative attitudes. Selye's book made Cousins think about the possible benefits of positive attitudes and emotions. He thought, "If negative emotions produce (negative) changes in the body, wouldn't positive emotions produce positive chemical changes? Is it possible that love, hope, faith, laughter, confidence, and the will to live have positive therapeutic value?"

[1] **arthritis:** a disease that causes pain and swelling in the joints of the body
[2] **immobilized:** not able to move
[3] **diagnosis:** identification of what illness a person has

(continued on next page)

3   He decided to concentrate on positive emotions as a remedy to heal some of the symptoms of his ailment. In addition to his **conventional** medical treatment, he tried to put himself in situations that would **elicit** positive emotions. "Laughter Therapy" became part of his treatment. He scheduled time each day for watching comedy films, reading humorous books, and doing other activities that would bring about laughter and positive emotions. Within eight days of starting his "Laughter Therapy" program, his pain began to decrease, and he was able to sleep more easily. His body chemistry even improved. Doctors were able to see an improvement in his condition! Within a few months' time, he was able to walk wearing a metal brace. Soon after that, he was able to return to work. He actually reached complete recovery in a few years. He lived for 26 years after he became ill. He died in 1990 at the age of 75.

4   **Skeptical** readers may question the doctor's preliminary diagnosis, but Cousins believed his recovery was the result of a mysterious mind-body interaction. His "Laughter Therapy" is a good example of one of the many **alternative**, or nonconventional, medical treatments people look to today.

COMPREHENSION

Write answers to the questions. Use a separate piece of paper.

1. What was Norman Cousins' original diagnosis and how did he respond?

2. What is the connection between mind and body in Laughter Therapy?

3. What are some examples of Laughter Therapy?

4. How did Cousins benefit from his Laughter Therapy?

GO TO MyEnglishLab *FOR MORE VOCABULARY PRACTICE.*

READING SKILL

1 In Reading Two, the author describes a number of events that take place around the year 1964: Cousins's diagnosis with arthritis, his reading books by Hans Selye, his invention of Laughter Therapy, etc. What is the order in which these different events take place? How do you know?

USING A TIMELINE TO ORGANIZE THE SEQUENCE OF EVENTS

Making a timeline of events in a narrative is a useful way to organize and remember information. This organization can help readers understand the text. In the article about Norman Cousins, a number of events happen before, during, and after the summer of 1964.

Look at paragraph 3. The author states, "Within eight days of starting his 'Laughter Therapy' program [later in the summer of 1964], his pain began to decrease, and he was able to sleep more easily. His body chemistry even improved."

How would you complete the timeline?

Later in the summer of 1964	
8 days later	

What happened later in the summer of 1964?
Cousins was diagnosed with a severe form of arthritis and started his Laughter Therapy program.

What happened eight days later?
Cousins's pain decreased, he was able to sleep better, and his body chemistry improved.

Understanding how events are related chronologically can increase the comprehension and retention of the information you read. Using a timeline is one way to do this.

2 Go back to Reading Two. Complete the timeline using information from the article.

Sometime before the summer of 1964	
Summer 1964	
Later in the summer of 1964	Cousins was diagnosed with a severe form of arthritis and started his Laughter Therapy program.
8 days later	Cousins's pain decreased, he was able to sleep better, and his body chemistry improved.
A few months later	
Soon after that	
A few years later	
1990	

GO TO MyEnglishLab *FOR MORE SKILL PRACTICE.*

STEP 1: Organize

You have read about genetic testing in Reading 1 (R1) and Norman Cousins's Laughter Therapy in Reading 2 (R2). What are the similarities and differences between them? Complete the Venn diagram with information from both readings. In the left circle, write notes that are true only about the genetic testing. In the right circle, write notes that are true only about Norman Cousins. In the middle, write notes that are true for both.

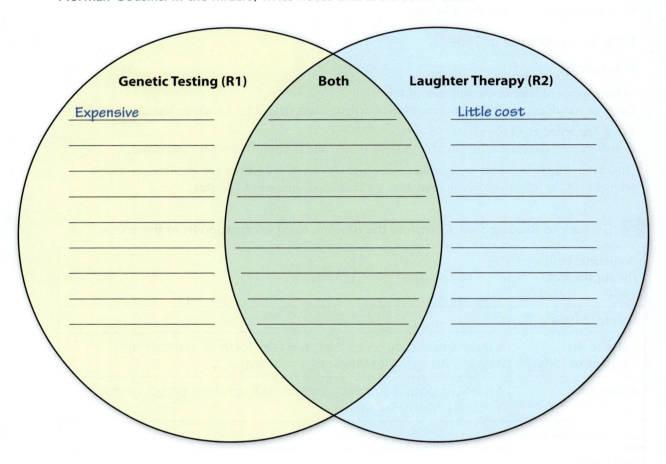

Genetic Testing (R1)

Expensive

Both

Laughter Therapy (R2)

Little cost

STEP 2: Synthesize

On a separate piece of paper, write a short paragraph explaining the similarities and differences between the genetic testing story and Norman Cousins's story. Use the information from Step 1.

GO TO MyEnglishLab *TO CHECK WHAT YOU LEARNED.*

3 FOCUS ON WRITING

VOCABULARY

REVIEW

Complete the paragraph using the words in the boxes.

advocates	impact	potential	revolutionize	risk factors

Many people believe that genetic testing will _____ the

practice of medicine. These _____, who support genetic testing,

1.

believe it has the _____ to save many lives. They point out that

2.

the _____ indicated by genetic test results can help patients

3.

choose an appropriate treatment plan. These supporters acknowledge that the

4.

_____ of a positive test could be devastating, but point out that with

5.

proper counseling this negative aspect of genetic testing will not be a problem.

consult	environment	linked	reliable	skeptical

However, others are _____ of the value of genetic testing. For

6.

one thing, some people don't believe it is _____. In addition,

7.

they note that without professional help to interpret the results, patients may

experience more harm than good from the tests. Of course, if patients were required to

_____ with their doctors about the results, this problem would be

8.

eliminated. Another problem they see is that some diseases are not caused by genetics.

They are _____ to the _____.

9.   10.

(continued on next page)

alternative	consensus	conventional	interaction

A further area of concern is that doctors still do not fully understand the

_____ between specific genes and how this affects the possibility
11.

for disease. Although there may never be _____ on the value
12.

of genetic testing, the way the public and the medical establishment view specific

treatments and therapies may change over time. Don't forget that when Norman

Cousins first used Laughter Therapy in the summer of 1964, it was definitely viewed as

a(n) _____ therapy. Nowadays, it is used in many hospitals around
13.

the world, and has entered the realm of _____ medicine.
14.

EXPAND

1 Work with a partner. Write **S** if the word pairs have a similar meaning and **D** if they have a different meaning.

1. reliable / dependable __S__

2. impact / interaction _____

3. conventional / alternative _____

4. interpret / elicit _____

5. revolutionize / change _____

6. environment / surroundings _____

7. treatment / diagnosis _____

8. linked / connected _____

9. elicit / produce _____

10. consensus / disagreement _____

11. consulted / asked advice of _____

12. potential / ability _____

13. aspect / factor _____

14. skeptical / doubtful _____

15. advocate / supporter _____

2 Write the word that best completes each sentence.

1. The _____ (impact / interaction) of a positive test result can be devastating for a patient.

2. A medical professional can help a patient _____ (elicit / interpret) genetic test results.

3. After the doctor told Norman Cousins he was suffering from ankylosing spondylitis, Cousins had to decide on his _____ *(treatment / diagnosis)*.

4. The idea of genetic testing is still a controversial topic. There is ongoing – *continuos progresive* _____ *(disagreement / consensus)* on when it should be used.

5. When Norman Cousins first used Laughter Therapy, it was considered a(n) _____ *(alternative / conventional)* treatment.

6. Norman Cousins watched comedy films as a way to _____ *(revolutionize / elicit)* positive emotions.

7. Some people are skeptical of Cousins's original _____ *(diagnosis / treatment)*. They don't think he was really suffering from a severe form of arthritis.

CREATE

Imagine that you are going to interview Kristen Powers or Norman Cousins. On a separate piece of paper, write four interview questions that you would like to ask. Use at least one word from the box in each question. Then work with a partner. Answer each other's questions as if you were Kristen Powers or Norman Cousins.

advocate	consensus	elicit	impact	link	revolutionize
alternative	consult	environment	interaction	potential	skeptical
aspect	conventional	factor	interpret	reliable	

■■■■■■■■■■■■■■■■■■■■■■■■■■ **GO TO** MyEnglishLab **FOR MORE VOCABULARY PRACTICE.**

GRAMMAR

1 Examine the sentences with a partner. Write **T** (true) or **F** (false) for the statements that follow the sentences.

    a. If Kristen Power's mother **hadn't died** of Huntington's disease, Kristen **might not have wanted** to be tested.

T as T   **b.** If Kristen's mother **had been** closer to her biological father, Kristen **could have known** that Huntington's disease ran in her family.

F as T.   **c.** If Norman Cousins **hadn't read** Hans Selye's book, Cousins **wouldn't have invented** Laughter Therapy.

(continued on next page)

1. In sentence *a*: Kristen's mother died. _____

   Kristen didn't want to be tested. _____

2. In sentence *b*: Kristen's mother wasn't close to her father. _____

   Kristen didn't know Huntington's disease ran in her family. _____

3. In sentence *c*: Norman Cousins didn't read Hans Selye's book. _____

   Norman Cousins invented Laughter Therapy. _____

PAST UNREAL CONDITIONALS

1. A **past unreal conditional** sentence has two clauses: the *if* **clause**, which gives the condition, and the **result clause**, which gives the result. The sentence can begin with the *if* clause or the result clause, and the meaning is the same.

2. There are two important things to notice in past unreal conditional sentences:
   - the use of the comma when the *if* clause comes at the beginning of the sentence
   - the verb forms used in each clause

If Clause	Result Clause
If + subject + past perfect,	subject + *would (not) have* + past participle *could (not) have* *might (not) have*
If Kristen's father **hadn't supported** her,	she **might not have wanted** a genetic test.

Result Clause	*If* Clause
Subject + *would (not) have* + past participle *could (not) have* *might (not) have*	*if* + subject + past perfect
Norman Cousins **might not have survived**	if he **hadn't used** Laughter Therapy.

3. The past unreal conditional talks about past unreal, untrue, or imagined conditions and their results. Both parts of the sentence describe events that are the opposite of what happened.

   Conditional statement: Kristen **could not have been tested if** the Human Genome Project **hadn't identified** all the genes in the human body.

   What really happened: Kristen was tested. The Human Genome Project did identify all the genes in the human body.

4. The past unreal conditional is often used to express regret about what really happened. In sentences like this, use *would have* in the result clause. To express possibility or uncertainty about the result, use *might have* or *could have* in the result clause.

2 Read the conditional sentences. Write **T** (true) or **F** (false) for each statement that follows the sentences.

1. If David Agus hadn't taken a genetic test, he wouldn't have discovered his risk for cardiovascular disease.

   __T__ He took a genetic test.

   __F__ He didn't discover his risk for cardiovascular disease.

2. If Norman Cousins had been healthy, he wouldn't have had to try Laughter Therapy.

   __F__ Norman Cousins was healthy.

   __F__ He didn't have to try Laughter Therapy.

3. Kristen's parents might not have been so worried if she had decided to go to a nearby college.

   __F__ Kristen decided to go to a nearby college.

   __T__ Her parents were worried.

4. The family wouldn't have understood Kristen's mother's symptoms if she hadn't been diagnosed with Huntington's disease.

   __T__ The family understood her symptoms.

   __F__ Kristen's mother was not diagnosed with Huntington's disease.

5. If there had been a famous advocate for Huntington's disease, Kristen might not have decided to make a documentary about her genetic testing.

   __T__ There is not a famous advocate for Huntington's disease.

   __T__ Kristen decided to make a documentary.

6. If Kristen hadn't had counseling, she might not have been prepared to deal with the test results.

   __F__ Kristen didn't have counseling.

   __T__ Kristen was prepared to deal with the test results.

7. If Norman Cousins hadn't survived for 26 more years, Laughter Therapy might not have received so much publicity.

   __T__ Norman Cousins survived for 26 more years.

   __T__ Laughter Therapy received a lot of publicity.

(continued on next page)

8. If Norman Cousins hadn't believed in a mind-body interaction, Laughter Therapy would not have been effective for him.

_F_ Norman Cousins didn't believe in a mind-body interaction.

_F_ Laughter Therapy didn't work for him.

3 Write a sentence about each situation. Use the past unreal conditional.

1. A female patient chose a treatment plan based on her genetic test results. She soon felt better. *If she hadn't chosen the correct treatment plan, she might not have felt better.*

2. Kristen Powers always wanted all the information available. She chose to be genetically tested. _____

_____

3. Norman Cousins read *The Stress of Life* by Hans Seyle. When Cousins was diagnosed with ankylosing spondylitis, he already had some ideas about the mind-body connection. _____

_____

4. Norman Cousins was sick. He tried to cure himself by using Laughter Therapy. He made a complete recovery. _____

_____

5. David Agus had a genetic test, and he found out that he was at risk for cardiovascular disease. His children made him change his diet. _If David hadn't had a genetic test, he wouldn't have found out, he was at risk_

6. Kristen's mom contacted her biological father. She learned that Huntington's disease ran in their family. _____

_____

7. Norman Cousins wasn't satisfied with his doctor's treatment plan. He developed his own Laughter Therapy treatment. _If Norman had been satisfied, he wouldn't have developed his own_

■■■■■■■■■■■■■■ **GO TO** MyEnglishLab **FOR MORE GRAMMAR PRACTICE AND TO CHECK WHAT YOU LEARNED.**

FINAL WRITING TASK

In this unit, you have read about genetic testing. Genetic testing can be ordered and interpreted by medical professionals. It can also be done at home by sending saliva samples to private companies. In these cases, there is often no consultation or interpretation offered.

You are going to *write a four-paragraph opinion essay expressing your opinion on making medical decisions based on genetic testing*. Use the vocabulary and grammar from the unit.*

PREPARE TO WRITE: Tree Mapping

Tree mapping helps you to organize ideas about a topic. The topic is written on the top line. Your ideas are written in branches leading from the topic. You can include reasons and evidence on smaller branches.

Complete the tree map. Then discuss your tree map with a partner. Notice how the ideas become more detailed as the branches extend.

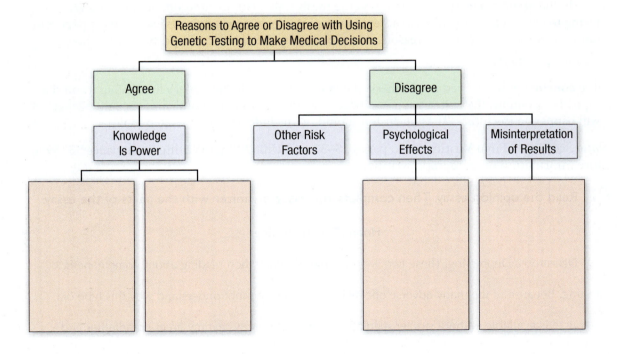

---

* For Alternative Writing Topics, see page 89. These topics can be used in place of the writing topic for this unit or as homework. The alternative topics relate to the theme of the unit but may not target the same grammar or rhetorical structures taught in the unit.

WRITE: An Opinion Essay

An **essay** is a group of paragraphs about one topic. An **opinion essay** is written to persuade or convince the reader that your opinion is "the right way of thinking." An opinion essay has three parts: the **introduction**, the **body**, and the **conclusion**.

INTRODUCTION

The **introduction** is the first paragraph of your essay. It includes a thesis statement that introduces the topic and states the main idea. The introduction should capture the readers' attention and make them want to read on. Many introductions begin with general background information on the topic and often end with the thesis statement as the last sentence of the paragraph. In an opinion essay, the thesis statement should state your opinion about the topic. *Tip*: Some writers find it helpful to write their introductory paragraph after they have completed their essay.

BODY

The **body** is one to three paragraphs. The body supports the thesis statement by giving examples, details, reasons, and facts to support the thesis statement. Each paragraph should start with a clearly stated topic sentence that relates to the thesis statement. In addition, because you are trying to convince your readers to accept your opinion, you need to give evidence to support your opinion. You also need to give reasons that explain why the evidence supports your opinion.

CONCLUSION

The **conclusion** should restate the thesis statement and include the writer's final thoughts on the topic. For example, the writer can give advice, suggest a solution to a problem, or predict what will happen in the future. The conclusion should not include new or unrelated topics.

Note: See Unit 1 Final Writing Task, pages 25–32 and Unit 2 Final Writing Task, pages 55–59 for more information on paragraph writing.

1 Read the opinion essay. Then complete the essay organizer with the parts of the essay.

Home Genetic Testing

Disastrous. Depressing. These two words come to mind when reading about home genetic testing. Because of the many adverse effects it can cause, I cannot understand why this type of 'service' is available without stricter regulations. First, let me say that my great-grandfather and my grandmother both suffered from Huntington's disease. I am a well-educated college graduate with a Master's degree in biology. I am thirty years old and so far show no signs of developing Huntington's. I don't think knowing whether I have the potential to develop an incurable disease will, in any way, enhance the quality of my life, nor would I be able to interpret the test results without the help of a medical professional. From this personal perspective, I believe that home genetic testing should be much more strictly regulated, if not prohibited all together.

I have witnessed the devastating effects that home genetic testing can have. A 55 year-old co-worker of mine whose family had a history of cancer submitted a DNA sample to an Internet genetic testing company. He was told that he had an 83% chance of developing colon cancer. He was convinced that because of this test result, he was going to die. After the test, this was all he could think about. This fear of impending tragedy made it impossible for him to concentrate on his work. As a result, his work suffered, and eventually he was let go. Finally, he went to a doctor and was retested. The doctor was able to interpret the results and explain to him that by taking the correct medications and changing his lifestyle, he could expect to live for many more years and very possibly never develop colon cancer. This is exactly why genetic testing must have stricter regulations.

The results of genetic testing are seen as infallible and definitive. Neither of these assumptions is true. Genetic testing is currently in its infancy, and even doctors and researchers do not fully understand the interaction between different genes. Very few diseases can be indicated by a single gene, so, until the link between diseases and multiple genes has been further studied, there is the potential for false positives and false negatives. In addition, environmental factors play a large part in who develops a disease and who doesn't. DNA is not the only factor affecting disease. For example, some cancers and other diseases are caused by exposure to chemicals or even to the sun. They have nothing to do with genetics. Knowledge is power, but it is important that that knowledge be accurate.

If we, as a society, truly believe that genetic testing has more benefits than negative effects, it is our responsibility to regulate it so all testing includes counseling and interpretation by professionals. In this way, patients can choose the treatment that is appropriate and effective for their genetic profile and lifestyle. Do we, as a society, truly believe that home genetic testing can be an effective method of choosing treatment without this professional counseling and interpretation?

Remember, the key is that to truly be able to make the best medical choices, medical professionals need to be involved in any decision.

2 Create an essay organizer like the one below with information for your opinion essay about making medical decisions based on genetic testing.

THREE PARTS OF AN ESSAY	NOTES
I. Introduction Thesis Statement:	**Background Information:**
II. Body Paragraph 1 Topic: **Body Paragraph 2** Topic:	**Body Paragraph 1** Support/Evidence: **Body Paragraph 2** Support/Evidence:
III. Conclusion Restate the Thesis: Final Thought/Wrap Up:	

3 Now write the first draft of your opinion essay. Use the information from Prepare to Write and your essay organizer to plan your essay. Make sure you have four paragraphs: an introductory paragraph, two body paragraphs, and one concluding paragraph. Be sure to use grammar and vocabulary from the unit.

REVISE: Writing Introductions and Hooks

The **introductory paragraph** is very important in all essays. The reader will decide whether or not your essay is worth the time and effort to read, depending on how interesting your introductory paragraph is. The introduction for an opinion essay should:

- state who you are and why your opinion matters;
- provide background information about the topic;
- provoke the reader's interest with a hook;
- include a thesis statement.

A **hook** is a sentence or two meant to grab the reader's attention. The hook could be:

- a shocking or surprising sentence;
- an anecdote (story);
- an interesting point;
- a quote.

1 Is there a hook in the essay "Home Genetic Testing" on page 84? What is it? Is it effective? Why or why not? Share your answer with a partner.

2 Read the hooks from introductions of opinion essays. Check (✓) the hooks you think are effective. Discuss your answers with a partner.

1. _____ "Genetic testing definitely saved my life! If I hadn't been tested, I would never have known that I had an elevated risk of type-2 diabetes. Because of my test results, I was able to change my lifestyle before developing the disease," says Dr. Neville Clynes of Columbia Presbyterian Hospital.

2. _____ People are becoming more interested in genetic testing. Genetic testing can be very useful in making medical decisions.

3. _____ Stop! Don't go to the doctor! You can cure all problems with genetic testing. Or at least that's what people who believe in genetic testing would have you believe.

4. _____ People should stick with conventional medicine because it has been proven. There is no proof that genetic testing is an effective tool in making medical decisions.

5. _____ There are some studies that prove genetic testing can help with medical decision-making. This is why genetic testing should be a regular part of medical treatment.

6. _____ Dr. Robert Grasberger finally, after almost 3 months of consultation, understood what was wrong with his patient. What had he done? He had ordered a genetic test; the results explained everything.

7. _____ Imagine a world in which people are given jobs entirely based on their genes. Marriages are permitted only between couples whose genetic matchup ensures a "perfect" child. This is the future genetic testing will bring! Is this the future you want?

3 Look at the introductory paragraph in your first draft. Make sure you have all the parts of an effective introduction. If you don't have a hook, add one.

GO TO MyEnglishLab *FOR MORE SKILL PRACTICE.*

EDIT: Writing the Final Draft

Go to MyEnglishLab and write the final draft of your essay. Carefully edit it for grammatical and mechanical errors, such as spelling, capitalization, and punctuation. Make sure you use some of the grammar and vocabulary from the unit. Use the checklist to help you write your final draft. Then submit your essay to your teacher.

FINAL DRAFT CHECKLIST

❏ Does the essay have an introduction, two body paragraphs, and a conclusion?

❏ Does the introduction include a thesis statement, background information about the topic, and a hook?

❏ Does each paragraph have a topic sentence?

❏ Do all the topic sentences support the thesis statement?

❏ Does the essay have a conclusion that restates the thesis and includes a final thought?

❏ Did you use the past unreal conditional correctly?

❏ Have you used vocabulary from the unit?

UNIT PROJECT

In this unit, you have read about using genetic testing to make medical decisions. Genetic testing is also used for a variety of other reasons. You are going to research two genetic testing companies and find out what services they offer. Do they provide information about ancestry, ethnicity, paternity, or different health-related issues? Follow these steps:

STEP 1: In small groups, report on two genetic testing companies. Do research on the Internet to complete the following information.

DOES THE COMPANY TEST FOR:	COMPANY #1: _____	COMPANY #2: _____
ANCESTRY?		
ETHNICITY?		
HEALTH? (EXPLAIN)		
PATERNITY?		
OTHER? _____		
MORE QUESTIONS		
WHAT IS THE COST?		
IS THE COST DIRECT TO CONSUMERS?		
HOW IS DNA COLLECTED AND SUBMITTED?		
IS COUNSELING AND INTERPRETATION PROVIDED?		
WHEN WAS THE COMPANY ESTABLISHED?		

STEP 2: Compile your information and prepare a poster or PowerPoint™ presentation with your findings. Present the information to the class.

ALTERNATIVE WRITING TOPICS

Write an essay about one of the topics. Use the vocabulary and grammar from the unit.

1. Ethicists worry that genetic testing will be used not just to help make medical decisions, but to discriminate against people. They foresee a world in which test results could prevent people from getting high-paying jobs, insurance and welfare benefits, and even being able to marry. Do you believe such uses of test results will happen and be a problem? If so, does this issue outweigh the potential medical benefits of genetic testing?

2. What do you think of Norman Cousins's Laughter Therapy? Do you think there is any truth to the idea of a mind-body interaction? Have you, or someone you know, had a medical experience where the mind was stronger than the body?

GO TO MyEnglishLab *TO WRITE ABOUT ONE OF THE ALTERNATIVE TOPICS, WATCH A VIDEO ABOUT A SLEEP CLINIC, AND TAKE THE UNIT 3 ACHIEVEMENT TEST.*

INSTINCT OR
Intellect?

1 FOCUS ON THE TOPIC

1. Do you think an animal's ability to imitate human behavior is a sign of high intelligence? Explain.

2. Do you think domesticated animals (dogs, horses, monkeys, parrots) that can be trained are more intelligent than animals living in the wild?

3. Work in a small group. Think of three animals you believe are intelligent. What do they do that makes them seem intelligent?

GO TO MyEnglishLab *TO CHECK WHAT YOU KNOW.*

VOCABULARY

Reading One is an excerpt from the book *Animals in Translation* by Temple Grandin. In this excerpt, the author discusses animal intelligence. Many other scientists and researchers are also studying animal intelligence.

Read the imaginary interview with Dr. Clara Bell, a noted researcher in animal intelligence. Complete the interview with synonyms for the words in parentheses. Use the words in the box.

achieve	approach	cognition	perception
acquired	behavior	controversy	unconscious
apparently	category	obvious	unique

Reporter: Dr. Bell, can you tell us a little bit about your work studying animal intelligence?

Dr. Bell: Sure, but let me start by saying that there has always been _____ about
1. (serious disagreement)

exactly what animal intelligence is. For many years, those animals that could act most human were

put into the _____ of 'intelligent.'
2. (group)

R: But that is not really the case, is it? Maybe you could give us some historical background.

Dr. B.: Well, during the 19th and early 20th centuries, people believed animals possessed

human emotions and mental abilities. Those animals that could be trained to imitate human

_____ were judged to be intelligent. In fact, shows involving these trained
3. (conduct)

animals were very popular. One such animal was the famous horse, Clever Hans, who seemed to

be able to solve mathematical problems. The _____ conclusion was that he was
4. (clear)

intelligent. Actually, Clever Hans was reacting to _____ movements made by
5. (done without realizing it)

people watching him. His answers had nothing to do with a knowledge of mathematics.

R: But doesn't the fact that an animal can be trained show that it is intelligent?

Dr. B.: Not really. When trying to assess animal intelligence, it is easy to confuse trainability with

_____. However, just because you can train an animal to perform certain
   6. (thinking)
behaviors doesn't mean it really knows what it is doing. Dogs at John F. Kennedy Airport in New

York sniff suitcases and signal their handlers when they perceive illegal drugs. These dogs are

_____ behaving in an intelligent manner, but they have no concept of drugs
   7. (seeming to be true)
being illegal.

R: So, what is actually happening?

Dr. B.: These dogs possess extreme _____ with their sense of smell, but this
                                           8. (use of senses)
doesn't necessarily make them intelligent. In fact, smell is not the only sense in which animals

outdo humans. For example, eagles can clearly see a rabbit when flying almost a mile above it.

They also see more colors than humans. In fact, eagles are not _____ in regard
                                                                    9. (special)
to extreme vision. Hammerhead sharks have a visual field of 360 degrees. In other words, they can

see fish both in front of and behind them, but again, this alone does not make them intelligent.

R: So, how can we really know if an animal is intelligent?

Dr. B.: As Albert Einstein said, "Everybody is a genius. But, if you judge a fish by its ability to

climb a tree, it'll spend its whole life believing it is stupid." Therefore, in order to assess animal

intelligence, it is important to test the animal in ways that are meaningful for their lives. This is the

_____ most researchers are using in the 21st century.
   10. (method)
R: Using this method, how do researchers today define intelligence?

Dr. B.: First of all, it is necessary to separate what animals are born with, instinct, from what they

have _____ by learning. Learning how to respond to new situations in ways
   11. (developed/obtained)
that allow them to _____ the goals that are important in their lives is the most
                      12. (accomplish)
effective measure of their intelligence.

■■■■■■■■■■■■■■■■■■■■■■■■■■■■■■■■■■■■■■ *GO TO* MyEnglishLab *FOR MORE VOCABULARY PRACTICE.*

PREVIEW

In Reading One, Temple Grandin talks about animals that are considered intelligent. She mentions two types of dogs that help people with medical problems, seizure[1] alert dogs and seizure response dogs. She also gives her own definition of what animal intelligence is.

Answer the questions with a partner.

1. What do you think the difference is between a seizure response dog and a seizure alert dog?

   _____

   _____

   _____

2. Which of these dogs might the author think is showing more intelligence?

   _____

   _____

   _____

3. How do you think Temple Grandin defines intelligence in animals?

   _____

   _____

   _____

Now read the article about animal intelligence.

---

[1] **seizure:** a short time when someone is unconscious and cannot control the movements of his or her body

EXTREME PERCEPTION AND ANIMAL INTELLIGENCE
By Temple Grandin and Catherine Johnson
(from *Animals in Translation*)

1   Many animals have extreme **perception**. Forensic[1] dogs are three times as good as any X-ray machine at sniffing out contraband,[2] drugs, or explosives, and their overall success rate is 90 percent.

2   The fact that dogs can smell things a person can't doesn't make him a genius; it just makes him a dog. Humans can see things dogs can't, but that doesn't make us smarter. But when you look at the jobs some dogs have invented for themselves using their advanced perceptual abilities, you're moving into the realm of true **cognition**, which is solving a problem under novel conditions. The seizure alert dogs are an example of an animal using advanced perceptual abilities to solve a problem no dog was born knowing how to solve. Seizure alert dogs are dogs who, their owners say, can *predict* a seizure before it starts. There's still **controversy** over whether you can train a dog to predict seizures, and so far people haven't had a lot of luck trying. But there are a number of dogs who have figured it out on their own. These dogs were trained as seizure response dogs, meaning they can help a person once a seizure has begun. The dog might be trained to lie on top of the person so he doesn't hurt himself, or bring the person his medicine or the telephone. Those are all standard helpful **behaviors** any dog can be trained to perform.

Seizure alert dog with owner Donna Jacobs

3   But some of these dogs have gone from responding to seizures to perceiving signs of a seizure ahead of time. No one knows how they do this because the signs are invisible to people. No human being can look at someone who is about to have a seizure and see (or hear, smell, or feel) what's coming. Yet one study found that 10 percent of owners said their seizure response dogs had turned into seizure alert dogs.

4   The *New York Times* published a terrific article about a woman named Connie Standley, in Florida, who has two huge Bouvier de Flandres dogs who predict her seizures about thirty minutes ahead of time. When they sense Ms. Standley is heading into a seizure, they'll do things like pull on her clothes, bark at her, or drag on her hand to get her to someplace safe so she won't get hurt when the seizure begins. Ms. Standley says they predict about 80 percent of her seizures. Ms. Standley's dogs **apparently** were trained as seizure alert dogs before they came to her, but there aren't many dogs in that **category**. Most seizure alert dogs were trained to respond to seizures, not predict seizures.

(continued on next page)

---

[1] **forensic:** relating to methods for finding out about a crime
[2] **contraband:** goods that are brought into or taken out of a country illegally

5   The seizure alert dogs remind me of Clever Hans. Hans was the world-famous German horse in the early 1900s whose owner, Wilhelm von Osten, thought he could count. Herr von Osten could ask the horse questions like, "What's seven and five?" and Hans would tap out the number twelve with his hoof. Hans could even tap out answers to questions like, "If the eighth day of the month comes on Tuesday, what is the date for the following Friday?" He could answer mathematical questions posed to him by complete strangers, too.

6   Eventually, a psychologist named Oskar Pfungst managed to show that Hans wasn't really counting. Instead, Hans was observing subtle, **unconscious** cues the humans had no idea they were giving off. He'd start tapping his foot when he could see it was time to start tapping; then he'd stop tapping his foot when he could see it was time to stop tapping. His questioners were making tiny, unconscious movements only Hans could see. The movements were so tiny the humans making them couldn't even *feel* them.

7   Dr. Pfungst couldn't see the movements, either, and he was looking for them. He finally solved the case by putting Hans's questioners out of view and having them ask Hans questions they didn't know the answers to themselves. It turned out Hans could answer questions only when the person asking the question was in plain view and already knew the answer. If either condition was missing, his performance fell apart.

8   Psychologists often use the Clever Hans story to show that humans who believe animals are intelligent are deluding themselves. But that's not the **obvious** conclusion as far as I'm concerned. No one has ever been able to *train* a horse to do what Hans did. Hans trained himself. Is the ability to read a member of a different species as well as Hans was reading human beings really a sign that he was just a "dumb animal" who'd been classically conditioned to stamp his hoof? I think there is more to it than that.

9   What makes Hans similar to seizure alert dogs is that both Hans and the dogs **acquired** their skills without human help. As I mentioned, to my knowledge, so far no one has figured out how to take a "raw" dog and teach it how to predict seizures. About the best a trainer can do is reward the dogs for helping when a person is having a seizure and then leave it up to the dog to start identifying signs that predict the onset of a seizure on his own. That **approach** hasn't been hugely successful, but some dogs do it. I think those dogs are showing superior intelligence the same way a human who can do something few other people can do shows superior intelligence.

10   What makes the actions of the seizure alert dogs, and probably of Hans, too, a sign of high intelligence—or high talent—is the fact that they didn't have to do what they did. It's one thing for a dog to start recognizing the signs that a seizure is coming; you might chalk that up to **unique** aspects of canine hearing, smell, or vision, like the fact that a dog can hear a dog whistle while a human can't. But it's another thing for a dog to start to recognize the signs of an impending seizure and *then decide to do something about it*. That's what intelligence is in humans; intelligence is people using their built-in perceptual and cognitive skills to **achieve** useful and sometimes remarkable goals.

MAIN IDEAS

1 Look again at your answers to the Preview questions on page 94. Were they correct? How did they help you understand the story?

2 Work with a partner. Read the statements and decide which three represent the main ideas of Reading One. Then discuss the reasons for your choice.

1. Many animals have extreme perception.

2. The author believes that true cognition, or intelligence, is defined as solving problems under novel conditions.

3. Ms. Standley's seizure alert dogs are able to predict about 80 percent of her seizures before they happen.

4. Some psychologists believe animals like Clever Hans are not really intelligent.

5. Some animals are able to read human behavior by observing subtle signs that even humans don't recognize.

6. The psychologist Oskar Pfungst was able to show that Hans wasn't really counting.

7. For Clever Hans to correctly answer a question, two conditions had to be met. He had to be able to see the person asking the question, and the person had to know the answer to the question.

8. The author believes seizure alert dogs and Clever Hans are showing high intelligence because they are able to recognize a sign and then choose to do something about it.

DETILS *Homework*

Reading One mentions many people and animals connected with animal intelligence. Match these people and animals with their descriptions.

1. __F__ Forensic dogs

2. __c__ Seizure response dogs

3. __d__ Seizure alert dogs

4. __b__ Ms. Connie Standley

5. __a__ Wilhelm von Osten

6. __g__ Oskar Pfungst

7. __e__ Clever Hans

a. Clever Hans's owner who thought he could count

b. Owner of two seizure alert dogs

c. Dogs that have been trained to help people once their seizures have started

d. Dogs that are able to predict seizures before they happen and warn their owners

e. German horse who apparently could count and answer questions

f. Dogs that use their sense of smell to find contraband such as drugs or explosives

g. Psychologist who proved that Clever Hans wasn't really counting

MAKE INFERENCES

HEDGING

Sometimes authors employ cautious language, called hedging, when they are not entirely sure that their information is supported by facts. This caution can be denoted by verb choice (*seem, look like, say, indicate, suggest, think, believe*), the use of modals (*might, may, could*), adverbs (*really, sometimes, possibly, perhaps, apparently*), adjectives (*most, some, obvious*), or certain phrases (*to my knowledge, as far as I'm concerned*).

Look at the example and read the explanation.

Look at the excerpt from paragraph 2. What cautious language does Temple Grandin use to show that the information may not be factual?

"The seizure alert dogs are an example of an animal using advanced perceptual abilities to solve a problem no dog was born knowing how to solve. Seizure alert dogs are dogs who, their owners say, can predict a seizure before it starts."

She doesn't say that seizure alert dogs *can* predict seizures, but rather that *their owners say* that they can.

Why does she include the phrase "their owners say"? She does not have scientific proof but only anecdotal evidence.

It is important to recognize hedging language as it indicates that the author is not 100 percent certain of the information he or she writes.

Look at the indicated paragraphs in Reading One and write the words or phrases used by the author that indicate hedging. Compare your answers with a partner's.

1. *Paragraph 4*

   What hedging language does the author use? _____

   Why does the author use this hedging language? _____

2. *Paragraph 5*

   What hedging language does the author use? _____

   Why does the author use this hedging language? _____

3. *Paragraph 6*

   What hedging language does the author use? _____

   Why does the author use this hedging language?_____

4. *Paragraph 8*

   What hedging language does the author use? _____

   Why does the author use this hedging language? _____

5. *Paragraph 9*

   What hedging language does the author use? _____

   Why does the author use this hedging language? _____

EXPRESS OPINIONS

Discuss the questions with a partner.

1. Oskar Pfungst proved that Clever Hans wasn't able to solve mathematical problems. Do you still believe that Hans showed intelligence by learning to "read" the movements of his questioners and audience members?

2. Temple Grandin feels that seizure alert dogs are showing signs of high intelligence. Others may say that what they do is really just an example of animals reacting based on instinct. What is your opinion? Explain.

3. Share examples of animal behavior you have witnessed that you think exhibit intelligence. Do these examples relate to Temple Grandin's idea of what animal intelligence is?

■ ■ ■ ■ ■ ■ ■ ■ ■ ■ ■ ■ ■ ■ ■ ■ ■ ■ ■ **GO TO** MyEnglishLab **TO GIVE YOUR OPINION ABOUT ANOTHER QUESTION.**

READ

Reading Two talks about why it is difficult to judge animal intelligence. One problem is that we often use human standards to evaluate animal intelligence.

1 Look at the boldfaced words in the reading and think about the questions.

1. Which words or phrases do you know the meanings of?

2. Can you use any of the words or phrases in a sentence?

2 Read the article, *How smart are animals?* As you read, notice the boldfaced vocabulary. Try to guess its meaning from the context.

How smart are animals?
By Gita Simonsen

1 We think that crows are smart, but what do we really know? Intelligence takes on diverse meanings for different species, and researchers think we are too prone to use human standards.

2 We've all heard talk of animal intelligence. We speak of crafty crows, clever foxes, discerning dolphins, and brilliant squids, but can we really use the word intelligence with regard to animals?

3 Researchers are concerned with learning mechanisms and other cognitive abilities—thinking, acquiring knowledge, **sensory** perception, memory, and language. These are the thought processes which form the basis for what we experience and comprehend of the world around us.

4 The problem is that we often look for human traits when we study animal behaviour. But what may be clever for us needn't be a **viable** attribute in other members of the animal kingdom.

5 "Animals are often given tasks based on human behaviour, such as the use of tools," says Peter Bøckman, a zoologist at the Natural History Museum in Oslo.

6 "If you turn it around and visualise a flock[1] of screaming chimpanzees hauling you up into a treetop and **confronting** you with a complicated problem involving nuts, how intelligently do you think you would perform?" he asks.

[1] **flock:** group

7   Indeed, we can easily fail to notice animal intelligence if we only look for human qualities, says Bjarne Braastad, an animal behaviourist at the Norwegian University of Life Sciences.

8   "It can be limiting if your point of departure is human traits. Animals have other abilities and can have elements of intelligence that humans lack," he says.

IQ by the kilo

9   We often measure intelligence, particularly in mammals, in accordance with how much the brain weighs in relation to total body weight. Humans lead by a long shot on this list, and the animal right behind us is not one of the apes—it's the dolphin.

10   Dolphins can thus be said to have the potential for very high intelligence, but we can't measure this optimally. Dolphins come from a completely different world, in a way, and have a language we can't fathom.[2] Communication is definitely a great barrier in the understanding of animal behaviour.

11   "Human intelligence is strongly linked to the language we use to communicate with one another," says Bøckman. "As long as we can't communicate with animals, it's really hard to decide how smart they are."

12   "Language is such an integral part of being human, and that makes it hard to avoid using human traits as a framework for considering the intelligence of animals."

Bees smarter than babies?

13   A group of scientists from Queen Mary University in London examined studies of animal intelligence to find out what scientists currently think about comparable cognition in different species.

14   They found that concepts and terms used to calculate the intelligence of animals are often borrowed from studies of human psychology.

15   One recent study charting the learning speed of bees, human infants, birds, and fish ended with the bees on top and our offspring[3] at bottom. So the researchers behind the experiment concluded that learning speed couldn't be used to measure intelligence— because humans weren't first across the finish line.[4]

16   The British scientists point out that the bees beat the babies in a learning test because the lab tested characteristics that bees have been perfecting during aeons[5] of evolutionary development.

17   In comparisons of intelligence among species, it's hard to avoid dealing trump cards[6] to one species or another.

18   "It's difficult to **discern** between reasoning, learned reflexes, and pure instincts. This makes it challenging for humans to create tests that don't remind animals of their natural behaviour," says Bøckman.

(continued on next page)

---

[2] **fathom:** understand what something means after thinking about it carefully

[3] **offspring:** someone's child or children

[4] **first across the finish line:** the winner

[5] **aeons:** extremely long periods of time

[6] **dealing trump cards to:** giving an advantage to

Bottom-up

19 The British scientists suggest what they term a bottom-up method. This differs from what they regard as top-bottom studies in animal behaviour research. In these, researchers pick out a cognitive **trait** and investigate how the animal's nerve system guides this trait.

20 With more emphasis on a bottom-up method, they would study the species' neural networks in attempts to perceive what uses these networks can have.

21 "The advantage of the bottom-up methods is that we can find traits that we didn't know existed in animals," says Braastad.

22 Bøckman comments that one of the challenges of this method is the extreme difficulty of investigating tiny neural circuitry in minuscule brains, such as in small insects.

Better tools required

23 There are now numerous studies that compare the cognitive capabilities of various species through investigations of their brains' neural circuitry. This has contributed toward answering questions about whether some of our human qualities can also exist in other species and help lay the groundwork for better comparisons.

24 For instance, multiple studies have been conducted with regard to facial recognition, imitation, social behaviour and empathy, and these can be found among many of our animal cousins.

25 "If the neural paths that are active in animals are the same ones acting in humans, we could have kindred[7] abilities," says Bøckman.

26 Gro Amdam conducts research on bees and what happens to their brains as they age. She is a professor at Arizona State University, and a researcher at the Norwegian University of Life Sciences.

27 "Scientists need to develop better tools, methods, and theories for comparing the brain skills in different species, but we are well on our way," she says.

---

[7] **kindred:** of the same family

COMPREHENSION

Two of the three answers for each question are correct. Cross out the answer that is incorrect.

1. It is difficult to define animal intelligence because

    a. animals have extreme sensory perception.

    b. intelligence has different meanings depending on the species of animal.

    c. what is intelligent for one species may not be for another.

2. The presence of human traits in animal behavior may not be a good indicator of animal intelligence because

    a. an animal's ability to imitate human behavior may have no value in its own life.

    b. animals may have other types of intelligence that humans lack.

    c. animals are given tasks based on human behavior.

3. Despite the fact that dolphins apparently are very intelligent based on their brain size, we cannot optimally measure their intelligence because

    a. we cannot use language to communicate.

    b. the concepts and terms used to calculate animal intelligence are often borrowed from human psychology.

    c. they live in a very different environment.

4. If humans do not come out on top in intelligence tests compared to animals, then researchers assume that

    a. it is due to comparable cognition in different species.

    b. there is something wrong with the assessment.

    c. the test must have been similar to the animal's, and not the human's, natural environment.

5. A new way of assessing animal intelligence, the bottom-up method, involves finding a cognitive trait and investigating how the neural system guides this trait. An advantage of this method is that

    a. many animals have minuscule brains.

    b. researchers can find traits they didn't even know existed in animals.

    c. it allows researchers to understand the use of neural networks.

6. For scientists to eventually be able to effectively assess animal intelligence, they need to

    a. develop better tools and methods.

    b. develop new theories.

    c. develop facial recognition.

■■■■■■■■■■■■■■■■■■■■■■■■■■■■■■■ *GO TO* MyEnglishLab *FOR MORE VOCABULARY PRACTICE.*

READING SKILL

1 Look at paragraphs 6–8 of Reading Two. The author uses a quotation in paragraph 8 to support a point she has made previously in the article. Which of her points is she supporting?

RECOGNIZING THE ROLE OF QUOTED SPEECH IN A READING

One way that authors use quotations is to support a point they are trying to make. By doing this, they are giving the reader an example of why their assertion is correct. Seeing how the quotation is related to an author's point helps the reader to understand the author's point and its importance.

In paragraph 11, the author quotes Peter Bøckman, a zoologist, who says, "As long as we can't communicate with animals [dolphins], it's really hard to decide how smart they are."

Which of the author's points does this quotation support?

Look at paragraph 10:

"Dolphins can thus be said to have the potential for very high intelligence, but we can't measure this optimally. Dolphins come from a completely different world, in a way, and have a language we can't fathom. Communication is definitely a great barrier in the understanding of animal behaviour."

The author's assertion that the quotation supports is "Communication is definitely a great barrier in the understanding of animal behaviour."

In fact, this statement is a paraphrase of the quotation that the author included for support. Seeing the connection between an author's point and the quotations he or she uses as support can give you a deeper understanding of the ideas that the author is presenting.

2 In Reading Two, Gita Simonsen often makes a statement about animal intelligence and then supports it with an appropriate quotation. Look at the quotations in the paragraphs indicated. Then look at the preceding paragraph(s) and underline the author's words that the quotations support. Compare your answers with a partner's.

1. *(paragraph 6):* "If you turn it around and visualise a flock of screaming chimpanzees hauling you up into a treetop and confronting you with a complicated problem involving nuts, how intelligently do you think you would perform?"

2. *(paragraph 18):* "It's difficult to discern between reasoning, learned reflexes and pure instincts. This makes it challenging for humans to create tests that don't remind animals of their natural behaviour."

3. *(paragraph 21):* "The advantage of the bottom-up method is that we can find traits that we didn't know existed in animals."

4. *(paragraph 25):* "If the neural paths that are active in animals are the same ones acting in humans, we could have kindred abilities."

GO TO MyEnglishLab *FOR MORE SKILL PRACTICE.*

STEP 1: Organize

Both Reading One (R1) and Reading Two (R2) talk about what intelligence is for animals, how it differs from instinct and learned reflexes, and the problems associated with assessing animal intelligence. Complete the chart with examples from each reading. Use the information in the box.

For humans, intelligence is linked to language, but we can't understand animal language. (dolphins)	Extreme perception	Using human standards (Clever Hans can count→ he is smart; He is not really counting→ he is a dumb animal.)
Looking for human traits and qualities (the use of tools)	Using extreme perception to invent jobs (Recognizing something and then deciding to act)	Learned reflexes
Diverse meanings for different species	Instinct	Brain weight of mammals

	R1	R2
WHAT IS INTELLIGENCE?		
PROBLEMS WITH ASSESSING ANIMAL INTELLIGENCE		1. 2. 3.
OTHER ABILITIES VS. INTELLIGENCE	Forensic dogs: Clever Hans:	Bees:

STEP 2: Synthesize

Read the imaginary interview with the authors of Reading One and Reading Two. Complete the interview using information from Step 1 and from the readings.

REPORTER: Today we are lucky to have with us two animal experts, Temple Grandin and Gita Simonsen. They are both especially interested in the question of animal intelligence. Ms. Grandin, how would you define animal intelligence?

TEMPLE GRANDIN: Let me start by saying that many people confuse extreme perception with intelligence. Many animals have extreme perception at least compared to humans, but that alone _____. I think seizure alert dogs are a good example of animal intelligence because

_____.

This is not something they need to do or have been taught to do, but something that _____.
This is what shows intelligence.

GITA SIMONSEN: I definitely agree that seizure alert dogs are showing intelligence, but, in my opinion, what can be considered intelligence in animals

_____.

REPORTER: How can animal intelligence be assessed?

TEMPLE GRANDIN: One problem that we have in assessing animal intelligence is that

_____

_____.

GITA SIMONSEN: Yes, I agree. For example, _____

_____.

TEMPLE GRANDIN: In the case of the "counting" horse, Clever Hans, many people judged him to be intelligent when _____

_____. However, as soon as they realized that he was getting unconscious cues from the audience, then _____. I don't agree with them. I think Clever Hans was showing intelligence because _____

_____.

GITA SIMONSEN: That's a good point. However, let me say one more thing about the problems with assessing animal intelligence. Because for humans intelligence is so linked to language, the fact that we don't understand animal language _____.

REPORTER: Are all of these apparently amazing things that animals are capable of doing really a sign of intelligence, or are there other explanations for their actions?

TEMPLE GRANDIN: Sometimes there are other explanations. For example, forensic dogs that work at airports looking for explosives or illegal drugs _____

_____.

GITA SIMONSEN: Yes, similarly, a recent test of intelligence across species (including humans) found bees to be smarter than all other species including humans. However, the explanation might not be intelligence, but rather _____.

REPORTER: Thank you both very much. I am afraid we have run out of time. I know I have learned a lot, and I am sure our viewers have, too. Thanks again.

■■■■■■■■■■■■■■■■■■■■■■■■■■■■■■■■■■ *GO TO* MyEnglishLab *TO CHECK WHAT YOU LEARNED.*

VOCABULARY

REVIEW

Two of the three words in each row have similar meanings to the boldfaced word from the reading. Cross out the word that does not belong. If you need help, use a dictionary.

READING ONE

1. **achieve**	assess	accomplish	attain
2. **acquire**	obtain	need	gain
3. **apparently**	seemingly	allegedly	visually
4. **approach**	method	attempt	procedure
5. **behavior**	ability	action	conduct
6. **category**	section	group	aspect
7. **cognition**	understanding	instinct	intelligence
8. **controversy**	consensus	disagreement	debate
9. **obvious**	clear	evident	possible
10. **perception**	thought	awareness	observation
11. **unconscious**	cautious	involuntary	unintentional
12. **unique**	singular	normal	solitary

READING TWO

13. **confront**	remind	challenge	present
14. **discern**	differentiate	figure out	dislike
15. **sensory**	auditory	visual	habitual
16. **trait**	characteristic	path	feature
17. **viable**	usable	applicable	achievable

EXPAND

Many academic words, especially those used in the sciences, have Latin or Greek roots. For example, the word *psychologist* comes from the Greek root, *psych*, meaning *mind*. A **psych**ologist is someone who is trained to study the mind and how it works.

Work with a partner to complete the chart.

1. For each root (column 1), find a word with that root in the reading(s) and paragraph(s) indicated.

2. Write the word in column 4.

3. Guess the meaning of the word using the meaning of the root and the context of the sentence in which you found the word. Write the meaning in column 5.

4. In the last column, write other words you can think of with the same root. If you need help, use a dictionary. Share your answers with the class.

1 ROOT	2 MEANING	3 READING and PARAGRAPH(S)	4 WORD	5 MEANING	6 OTHER WORDS WITH THE SAME ROOT
1. PSYCH-	mind	R1-6	psychologist	Someone who is trained to study the mind	psychic
2. COGNI-	know / learn	R1-2, 10			
		R2-3, 13			
3. DICT-	say / tell	R1-2			
4. ACT-	do	R1-10			
		R2-25			
5. CEPT-	taken	R1-2			
		R2-14			
6. NUMER-	number	R2-23			
7. NOV-	new	R1-2			
8. SENS-	feeling	R1-4			
		R2-3			
9. CENT-	one hundred	R1-3			
10. SCI-	know	R1-6			
		R2-7			
11. NEUR-	nerve	R2-20			

CREATE

On a separate piece of paper, write five questions about Clever Hans. Use at least one word from the Review or Expand sections in each question. Then exchange papers with a partner and answer the questions. You can write or discuss your answers.

GO TO MyEnglishLab *FOR MORE VOCABULARY PRACTICE.*

GRAMMAR

1 Examine the sentences and answer the questions with a partner.

    a. Animals have other abilities and can have elements of intelligence **that humans lack**.

    b. No human being can look at someone **who is about to have a seizure** and see (or hear, smell, or feel) what's coming.

    c. Oskar Pfungst thought back proudly on the afternoon **when he was finally able to figure out how Clever Hans was able to answer the questions**.

  1. In sentence *a*, what elements of intelligence is the writer describing?

  2. In sentence *b*, what type of person does the writer say no human being can look at and see what's coming?

  3. In sentence *c*, which afternoon is the writer describing?

  4. What words begin the boldfaced phrases? Are the words that come just before these phrases verbs, adjectives, nouns, or adverbs?

IDENTIFYING ADJECTIVE CLAUSES

1. Identifying adjective clauses, sometimes called restrictive relative clauses, are groups of words (phrases) that act as adjectives to describe or identify a noun. These phrases come directly after the nouns they describe and begin with relative pronouns that refer to the noun. Sentences with adjective clauses can be seen as a combination of two shorter sentences about the same noun.

He had **a horse**. + **The horse** could answer mathematical questions.
= He had **a horse that could answer mathematical questions**.

Clever Hans lived in **a small town**. + **The small town** was in Germany.
= **The small town where Clever Hans lived** was in Germany.

2. Identifying adjective clauses begin with a **relative pronoun**. The noun that the clause describes determines the choice of pronoun.

who = person or people (and sometimes animals)
which = thing or things
that = thing, things, person, or people (less formal than *which* or *who*)
when = a time or times
where or *in which* = a place or places
whose or *in whose* = possession

3. Remember that the relative pronoun replaces the noun it describes; the noun is not repeated.

I saw **the horse**. + The scientist was testing **the horse**.
= I saw **the horse** *that* the scientist was testing.

INCORRECT: I saw **the horse** *that* the scientist was testing **the horse**.

2 Read the sentences and circle *Correct* or *Incorrect* for the underlined relative pronouns. If the pronoun is correct, add an alternative, or other, pronoun that could also be used. If the pronoun is incorrect, write one or two pronouns that could be used.

1. The scientist <u>which</u> observed Clever Hans wrote a book.

   Correct   Alternative: _____

   (Incorrect)   Correction(s): _____*who or that*_____

2. The museum <u>where</u> Peter Bøckman works is in Oslo, Norway.

   Correct   Alternative: _____

   Incorrect   Correction(s): _____

3. Seizure alert dogs are dogs <u>whose</u> can predict a seizure before it starts.

   Correct   Alternative: _____

   Incorrect   Correction(s): _____

4. Hans was the world-famous horse <u>which</u> owner, Wilhelm von Osten, was a retired school teacher.

   Correct   Alternative: _____

   Incorrect   Correction(s): _____

5. On the day <u>when</u> Oskar Pfungst discovered Clever Hans's secret, Wilhelm von Osten was visiting his sister.

   Correct   Alternative: _____

   Incorrect   Correction(s): _____

6. Zoologists are now developing tests <u>that</u> assess animal intelligence more accurately.

   Correct   Alternative: _____

   Incorrect   Correction(s): _____

7. Many people <u>when</u> study animals are convinced that they are able to understand some human language.

   Correct   Alternative: _____

   Incorrect   Correction(s): _____

(continued on next page)

8. Oskar Pfungst put the questioners in a place <u>which</u> they could not be seen by Clever Hans.

Correct   Alternative: _____

Incorrect   Correction(s): _____

3 Combine each pair of sentences into one sentence using an identifying adjective clause.

  1. **a.** Clever Hans was trained by a retired school teacher.

    b. The school teacher had taught science for many years.

    Clever Hans was trained by a retired school teacher who had taught science for many years.

  2. **a.** The afternoon was cold and rainy.

    b. That afternoon Clever Hans was ready to perform in front of an audience.

    The afternoon when Clever Hans was ready to perform in front of an audience was cold and rainy.

  3. **a.** Binti the gorilla is best known for an amazing incident.

    b. The incident occurred on August 16, 1996.

    _____

    _____

  4. **a.** I spoke with a man.

    b. The man had trained dolphins and killer whales.

    _____

    _____

  5. **a.** Psychologists study many animals.

    b. Animals live in zoos.

    _____

    _____

  6. **a.** I saw my friend.

    b. Her dog could predict seizures before they started.

    _____

    _____

7. a. We saw the dolphin.

   b. The dolphin performed some spectacular feats.

   _____

   _____

8. a. The psychologist had studied at the University of Berlin.

   b. The psychologist developed a new test of animal intelligence.

   _____

   _____

9. a. The morning was sunny and hot.

   b. That morning the dogs saved Ms. Standley.

   _____

   _____

10. a. The contraband was in an old brown suitcase.

   b. It was discovered by the forensic dog.

   _____

   _____

■ ■ ■ ■ ■ ■ ■ ■ ■ ■   *GO TO* MyEnglishLab *FOR MORE GRAMMAR PRACTICE AND TO CHECK WHAT YOU LEARNED.*

FINAL WRITING TASK

In this unit, you read two passages on animal intelligence. How would you summarize the important information from one of the readings?

You are going to **write a summary of Reading One as if you were a journalist writing for a newspaper or magazine**. Use the vocabulary and grammar from the unit.*

PREPARE TO WRITE: Asking and Answering Wh- Questions

To help you to plan your summary of Reading One, you will **ask and answer the Wh- questions Who, What, Where, When, Why,** and **How**. Many writers, especially journalists, use the Wh-questions when they are writing a summary of an important story or news event.

---

* For Alternative Writing Topics, see page 121. These topics can be used in place of the writing topic for this unit or as homework. The alternative topics relate to the theme of the unit but may not target the same grammar or rhetorical structures taught in the unit.

Write one or two questions for each *Wh-* question. Share your questions with a partner and answer them.

Q: What: What is the main idea (paragraph) or thesis (essay or longer article)? What does the person have to say? What issues are discussed?

A: _____

_____

Q: Who: Who wrote the article or passage?

 A: _____

_____

Q: When: _____

_____

A: _____

_____

STORY

Q: Where: _____

_____

A: _____

_____

Q: Why: _____

_____

A: _____

_____

Q: How: _____
A: _____

WRITE: A Summary

A **summary** is a shortened version of a text that focuses on the thesis or main idea. It does not include many details or examples. It does not include personal opinions. Here are some important points:

1. **Read and reread the text**. As you read, think about the *Wh-* questions. Make sure you understand the text.

2. **Highlight or underline the thesis**. To find the thesis, think about the purpose of the text. What is the author's main idea?

3. **Rewrite the thesis in one sentence**. Use your own words.

4. **Continue reading**. Highlight the main idea and key words and phrases for each paragraph. Write one-sentence summaries in your own words for each paragraph.

5. **Check your sentences against the text**. Again, use your own wording.

6. **Make sure you have not included irrelevant examples or your own opinion**.

7. **Write your summary**.

8. **Return later and check it again** with fresh eyes.

9. **Polish summary for flow**; it needs to read well.

1 Read the summary of Reading Two and answer the questions.

In *How smart are animals?*, author Gita Simonsen discusses the problems scientists face in assessing animal intelligence. The first problem is defining animal intelligence. Too often our tests of animal intelligence are based on how well animals can imitate human behavior. This method does not recognize other elements of intelligence that animals use in their own lives that humans may not possess.

Another method that scientists use with mammals is brain weight as a proportion of total weight. This measurement finds dolphins high in intelligence. However, since human intelligence is linked to language, and we can't communicate with dolphins, or other animals, it is not possible to fully assess their intelligence.

A further problem of animal intelligence testing, especially when comparing intelligence across species, is the assumption that humans must be smarter than any other animal. In a study where bees outperformed human babies, scientists reassessed the test itself. They concluded that the test must have been flawed, and the bees came out on top because of instinct, not intelligence.

A new method of assessment involves studying animals' neural networks and trying to figure out what traits they are designed to allow. This helps scientists to identify traits they had not even thought about. Nevertheless, the minuscule size of some animal brains makes this method very challenging.

Simonsen concludes by quoting Gro Amdam, a professor at Arizona State University, who states, "Scientists need to develop better tools, methods, and theories for comparing the brain skills in different species, but we are well on our way."

1. Who is the author? What is the title of the article? _____

   _____

2. What is the thesis? _____

   _____

(continued on next page)

3. What are some of the problems of testing an animal's intelligence? _____

_____

_____

4. What is the author's conclusion about testing animal intelligence? _____

_____

_____

2 Before you begin to write a summary of Reading One, practice by summarizing sections of the reading, individual paragraphs, or groups of paragraphs. For paragraphs 1–7, circle the sentence that best describes the main idea. For paragraphs 8–10, write the one-sentence summary yourself. Check your answers with a partner's.

1. Read paragraph 1 of Reading One. Which statement best describes the main idea of the paragraph?

   a. Animals that display a deep understanding of the world around them are plentiful.

   b. There are some dogs that can sniff out dangerous materials at a very successful rate.

   c. Some forensic dogs are so good at their jobs that they are much better than X-ray machines.

2. Read paragraph 2. Which statement best describes the main idea of the paragraph?

   a. Some seizure response dogs have trained themselves to be seizure alert dogs.

   b. Dogs who are truly intelligent will apply their thinking skills to new situations.

   c. Seizure response dogs are trained to save their owners' lives.

3. Read paragraphs 3 and 4. Which statement best describes the main idea of the paragraphs?

   a. Connie Standley's dogs predict her seizures before they happen.

   b. No one knows how seizure response dogs read signs given off by humans before a seizure.

   c. Some seizure response dogs have become seizure alert dogs without any training.

4. Read paragraphs 5, 6, and 7. Which statement best describes the main idea of the paragraphs?

    a. Clever Hans was not really counting but was able to detect and understand human signs that even humans could not see, just as seizure alert dogs can.

    b. Oskar Pfungst, a psychologist, eventually proved that Clever Hans was not really counting.

    c. Clever Hans looked like he was counting but was really just tapping his foot until he knew to stop.

5. Read paragraph 8. Write a one-sentence summary of the main idea.

_____

_____

6. Read paragraphs 9 and 10. Write a one-sentence summary of the main idea.

_____

_____

3 Now write your first draft of your summary of Reading One. Use the information from Prepare to Write and Write to plan your summary. Make sure you state the thesis and eliminate any unimportant details. Be sure to use grammar and vocabulary from the unit.

REVISE: Paraphrasing

Summary writing often requires the writer to restate an author's ideas. It is very important to restate the author's ideas in your own words while keeping true to the author's ideas. This is called **paraphrasing**. (*Note:* When you choose to use an author's direct words, you must use quotation marks.)

AUTHOR'S OWN WORDS	PARAPHRASED TEXT
"A group of scientists from Queen Mary University in London examined studies of animal intelligence to find out what scientists currently think about comparable cognition in different species. One recent study, charting the learning speed of bees, human infants, birds and fish, ended with the bees on top and our offspring at bottom. So the researchers behind the experiment concluded that learning speed couldn't be used to measure intelligence—because humans weren't first across the finish line. The British scientists point out that the bees beat the babies in a learning test because the lab tested characteristics that bees have been perfecting during aeons of evolutionary development."	A further problem of animal intelligence testing is comparing intelligence across species. Scientists from Queen Mary University in London recently studied the learning speed of different species. When bees outperformed all the other species, including human babies, scientists reassessed the test itself. They concluded that the test must have been flawed and the bees came out on top because of instincts they had developed over millions of years, not intelligence.

When using a direct quote, use these punctuation rules:

1. Lift the quote directly as is from the text. Do not change the capitalization or punctuation.

2. Place a comma before the quote: Simonsen concludes by quoting Gro Amdam who states, "Scientists need to develop better tools, methods, and theories for comparing the brain skills in different species, but we are well on our way."

3. Place the final punctuation mark at the end of the sentence before the final quotation mark: Simonsen concludes by quoting Gro Amdam who states, "Scientists need to develop better tools, methods, and theories for comparing the brain skills in different species, but we are well on our way."

When paraphrasing or quoting, use a variety of reporting verbs to introduce an author's ideas:

says	*notes*
tells	*mentions*
acknowledges	*thinks*
concedes	*writes*
states	*believes*
explains	*concludes*

When paraphrasing, first think of the main idea or what the author is trying to tell you. Think of ways to say the same thing using your own words. Do not just replace words in a sentence with synonyms.

Original	**Incorrect Paraphrase**
Many animals have extreme perception.	Many animals have excellent awareness.

Rules for Paraphrasing

1. Read the original text. Make sure you understand it. Highlight the main idea and key words or phrases.

2. Read the text again. Put the text aside.

3. Write the idea in your own words without looking at the text. Try to use different words than the text.

4. Try to reorder the ideas in the sentence. Start with the middle or the end. Put the paraphrased text aside for a while.

5. With fresh eyes, check your paraphrased sentence against the original. Make sure it is not too close to the original.

Original	**Correct Paraphrase**
Many animals have extreme perception.	Animals that display a deep understanding of their world are common.

1 Paraphrase the sentences from Reading Two in your own words.

1. The problem is that we often look for human traits when we study animal behaviour. But what may be clever for us needn't be a viable attribute in other members of the animal kingdom.

   _____

   _____

2. "Human intelligence is strongly linked to the language we use to communicate with one another," says Bøckman. "As long as we can't communicate with animals, it's really hard to decide how smart they are."

   _____

   _____

(continued on next page)

3. There are now numerous studies that compare the cognitive capabilities of various species through investigations of their brains' neural circuitry. This has contributed toward answering questions about whether some of our human qualities can also exist in other species and help lay the groundwork for better comparisons.

_____

_____

2 Look at your first draft. Make sure you have paraphrased the author of Reading One using your own words. Check against the original text and make any changes necessary. Add a quote if you think it will be effective. Watch your punctuation with your quote!

GO TO MyEnglishLab FOR MORE SKILL PRACTICE.

EDIT: Writing the Final Draft

Go to MyEnglishLab and write the final draft of your summary. Carefully edit it for grammatical and mechanical errors, such as spelling, capitalization, and punctuation. Make sure you use some of the grammar and vocabulary from the unit. Use the checklist to help you write your final draft. Then submit your essay to your teacher.

FINAL DRAFT CHECKLIST

❑ Does the summary include the author's name and the title of the reading?

❑ Does the summary include a thesis statement?

❑ Does the summary answer some of the _Wh-_ questions?

❑ Is the summary in your own words?

❑ Did you use a variety of reporting verbs?

❑ If you are using quotes, are they properly punctuated?

❑ Did you use identifying adjective clauses?

❑ Have you used the vocabulary from the unit?

UNIT PROJECT

In this unit, you have read about animal intelligence and a few specific "intelligent" animals: Clever Hans and Connie Standley's dogs. Other famous animals have equally remarkable abilities. From the list below, choose an "intelligent" animal to research. Take notes and write a report based on your findings. Follow these steps:

STEP 1: Use the Internet and other sources to research an animal from the list.

Koko the gorilla	Twiggy the squirrel
Bimbo the killer whale	Jonathan and Chantek the orangutans
Betty the crow	Lulu the pig
Ruby the elephant	Washoe the chimpanzee
Akeakemai the dolphin	Siri the elephant
Michael the gorilla	Orky and Corky the killer whales
Alex the parrot	Willow the dog
Rio the sea lion	

STEP 2: Write a summary of the information you find, including answers to some of the *Wh-* questions. Conclude by explaining whether you think the animal is exhibiting intelligence and why.

STEP 3: Combine your research with all of your classmates' research and create a class book.

ALTERNATIVE WRITING TOPICS

Write an essay about one of the topics. Use the vocabulary and grammar from the unit.

1. Noted animal intelligence expert Dorothy Hinshaw believes, "The things that are important to animals can be different than those that matter to humans. When studying animals, we must test them in situations that have meaning for their lives, not ours, and not just look to see how much they resemble us." Think of a specific animal or group of animals. What situations would have meaning for them? Why? How could you test them in these situations?

2. "If a rabbit defined intelligence the way man does, then the most intelligent animal would be a rabbit, followed by the animal most willing to obey the commands of a rabbit."
   —Robert Brault (writer, born 1938)

   How does the quotation apply to the problems of testing animal intelligence that is discussed in Reading One and Reading Two?

■■■■■■■■■■■■■■■■■■■ *GO TO* MyEnglishLab *TO WRITE ABOUT ONE OF THE ALTERNATIVE TOPICS, WATCH A VIDEO ABOUT TALKING TO ANIMALS, AND TAKE THE UNIT 4 ACHIEVEMENT TEST.* ■■■■■■■■■

TOO MUCH OF A GOOD Thing?

1. It has been projected that by the year 2050, the average lifespan will reach 125, and by 2087 it will be 150! Do you think living longer is a good thing? Why or why not? Think about how such issues as relationships, marriage, family structure, and career might be affected.

2. Immortality means living forever. Do you know stories or myths about the desire or search for immortality?

3. If scientists could create a pill that would allow you to live twice as long while staying healthy, would you take it?

GO TO MyEnglishLab *TO CHECK WHAT YOU KNOW.*

READING ONE DEATH DO US PART

VOCABULARY

Reading One is a story about Marilisa and her husband, Leo. Read the letter Marilisa wrote to a friend about Leo. Then choose the definition that best defines each boldfaced word.

1. **a.** mean
   b. energetic
   c. lazy

2. **a.** on time
   b. well dressed
   c. considerately

3. **a.** understandably
   b. incredibly
   c. to some extent

4. **a.** difficult
   b. fascinating
   c. different

5. **a.** slightly
   b. always
   c. completely

6. **a.** complicated
   b. impressive
   c. terrible

7. **a.** doing things slowly after much thinking
   b. doing things because somebody said to
   c. doing things quickly without thinking

Dear Joan,

I know you're worried about my marrying Leo, but please realize that he has many good qualities. For example, he is quite **(1) vigorous**. Despite his age, he still exercises for hours and then works in the garden. In addition, he's very thoughtful. Unlike some of my friends, he always arrives **(2) punctually**. If he says he'll meet me at 10 o'clock, he'll be there exactly at 10.

He is also **(3) immeasurably** wise. He has so much knowledge and experience and is interested in so many **(4) disparate** subjects like Greek history, diamond mining, dinosaurs, and alternative medicine. Even though they're not related, he enjoys them all. I find this quality **(5) utterly** fascinating, and I'm totally amazed by his vast knowledge. Leo really has had an **(6) awesome** life when you think about everything he's done. It's so exciting living with someone who has had so many incredible experiences.

However, I'm not claiming that Leo is perfect. For one thing, he can be very **(7) impetuous**. Just last week, he bought a new car. He didn't even think about the fact that we needed that money to pay our credit card bills!

8. **a.** annoying
   b. friendly
   c. interesting

9. **a.** pleasant
   b. very unfriendly
   c. unhappy

10. **a.** rude or arrogant
    b. modest or shy
    c. admired or respected

11. **a.** accustomed to
    b. feeling love or
       affection for
    c. drawn toward

12. **a.** maybe
    b. currently
    c. in the end

Furthermore, at times, he can be **(8) insufferable**. I was trying to watch television last night, and he was constantly interrupting me to ask questions. Couldn't he understand that I was trying to concentrate on the show? His family is another problem. Take his ex-wife, Katrin, for example. I don't understand why he ever married her. Leo, of course, is very nice and friendly to everyone.

She, however, always seems very **(9) chilly**, especially toward me. Also, one of his sons from a previous marriage can be very **(10) presumptuous**. He expects me to do things for him just because I am now married to his father . . . even though I barely know him! His daughter, however, is lovely. I am really quite **(11) fond of** her. I think you would really like her, too.

Despite my complaints, I know that Leo is **(12) ultimately** the best first husband I could ever wish for, so don't worry. I'm sure we'll always be happy together. Joan, I hope all is well with you.

Love,

Marilisa

GO TO MyEnglishLab **FOR MORE VOCABULARY PRACTICE.**

You are going to read a science fiction story. Science fiction is a genre of writing that describes imaginary future developments in science and technology and their effects on people. It often includes elements that seem familiar to our lives today, making the story seem "real."

Read the first two paragraphs of *Death Do Us Part*. Then work with a partner to answer the questions.

1. What do you think was "her first, his seventh"?

2. What is happening with Marilisa and Leo?

3. Where and when do you think this story takes place?

4. What seems real?

5. What seems unreal?

6. What do you think "the Process" is?

Now read the rest of the story.

DEATH DO US PART

By Robert Silverberg

1   It was her first, his seventh. She was thirty-two, he was three hundred and sixty-three: the good old May/December[1] number. They honeymooned in Venice, Nairobi, the Malaysia Pleasure Dome, and one of the posh[2] L-5 resorts, a shimmering glassy sphere with round-the-clock sunlight and waterfalls that tumbled like cascades of diamonds, and then they came home to his lovely sky-house suspended on tremulous guy-wires[3] a thousand meters above the Pacific to begin the everyday part of their life together.

2   Her friends couldn't get over it. "He's ten times your age!" they would exclaim. "How could you possibly want anybody that old?" Marilisa admitted that marrying Leo was more of a lark[4] for her than anything else. An impulsive thing: a sudden **impetuous** leap. Marriages weren't forever, after all—just thirty or forty years and then you moved along. But Leo was sweet and kind and actually

---

[1] **May/December:** term used to describe a romantic relationship where there is a big difference in the ages of the two people
[2] **posh:** expensive and used by rich people
[3] **tremulous guy-wires:** shaking cables (metal ropes)
[4] **lark:** something you do to amuse yourself or as a joke

quite sexy. And he had wanted her so much. He genuinely did seem to love her. Why should his age be an issue? He didn't appear to be any older than thirty-five or so. These days you could look as young as you like. Leo did his Process faithfully and **punctually**, twice each decade, and it kept him as dashing and **vigorous** as a boy.

3   There were little drawbacks, of course. Once upon a time, long, long ago, he had been a friend of Marilisa's great-grandmother: They might have even been lovers. She wasn't going to ask. Such things sometimes happened, and you simply had to work your way around them. And then also he had an ex-wife on the scene, Number Three, Katrin, two hundred and forty-seven years old and not looking a day over thirty. She was constantly hovering[5] about. Leo still had warm feelings for her. "A wonderfully dear woman, a good and loyal friend," he would say. "When you get to know her, you'll be as **fond of** her as I am." That one was hard, all right. What was almost as bad, he had children three times Marilisa's age and more. One of them—the next-to-youngest, Fyodor—had an **insufferable** and **presumptuous** way of winking[6] and sniggering[7] at her. "I want you to meet our father's newest toy," Fyodor said of her once, when yet another of Leo's centenarian sons, previously unsuspected by Marilisa, turned up. "We get to play with her when he's tired of her." Someday Marilisa was going to pay him back[8] for that.

4   Still and all, she had no serious complaints. Leo was an ideal first husband: wise, warm, loving, attentive, and generous. She felt nothing but the greatest tenderness for him. And then too he was so **immeasurably** experienced in the ways of the world. If being married to him was a little like being married to Abraham Lincoln or Augustus Caesar, well, so be it: They had been great men, and so was Leo. He was endlessly fascinating. He was like seven husbands rolled into one. She had no regrets, none at all, not really.

5   In the spring of eighty-seven they go to Capri for their first anniversary. Their hotel is a reconstructed Roman villa on the southern slope of Monte Tiberio: alabaster wall frescoed in black and red, a brilliantly colored mosaic of sea-creatures in the marble bathtub, a broad travertine terrace that looks out over the sea. They stand together in the darkness, staring at the **awesome** sparkle of the stars. A crescent moon slashes across the night. His arm is around her; her head rests against his breast. Though she is a tall woman, Marilisa is barely heart-high to him.

Blue Grotto

6   "Tomorrow at sunrise," he says, "we'll see the Blue Grotto.[9] And then in the afternoon we'll hike down below here to the Cave of the Mater Magna. I always get a shiver when I'm there. Thinking about the ancient islanders who

(continued on next page)

---

[5] **hovering:** staying in the same place especially because you are waiting for something

[6] **winking:** closing and opening one eye quickly, usually to show that you are joking, being friendly, or telling a secret

[7] **sniggering:** laughing quietly in a way that is not nice

[8] **pay (someone) back:** to do something unpleasant to someone as a punishment because that person has done something unpleasant to you

[9] **Blue Grotto:** a famous sea cove on the coast of the Italian island of Capri

worshipped their goddess under that cliff, somewhere back in the Pleistocene. Their rites and rituals, the offerings they made to her."

7　　"Is that when you first came here?" she asks, keeping it light and sly. "Somewhere in the Pleistocene?"

8　　"A little later than that, really. The Renaissance, I think it was. Leonardo and I traveled down together from Florence-"

9　　"You and Leonardo, you were like *that*?"

10　　"Like that, yes. But not like *that*, if you take my meaning."

11　　"And Cosimo di'Medici. Another one from the good old days. Cosimo gave such great parties, right?"

12　　"That was Lorenzo," he says. "Lorenzo the Magnificent, Cosimo's grandson. Much more fun than the old man. You would have adored him."

13　　"I almost think you're serious when you talk like that."

14　　"I'm always serious. Even when I'm not." His arm tightens around her. He leans forward and down, and buries a kiss in her thick dark hair. "I love you," he whispers.

15　　"I love you," she says. "You're the best first husband a girl could want."

16　　"You're the finest last wife a man could ever desire."

17　　The words skewer[10] her. *Last* wife? Is he expecting to die in the next ten or twenty or thirty years? He is old—ancient—but nobody has any idea yet where the limits of the Process lie. Five hundred years? A thousand? Who can say? No one able to afford the treatments has died a natural death yet, in the four hundred years since the Process was invented. Why then does he speak so knowingly of her as his last wife? He may live long enough to have seven, ten, fifty wives after her.

18　　Marilisa is silent a long while.

19　　Then she asks him, quietly, uncertainly. "I don't understand why you said that."

20　　"Said what?"

21　　"The thing about my being your last wife."

22　　He hesitates[11] a moment. "But why would I ever want another, now that I have you?"

23　　"Am I so **utterly** perfect?"

24　　"I love you."

25　　"You loved Tedesca and Thane and Iavilda too," she says. "And Miaule and Katrin." She is counting on her fingers in the darkness. One wife is missing from the list. "And . . . Syantha. See, I know all their names. You must have loved them but the marriage ended anyway. They have to end. No matter how much you love a person, you can't keep a marriage going forever."

26　　"How do you know that?"

27　　"I just do. Everybody knows it."

28　　"I would like this marriage never to end," he tells her. "I'd like it to go on and on and on. To continue to the end of time. Is that all right? Is such a sentiment[12] permissible, do you think?"

29　　"What a romantic you are, Leo!"

30　　"What else can I be but romantic, tonight? This place, the spring night, the moon, the stars, the sea, the fragrance of the flowers in the air. Our anniversary. I love you. Nothing will ever end for us. Nothing."

---

[10] **skewer:** to hurt

[11] **hesitates:** pauses before doing or saying something because of uncertainty

[12] **sentiment:** an opinion or feeling that you have about something

31   "Can that really be so?" she asks.

32   "Of course. Forever and ever, as it is this moment."

33   She thinks from time to time of the men she will marry after she and Leo have gone their separate ways. For she knows that she will. Perhaps she'll stay with Leo for ten years, perhaps for fifty; but **ultimately**, despite all his assurances to the contrary,[13] one or the other of them will want to move on. No one stays married forever. Fifteen, twenty years, that's the usual. Sixty or seventy tops.

34   She'll marry a great athlete, next, she decides. And then a philosopher; and a political leader; and then stay single for a few decades, just to clear her palate, so to speak, an intermezzo[14] in her life, and when she wearies of that she'll find someone entirely different, a simple rugged man who likes to hunt, to work in the fields with his hands, and then a yachtsman with whom she'll sail the world, and then maybe when she's about three hundred she'll marry a boy, an innocent of eighteen or nineteen who hasn't even had his first Prep yet, and then—then a childish game. It always brings her to tears, eventually. The unknown husbands that wait for her in the misty future are vague **chilly** phantoms, fantasies, frightening, and inimical.[15] They are like swords that will inevitably fall between her and Leo, and she hates them for that.

35   The thought of having the same husband for all the vast expanse[16] of time that is the rest of her life, is a little disturbing—it gives her a sense of walls closing in, and closing and closing and closing—but the thought of leaving Leo is even worse. Or of his leaving her. Maybe she isn't truly in love with him, at any rate not as she imagines love at its deepest to be, but she is happy with him. She wants to stay with him. She can't really envision parting with him and moving on to someone else.

36   But of course she knows that she will. Everybody does in the fullness of time. *Everybody*.

37   Leo is a sand-painter. Sand-painting is his fifteenth or twentieth career. He has been an architect, an archeologist, a space-habitats developer, a professional gambler, an astronomer, and a number of other **disparate** and dazzling things. He reinvents himself every decade or two. That's as necessary to him as the Process itself. Making money is never an issue, since he lives on the compounding interest of investments set aside centuries ago. But the fresh challenge—ah, yes, always the fresh challenge.

38   Marilisa hasn't entered on any career path yet. It's much too soon. She is, after all, still in her first life, too young for the Process, merely in the Prep stage yet. Just a child, really. She has dabbled[17] in ceramics, written some poetry, composed a little music. Lately she has begun to think about studying economics or perhaps Spanish literature. No doubt her actual choice of a path to follow will be very far from any of these. But there's time to decide. Oh, is there ever time.

---

[13] **to the contrary:** showing that the opposite is true

[14] **intermezzo:** a short period of time between two longer periods

[15] **inimical:** harmful

[16] **vast expanse:** large, wide area

[17] **dabbled:** did something in a way that wasn't very serious

MAIN IDEAS

1 Look again at your predictions from the Preview on page 126. How did your answers to the questions help you understand the story?

2 Reading One discusses Marilisa's and Leo's views on marriage, family structure and relationships, careers, and longevity. Write sentences about how their views are different from the present-day society views described.

Marriage

Present-day society: *Marriage is seen as a lifelong commitment, although in some societies divorce is common. Some people may have more than one or two marriages.*

"Death Do Us Part": _____

_____

_____

Family structure / Relationships

Present-day society: *Three generations of a family living at the same time is common.*

"Death Do Us Part": _____

_____

_____

Careers

Present-day society: *Although many people have many different jobs throughout their lives, they don't frequently change careers.*

"Death Do Us Part": _____

_____

_____

Longevity

Present-day society: *The average lifespan varies around the world, but in developed countries the average lifespan is mid-seventies.*

"Death Do Us Part": _____

_____

_____

DETAILS

Marilisa and Leo have different perspectives on the topics in the chart. Complete the chart with examples of their differing views.

TOPIC	MARILISA	LEO
MARRIAGE	First marriage Assumes she'll be married again to a variety of men	
FAMILY STRUCTURE / RELATIONSHIPS		
CAREERS		
LONGEVITY		

MAKE INFERENCES

UNDERSTANDING CHARACTERS' ATTITUDES AND FEELINGS

Writers sometimes suggest relationships between characters in a story without stating them directly. We use inference to understand characters' attitudes and feelings on a deeper level.

Look at the example and read the explanation.

How does Marilisa feel about Leo? (*paragraph 2*)

a. That he is too old for her.

b. That he is a joke.

c. That he is youthful.

The best answer is *c*.

Evidence: In paragraph 2, we learn that Marilisa's friends are concerned about Leo's age. Marilisa doesn't seem as bothered because marriages aren't forever. We also learn that her marriage was a lark, but she doesn't say that Leo himself is a joke. He is actually sweet, kind, and sexy. This makes him appear youthful to Marilisa.

After reading the text closely, we can infer that Marilisa's strongest feeling about Leo is that he is youthful.

Circle the best answer. Refer to the paragraph in parentheses. Cite the evidence from the story that supports your answer.

1. How does Marilisa feel about Katrin? *(paragraph 3)*

    a. warm

    b. loyal

    c. jealous

    Evidence: _____

    _____

    _____

2. How does Fyodor feel toward Marilisa? *(paragraph 3)*

    a. playful

    b. disrespectful

    c. bored

    Evidence: _____

    _____

    _____

3. How does Leo feel about his marriage with Marilisa? *(paragraphs 23–32)*

    a. tired

    b. unclear

    c. secure

    Evidence: _____

    _____

    _____

4. How does Marilisa feel about her marriage to Leo? *(paragraphs 29–34)*

   a. It's romantic.

   b. She wants it to be permanent.

   c. She is resigned that it will end.

   Evidence: _____

   _____

   _____

5. Which best describes Marilisa's feeling about her marriage to Leo? *(paragraph 35)*

   a. conflicted

   b. committed

   c. insecure

   Evidence: _____

   _____

   _____

EXPRESS OPINIONS

Discuss the questions with a partner.

1. Leo was "ten times her age." Would you marry someone older than you? By how much? What possible advantages or disadvantages are there to marrying someone much older than you?

2. The story mentions that with the Process, "these days you could look as young as you like." What age would you choose to look if you were having the Process? Why?

3. Leo has had many different careers. "He reinvents himself every decade or two. That's as necessary to him as the Process itself." Why do you think he changes careers so often? Would you want to reinvent yourself every decade or two? Why or why not?

■■■■■■■■■■■■■■■■■■■■■■■■■■ *GO TO* MyEnglishLab *TO GIVE YOUR OPINION ABOUT ANOTHER QUESTION.*

Scientific understanding of aging at the cellular and molecular level may be the key to a longer lifespan. More and more scientists now believe that the human lifespan could be increased to 140 or more in the future. This may be achieved through genetic manipulation or caloric restriction (eating less). These strategies have proved effective with worms, flies, and mice. Maybe someday they will work on humans.

READD

1 Look at the boldfaced words in the reading and think about the questions.

1. Which words do you know the meanings of?

2. Can you use any of the words in a sentence?

2 Read *Toward Immortality: The Social Burden of Longer Lives*. As you read, notice the boldfaced vocabulary. Try to guess the meaning of the words from the context.

TOWARD IMMORTALITY: THE SOCIAL BURDEN OF LONGER LIVES

By Ker Than   LiveScience Staff Writer

A doubled lifespan

1   If scientists could create a pill that let you live twice as long while remaining free of infirmities,[1] would you take it?

2   If one considers only the personal benefits that longer life would bring, the answer might seem like a no-brainer[2]: People could spend more quality time with loved ones; watch future generations grow up; learn new languages; master new musical instruments; try different careers or travel the world.

3   But what about society as a whole? Would it be better off if lifespans were doubled? The question is one of growing relevance, and serious debate about it goes back at least a few years to the Kronos Conference on Longevity Health Sciences in Arizona. Gregory Stock, director of the Program on Medicine, Technology, and Society at UCLA's School of Public Health, answered the question with an **emphatic** "Yes." A doubled lifespan, Stock said, would "give us a chance to recover from our mistakes, lead us towards longer-term thinking and reduce healthcare costs by delaying the onset of expensive diseases of aging. It would also raise productivity by adding to our prime years."

---

[1] **infirmities:** sicknesses, diseases

[2] **no-brainer:** something that you do not have to think about because it is easy to understand

4   Bioethicist Daniel Callahan, a cofounder of the Hastings Center in New York, didn't share Stock's enthusiasm. Callahan's objections were practical ones. For one thing, he said, doubling lifespans won't solve any of our current social problems. "We have war, poverty, all sorts of issues around, and I don't think any of them would be at all helped by having people live longer," Callahan said in a recent telephone interview. "The question is, 'What will we get as a society?' I suspect it won't be a better society."

5   Others point out that a doubling of the human lifespan will affect society at every level. Notions[3] about marriage, family, and work will change in fundamental ways, they say, as will attitudes toward the young and the old.

Marriage and family

6   Richard Kalish, a psychologist who considered the social effects of life extension technologies, thinks a longer lifespan will **radically** change how we view marriage.

7   In today's world, for example, a couple in their 60s who are stuck in a **loveless** but **tolerable** marriage might decide to stay together for the remaining 15 to 20 years of their lives out of inertia[4] or familiarity. But if that same couple knew they might have to suffer each other's company for another 60 or 80 years, their choice might be different. Kalish predicted that as lifespans increase, there will be a shift in emphasis from marriage as a lifelong union to marriage as a long-term commitment. Multiple, brief marriages could become common.

8   A doubled lifespan will reshape notions of family life in other ways, too, says Chris Hackler, head of the Division of Medical Humanities at the University of Arkansas. If multiple marriages become the norm as Kalish predicts, and each marriage produces children, then half-siblings will become more common, Hackler points out. And if couples continue the current trend of having children beginning in their 20s and 30s, then eight or even ten generations might be alive simultaneously, Hackler said. Furthermore, if life extension also increases a woman's period of fertility, siblings could be born 40 or 50 years apart. Such a large age difference would radically change the way siblings or parents and their children interact with one another.

9   "If we were 100 years younger than our parents or 60 years apart from our siblings, that would certainly create a different set of social relationships," Hackler told *LiveScience*.

The workplace

10   For most people, living longer will **inevitably** mean more time spent working. Careers will necessarily become longer, and the retirement age will have to be pushed back, not only so individuals can support themselves, but to avoid overtaxing a nation's social security system.

11   Advocates of anti-aging research say that working longer might not be such a bad thing. With skilled workers remaining in the workforce longer, economic productivity would go up. And if people got bored with their jobs, they could switch careers.

12   But such changes would carry their own set of dangers, critics say. Competition for jobs would become fiercer as "mid-life re-trainees" beginning new careers vie with young workers for a limited number of entry-level positions. Especially **worrisome** is the

---

[3] **notions:** ideas, beliefs, or opinions
[4] **inertia:** the feeling that you do not want to do anything at all

(continued on next page)

problem of workplace mobility, Callahan said. "If you have people staying in their jobs for 100 years, that is going to make it really tough for young people to move in and get ahead," Callahan explained.

13   Callahan also worries that corporations and universities could become dominated by a few individuals if executives, managers, and tenured professors refuse to give up their posts.[5] Without a constant infusion of youthful talent and ideas, these institutions could stagnate.[6]

---

[5] **give up their posts:** leave their jobs
[6] **stagnate:** to stop developing or improving

Time to act

14   While opinions differ wildly about what the ramifications for society will be if the human lifespan is extended, most ethicists agree that the issue should be discussed now, since it might be impossible to stop or control the technology once it's developed. "If this could ever happen, then we'd better ask what kind of society we want to get," Callahan said. "We had better not go anywhere near it until we have figured those problems out."

COMPREHENSION

Discuss the questions with the class.

1. Some people in Reading Two think a longer lifespan is a good idea. Discuss the reasons.

2. Some people in Reading Two don't think a longer lifespan is a good idea. Discuss the reasons.

GO TO MyEnglishLab *FOR MORE VOCABULARY PRACTICE.*

READING SKILL

1   Go back to Reading Two. Did you look at the title and the headings before you read the article? If so, did they help you understand the article? Why or why not?

USING TITLES AND HEADINGS TO IMPROVE COMPREHENSION

The title of a reading and the headings give the reader information. Good readers use the clues provided by titles and headings to help them predict the content of the whole reading and the individual sections in the reading. Based on the title and headings, readers can ask themselves questions they think the reading or section will answer.

Think about the title, *Toward Immortality: The Social Burden of Longer Lives*. From this title, what questions would you expect this article to answer? Two of the choices are correct.

a. How long will people live in the future?

b. Why will there be fewer diseases in the future?

c. What problems may longer lives cause for society?

The best answers are *a* and *c*. Answer *a* is correct because the words "immortality" and "longer lives" are in the title. Therefore, we know that the author will probably mention how long people will live. Answer *c* is also correct because the words "social burden" suggest there will be problems or issues with longer lives. Answer *b* is not a good choice because there is no indication in the title that the article will discuss medical issues associated with longer lives.

Just as with titles, headings and subheadings also provide clues as to what you can expect to find in those sections of the text. Predicting content from headings can improve your reading comprehension.

2 Imagine that you are looking at the headings from Reading Two for the first time. For each heading, write two questions you might ask.

1. A doubled lifespan

_____

_____

2. Marriage and family

_____

_____

3. The workplace

_____

_____

3 Share your questions with a partner. Try to use these comprehension skills whenever you read a new article.

GO TO MyEnglishLab *FOR MORE SKILL PRACTICE.*

STEP 1: Organize

Reading One (R1) and Reading Two (R2) discuss both positive and negative effects of longer lifespans. Complete the cause and effect diagram with information from the readings.

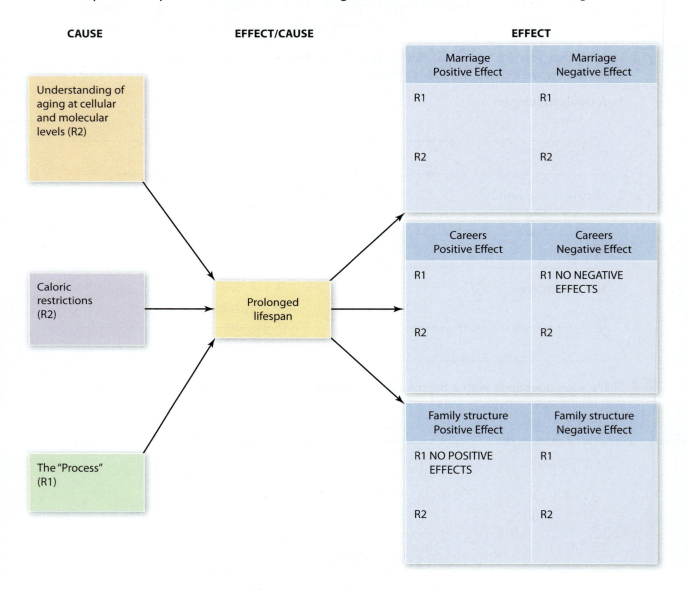

CAUSE   EFFECT/CAUSE   EFFECT

Understanding of aging at cellular and molecular levels (R2)

Caloric restrictions (R2)

The "Process" (R1)

Prolonged lifespan

Marriage Positive Effect	Marriage Negative Effect
R1	R1
R2	R2

Careers Positive Effect	Careers Negative Effect
R1	R1 NO NEGATIVE EFFECTS
R2	R2

Family structure Positive Effect	Family structure Negative Effect
R1 NO POSITIVE EFFECTS	R1
R2	R2

STEP 2: Synthesize

Bioethicist Daniel Callahan asked, when talking about the potential for doubled lifespans, "'What will we get as a society?' I suspect it won't be a better society." On a separate piece of paper, write a paragraph about whether you agree or disagree with his statement. Support your answer with at least three pieces of information from Step 1.

GO TO MyEnglishLab *TO CHECK WHAT YOU LEARNED.*

VOCABULARY

REVIEW

Work with a partner. Discuss the meanings of the adjectives and adverbs in the box. Decide if the words give you positive, negative, or neutral feelings. Then write the words in the chart. Note that some words can be interpreted in more than one way. Discuss why.

awesome	emphatic	impetuous	loveless	radically	utterly
chilly	fond	inevitably	presumptuous	tolerable	vigorous
disparate	immeasurably	insufferable	punctually	ultimately	worrisome

POSITIVE	NEGATIVE	NEUTRAL

EXPAND

ADJECTIVE SUFFIXES

Many adjectives are formed by combining a base word with a suffix. (*vigor* + *ous* = *vigorous*). Look at the boldfaced adjectives in the excerpts from the readings.

- They stand together in the darkness, staring at the **awesome** sparkle of the stars.
- A couple in their 60s who are stuck in a loveless but **tolerable** marriage might decide to stay together.
- Fyodor had a **presumptuous** way of winking and sniggering at her.

Suffixes can sometimes change the meaning of the base word.

- love → loveless (without love)
- care → careful (with care)
- tolerate → tolerable (able to be tolerated)

In addition, suffixes always change the form of the word.

- vigor (noun) → vigorous (adjective)

(continued on next page)

COMMON ADJECTIVE SUFFIXES					
-al	-ous	-ful	-able	-less	-ive
-ed	-ing	-ant	-ic	-ent	-ial
-ible	-ar	-en	-ical	-y	-ary
-ese	-ish	-some			

Adjective suffixes can be added to nouns or verbs.

adventure (n.) → adventurous   fascinate (v.) → fascinating

care (n.) → careful

Suffixes can also be added to base/root words. Sometimes there are spelling changes when a suffix is added.

- Leave out the final *e*.

    measure → measurable

- Double the final consonant.

    sun → sunny

- Leave out the final *s* before *-al*.

    politics → political

Complete the chart with synonyms from Reading One (R1) and Reading Two (R2) that have the suffixes listed. Then think of your own example of an adjective with the same suffix.

DEATH DO US PART (R1)			
SUFFIXES	EXAMPLE FROM TEXT	DEFINITION OR SYNONYM	EXAMPLE OF A NEW ADJECTIVE WITH THE SAME SUFFIX
Paragraphs 1–2			
-ing		sparkling	
-ive	*impulsive*	impetuous	*active*
Paragraphs 3–5			
-able		intolerable	
-al		perfect	
Paragraphs 6–15			
-ent		very old	
-ous		sincere	

Paragraphs 26–33			
-ible		allowable	
-ic		passionate	
Paragraphs 34–38			
-y		foggy	

TOWARD IMMORTALITY (R2)			
SUFFIXES	**EXAMPLE FROM TEXT**	**DEFINITION OR SYNONYM**	**EXAMPLE OF A NEW ADJECTIVE WITH THE SAME SUFFIX**
Paragraphs 1–2			
-al		individual	
Paragraphs 3–4			
-ic		forceful	
-ical		sensible	
Paragraphs 5–7			
-less		without love	
-ing		still left	
Paragraphs 10–13			
-ly		without doubt	
-ed		restricted	
-some		troublesome	
-ant		steady	
-ful		young	

CREATE

Imagine that you are either the bioethicist Daniel Callahan or Gregory Stock of UCLA's School of Public Health. On a separate piece of paper, write five questions for Leo (R1), about his extended lifespan. Use at least one word from the Review or Expand section in each question. Then exchange papers with a partner and answer the questions as if you were Leo.

GO TO MyEnglishLab *FOR MORE VOCABULARY PRACTICE.*

GRAMMAR

1 Examine the sentences and answer the questions with a partner.

> **a.** Marilisa and Leo **went** to Nairobi and Venice on their honeymoon three years ago.
>
> **b.** Leo **has been** an architect, an archeologist, a space-habitats developer, a professional gambler, an astronomer, and a number of other disparate and dazzling things.
>
> **c.** People **have been searching** for the "fountain of youth" since the beginning of recorded history.

1. In sentence *a*, is Leo and Marilisa's honeymoon over? How do you know?

2. In sentence *b*, is Leo still an architect, an archeologist . . . ? How do you know?

3. In sentence *c*, are people still searching for the fountain of youth? How do you know? When did people start searching?

4. What verb tenses are used in sentences *a, b,* and *c*?

CONTRASTING THE SIMPLE PAST, PRESENT PERFECT, AND PRESENT PERFECT CONTINUOUS

The Simple Past

1. Use the simple past for things that happened in the past and were completed.	Leo **watched** the movie. (*Leo is no longer watching the movie. He finished watching the movie.*)
2. Use past time expressions such as: *last, ago, in, on, at, yesterday, when* . . . to indicate that an action or event was completed at a definite time in the past.	Leo **watched** the movie **yesterday**. (*Leo is no longer watching the movie. He finished watching the movie yesterday.*)

The Present Perfect

3. Use the present perfect for completed actions that happened at an indefinite time in the past.	Marilisa **has eaten** breakfast. (*She has finished her breakfast, but we don't know exactly when she ate it, or it is not important.*)
4. You can also use the present perfect for repeated actions that were completed in the past, but that may happen again in the future.	Leo **has visited** Paris six times. (*Those six visits are finished. However, he may visit Paris again in the future.*)

5. Use the present perfect with *for* or *since* for actions that began in the past. These actions were not completed, have continued up to the present, and may continue into the future. Use *for* or *since* for this meaning especially with non-action verbs, such as *be, feel,* and *know*. *For* is followed by a length of time, for example, *six years*. *Since* is followed by a specific point in time, for example, *2099*.	Leo **has been** a sand painter **for** six years. *(Leo began to be a sand painter six years ago. He is still a sand painter today, and may continue to be a sand painter in the future.)* Leo **has been** a sand painter **since** 2099. *(Leo began to be a sand painter in 2099. He is still a sand painter today, and may continue to be a sand painter in the future.)*
6. Compare the present perfect without *for* or *since*.	Leo **has been** a sand painter. *(Leo was a sand painter at some time in the past, but he is not anymore. We don't know exactly when he was, or it is not important.)*

The Present Perfect Continuous

7. Use the present perfect continuous for actions that began in the past. These actions were not completed, have continued up to the present, and may continue into the future. The use of *for* or *since* with the present perfect continuous is optional. Using *for* or *since* gives additional information about when the action began or how long it has been in progress, but it does not change the meaning of the verb.	Daniel Callahan **has been studying** about the ramifications of increasing human lifespans. *(Daniel Callahan began studying sometime in the past. He is still studying and will probably continue to study in the future.)*
8. Non-action verbs are not usually used in the continuous. Use the present perfect with *for* or *since* for this meaning with a non-action verb.	Callahan **has been** at the Hastings Center **for** many years. Callahan **has been** at the Hastings Center **since** 1969.

2 Complete the conversations by circling the correct forms of the verbs.

Conversation 1

REPORTER: Our readers may already know about the "fountain of youth," but can you give us some historical perspective? Also, do you think scientific advancements will turn out to be a "fountain of youth," allowing people to live forever?

DANIEL CALLAHAN: People **(1) have been searching / searched** for the "fountain of youth" since the beginning of recorded history. People believed that drinking from this fountain would allow them to be healthy and vigorous forever. They would never get sick and would be full of energy. So far, the "fountain" **(2) has been / was** impossible to find. People **(3) have not been / were not** able to truly achieve eternal life. Human lifespans have been increasing, but we are still far from reaching immortality. Even considering the scientific advancements that **(4) have taken / took** place in the twentieth century, I, as a scientist, believe that ultimately the limit of human life will be no more than 150 years.

Conversation 2

DR. KALISH: I know you have been very busy attending conferences this month. I believe you have recently attended a conference on longevity. Did you learn a lot?

Dr. Gregory Stock: What a month! The conference on longevity I **(5) attended / have been attending** last week did not begin very punctually. It was supposed to begin at 9:00 A.M. but **(6) didn't actually start / hasn't actually started** until 9:45! On top of that, the first speaker was insufferable; he finished every sentence with, "you know." Luckily, I **(7) have gone / have been going** to three other conferences this month that had awesome speakers who provided us with lots of interesting facts and ideas about longevity. At the first conference, the speaker **(8) discussed / has been discussing** how restricting the amount of food eaten may increase lifespans. At the next conference, I learned about some ongoing research that Dr. Clynes **(9) did / has been doing** with mice that has ramifications for human longevity.

Conversation 3

Marilisa's Friend, Joan: Leo has such a large family. Now that you are married, how are you getting along with them?

Marilisa: Not as well as I would like, but I suppose the problems I am having are quite normal for a newlywed. I **(10) have had / had** problems with Leo's son, Fyodor, since the first time I met him, but I am willing to tolerate him for Leo's sake. Other than Fyodor, and one or two of Leo's ex-wives, I **(11) have enjoyed / enjoyed** getting to know Leo's family. I really like Leo's brother, Max. Max is a writer and scientist who **(12) has completed / completed** a book on "the Process" two years ago. Ever since that was published, he **(13) worked / has been working** on his autobiography.

3 Complete the sentences with the verb in the correct tense: simple past, present perfect, or present perfect continuous.

1. Leo (**meet**) _____ many important historical figures during his life, and he looks forward to meeting many more.

2. Marilisa and Leo (**visit**) _____ Capri in '87 on their first anniversary.

3. Leo (**have**) _____ at least 10 different careers so far.

4. Marilisa (**talk**) _____ to Fyodor for at least 30 minutes. Do you think they will be done soon?

5. Leo (**meet**) _____ Leonardo da Vinci over 500 years ago.

6. Doctors at the Hastings Center (**study**) _____ longevity for many years and plan to continue for many more years.

7. Daniel Callahan doesn't believe that scientists should continue working on extending lifespans until they (**figure**) _____ out the ramifications longer life will have for society.

8. The conference that Dr. Kalish (**attend**) _____ last August dealt with the future of marriage in a society with prolonged lifespans.

9. Dr. Chris Hackler (**do**) _____ research concerning family relationships of siblings born 40–50 years apart. He expects to finish his research next year.

10. Although it is only March, Gregory Stock (**write**) _____ four papers on how increased lifespans can decrease healthcare costs. He is expecting to write at least two more papers before the end of the year.

■■■■■■■■■■■■■■ *GO TO* MyEnglishLab *FOR MORE GRAMMAR PRACTICE AND TO CHECK WHAT YOU LEARNED.*

FINAL WRITING TASK

In this unit, you read about immortal life in the future. Imagine that scientists have discovered a way to make you immortal, and it is now the year 2175. What is your life like? What jobs have you had? What relationships have you had? Who have you married? What is your family like? What have been the advantages of living so long? What have been the disadvantages?

You are going to *write a descriptive essay about the positive and negative aspects of your life in 2175*. Use the vocabulary and grammar from the unit.*

PREPARE TO WRITE: Using an Idea Web

An **idea web** helps you see how different topics are related to one central theme.

Imagine your life in the year 2175. Look at the topics in the idea web. Close your eyes and try to create a mental picture of yourself and your life. Think about the topics in the circles as they relate to your life. Write your ideas about each topic in the circles. Be sure to include details and adjectives.

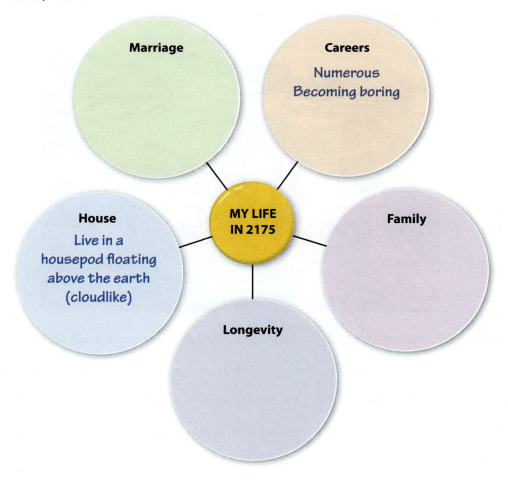

Marriage

Careers
Numerous
Becoming boring

House
Live in a housepod floating above the earth (cloudlike)

MY LIFE IN 2175

Family

Longevity

---

* For Alternative Writing Topics, see page 153. These topics can be used in place of the writing topic for this unit or as homework. The alternative topics relate to the theme of the unit but may not target the same grammar or rhetorical structures taught in the unit.

WRITE: A Descriptive Essay

A **descriptive essay** describes a place, person, or situation. The writer uses such vivid or descriptive language that the reader can create a clear mental picture of the description. Here are some important points:

1. **Have an introduction**. Capture the reader's attention by telling an interesting anecdote or story.

2. **Use strong imagery**. Try to create mental pictures for your reader by using descriptive adjectives and details.

3. **Rely on sensory details**. Create strong sensory images by describing smells, sights, sounds, tastes, and senses of touch.

4. **Have a conclusion**. Bring the ideas of the essay to a close by providing final thoughts or predictions.

1 Read the introductory paragraph from a descriptive essay about life in the future. Then answer the questions and share your answers with a partner.

I sleepily open my eyes as my alarm robot vigorously shakes me awake. I can smell the usual insufferable morning smells: bitter coffee made with sour milk and burnt toast. I haven't had time to reprogram my breakfast robot since the electric meteor shower last week blew out its motherboard with a loud *crack* that sounded as if my housepod had split in half. It's during these times that I fondly remember the simple days decades ago when I made my own breakfast and lived on Earth, not floating above it like a lonely cloud. No matter. I'll glide through a convenient coffee shop's hovercraft window on the way to work. Work. I used to be so punctual. "As utterly dependable as a Swiss watch," my bosses always said, even with a half a world commute every day. After more than 150 years of work, it's hard to get excited. But I am getting ahead of myself. In the past 200 years, I have had numerous wives, careers, countless numbers of children, and awesome experiences. My life has been an endless roller coaster ride filled with immeasurable happiness and sadness.

1. Circle the thesis statement.

2. What do you expect the next paragraphs of the essay will be about?

3. Descriptive essays often include sensory details and create mental imagery. What are some examples of sensory details in the paragraph above?

TOUCH	SMELL	SIGHT	TASTE	SOUND

4. What mental picture does this writing create? Underline the words or sentences in the paragraph that create these images for you.

2 Now write the first draft of your descriptive essay. Use your notes from Prepare to Write. Make sure you have multiple paragraphs and use descriptive language that includes adjectives and sensory details. Be sure to use grammar and vocabulary from the unit.

REVISE: Using Figurative Language

Many descriptive essays and stories include **figurative language**, such as **similes**, **metaphors**, and **personification**, to add depth and imagery.

A **simile** is a way of describing something through a comparison using *like* or *as*.

The comparison is with something not normally connected with the subject.

Simile: *The snow was like a blanket.*

Explanation: The subject, snow, is being compared to a blanket because it covers the ground in the same way a blanket covers a bed.

1 Look at the introductory paragraph in Write on pages 148–149. With a partner, find the two similes and complete the information.

_____ is being compared to _____ because _____

_____

_____ is being compared to _____ because _____

_____

2 Look at Reading One. With a partner find the similes and complete the information.

Paragraph 1: _____ are being compared to _____

because _____

Paragraph 2: _____ is being compared to _____

because _____

Paragraph 34: _____ are being compared to _____

because _____

A **metaphor** is another way of describing something through a comparison but without using *like* or *as*. Instead, the metaphor explicitly states what a thing "is." The subject and its complement are the same.

Metaphor: *The setting sun is a red ball of fire falling into the sea.*

Explanation: The sun is not *like* a red ball of fire, it **is** a red ball of fire.

3 Work with a partner. Look at Reading One, paragraph 34. What metaphor does Marilisa use to describe her unknown future husbands? Why does she use this metaphor?

Personification gives human qualities to animals or objects. This helps the reader better connect with the image.

Without Personification	With Personification
The leaves blew around in the wind.	The leaves danced in the wind.
The sun was shining in the sky.	The sun sang its happy summer song.

4 Look at Reading One, paragraph 17. Find an example of personification. With a partner, discuss how personification helps the description come alive.

5 Look at your first draft. Are your descriptions clear? Do they create vivid mental imagery? Add at least one simile, one metaphor, or one example of personification.

GO TO MyEnglishLab *FOR MORE SKILL PRACTICE.*

EDIT: Writing the Final Draft

Go to MyEnglishLab and write the final draft of your essay. Carefully edit it for grammatical and mechanical errors, such as spelling, capitalization, and punctuation. Make sure you use some of the grammar and vocabulary from the unit. Use the checklist to help you write your final draft. Then submit your essay to your teacher.

FINAL DRAFT CHECKLIST

❑ Does the essay have an interesting introduction?

❑ Does the essay have multiple paragraphs?

❑ Does the essay include clear descriptive language including lots of adjectives?

❑ Does the essay contain vivid mental imagery, including sensory details and a simile, a metaphor, or an example of personification?

❑ Does the essay have a conclusion?

❑ Did you use tenses correctly?

❑ Have you used the vocabulary from the unit?

UNIT PROJECT

In this unit, you have read a science fiction story about people living longer lives. Even today, there are areas of the world as well as specific groups of people who are already living lives that are significantly longer than average. Areas where these people live are called "blue zones." There are a number of reasons why people in these longevity hotspots seem to live longer than most people.

In a small group, research one of these areas. Compare your findings and write a report. Follow these steps:

STEP 1: Choose one of these blue zones:

Okinawa, Japan	Campodimele, Italy
Loma Linda, California, USA	Sardinia, Italy
Nicoya Peninsula, Costa Rica	Ikaria, Greece
Symi, Greece	Your own idea based on your research.
Hunza, Pakistan	

STEP 2: Do research on the Internet about the blue zone you chose. Read two or more articles describing the area or group you are studying. Answer the questions:

- How long do the people live?
- Where do they live, and what is their environment like?
- What is their diet?
- What is their lifestyle?
- What do they do that is different from what most people do?
- How do experts explain their longevity?
- What can we learn from these people?

STEP 3: Work in your small group to compare your findings and prepare a report for the class.

ALTERNATIVE WRITING TOPICS

Write an essay about one of the topics. Use the vocabulary and grammar from the unit.

1. If scientists created a pill that would allow you to live twice as long while remaining free of infirmities, would you take it? Why or why not?

2. As with all new medical technology, life extension technology will probably be very expensive, at least at first. Because of this, the people able to afford the treatments will be wealthy. How will this affect all areas of society? Think about politics, business, entertainment, the economy, and so on.

■■■■■■■■■■■■■■■■■■■■■■ *GO TO* MyEnglishLab *TO WRITE ABOUT ONE OF THE ALTERNATIVE TOPICS, WATCH A VIDEO ABOUT LONGEVITY, AND TAKE THE UNIT 5 ACHIEVEMENT TEST.* ■■■■■■■■■■■■■■■■■■

MAKING A
Difference

1. What do you think the people in the photo are doing?

2. Philanthropy is a way of showing concern for other people by giving money or volunteering (working without pay) to help people in need or organizations that help people in need. What do you think people can learn from volunteering?

3. Have you ever done any volunteering? If so, what motivated you to volunteer? What did you learn from this experience?

GO TO MyEnglishLab *TO CHECK WHAT YOU KNOW.*

VOCABULARY

1 Two of the three words in each row have meanings similar to the boldfaced word. Cross out the word that doesn't belong. If you need help, use a dictionary.

1. **passion**	enthusiasm	~~decision~~	interest
2. **proudly**	modestly	self-satisfyingly	contentedly
3. **challenge**	pride	test	demand
4. **satisfaction**	happiness	pleasure	amusement
5. **determined**	insistent	stubborn	uncertain
6. **proposal**	suggestion	order	recommendation
7. **donate**	contribute	give	sell
8. **admiring**	complimentary	approving	boring
9. **devote**	dedicate	appreciate	commit
10. **inspired**	saddened	encouraged	motivated
11. **manage**	handle	cope with	respond
12. **thrilled**	happy	scared	excited

Across the United States, more and more organizations—including corporate, educational, religious, and government groups—are supporting volunteer programs. In addition, more people are volunteering in a wide range of ways. People volunteer for many different reasons: some for political or religious reasons; some for personal or social reasons. Others volunteer because it's mandatory, or required, in certain situations, for example, as part of a school's curriculum or as a requirement for graduation.

2 Read what people say about volunteering. Complete each statement with the words in the boxes. Then write the reasons you think they volunteer. (Note: Not all words are used, and some people may have more than one reason.)

Reasons for Volunteering

environmental	medical research	political	aged care
mandatory	tutoring	personal	religious

1. Matt Olsen, age 60: Raised $2,000 for AIDS research in the annual Boston-to-New York AIDS bicycle ride

admiring	challenge	~~donate~~	manage

"I'm trying to raise money for AIDS research in memory of my brother. I'm hoping to _____*donate*_____ more than $2,000 this year. Maybe this way what happened to him won't happen to others. The ride is certainly a physical _____, especially since I hurt my leg last weekend. However, I still think I can _____ to finish the ride. In any case, I enjoy biking, and this way I can combine my favorite sport with a good cause."

Reasons: _*personal; medical research*_____

2. Steve Hooley, age 36: Donates his time as a Boy Scout leader

inspired	manage	passion	thrilled

"I've always loved the outdoors and camping. In fact, preserving the environment is a _____ for me. Therefore, I'm _____ to be a Scout leader. By being a Scout leader, I can do something I like and share my love of nature with the next generation. If they are _____, maybe they'll take better care of the environment than our generation has.

Reasons: _____

3. Hannah Bullard, age 27: Volunteers in a shelter for homeless women

inspired	passion	proudly	satisfaction

"I've always been taught that we should help those who are less fortunate than we are. Reverend Woodson spoke at church last Sunday about all the good work being done here. He spoke with such _____ that I knew I wanted to participate. It gives me a lot of _____ to work with these women. Some of them have been through so much: alcoholism, drug addiction, and in many cases, abuse. I am very _____ by how far some of them have come. Despite their many problems, many of these women have now taken back control of their lives."

Reasons: _____

(continued on next page)

4. Louisa Deering, age 17: Spends three hours a week playing guitar for senior citizens in a nursing home

determined	devoting	proposal	satisfaction

"I started coming here last year because it was a school requirement. After I completed my requirement, I didn't want to stop. In order to continue volunteering, I made a _____ to the director of the program—I asked him if I could come back again this year after school and on weekends because I really have a good time with the people. I want to continue _____ time to them because I truly enjoy being with them and I think they like to listen to my music, too."

Reasons: _____

5. Ted Sirota, age 23: Spends five hours a week volunteering at a politician's office

admiring	determined	donate	inspire

"I feel that this person is the best candidate. I find her truly amazing; she's someone I can really look up to and want to be like. However, I'm not just one of her _____ supporters. I also volunteer for her. By volunteering, I can do more than just vote. I am _____ to help her get elected. That way I can be more involved in the whole political process."

Reasons: _____

■■■■■■■■■■■■■■■■■■■■■■■■■■■■■■■ *GO TO* MyEnglishLab *FOR MORE VOCABULARY PRACTICE.*

PREVIEW

Justin Lebo is a boy who volunteers his time and energy to help others in a unique way.

Read the first two paragraphs of *Justin Lebo*. Work with a partner to answer the questions.

1. What condition is the bicycle in?

2. Why do you think Justin would be interested in a bike in that condition?

3. What do you think Justin will do with the bicycle?

Now read the rest of the article.

JUSTIN LEBO

BY PHILLIP HOOSE (from *It's Our World, Too*)

1   Something about the battered old bicycle at the garage sale[1] caught ten-year-old Justin Lebo's eye. What a wreck! It was like looking at a few big bones in the dust and trying to figure out what kind of dinosaur they had once belonged to.

2   It was a BMX bike with a twenty-inch frame. Its original color was buried beneath five or six coats of gunky paint. Everything—the grips, the pedals, the brakes, the seat, the spokes—was bent or broken, twisted and rusted. Justin stood back as if he were inspecting a painting for sale at an auction. Then he made his final judgment: perfect.

3   Justin talked the owner down to $6.50 and asked his mother, Diane, to help load the bike into the back of their car.

4   When he got it home, he wheeled the junker into the garage and showed it **proudly** to his father. "Will you help me fix it up?" he asked. Justin's hobby was bike racing, a **passion** the two of them shared. Their garage barely had room for the car anymore. It was more like a bike shop. Tires and frames hung from hooks on the ceiling, and bike wrenches dangled from the walls.

5   Now Justin and his father cleared out a work space in the garage and put the old junker up on a rack. They poured alcohol on the frame and rubbed until the old paint began to yield, layer by layer. They replaced the broken pedal, tightened down a new seat, and restored the grips. In about a week, it looked brand new.

6   Soon he forgot about the bike. But the very next week, he bought another junker at a yard sale[2] and fixed it up, too. After a while, it bothered him that he wasn't really using either bike. Then he realized that what he loved about the old bikes wasn't riding them: It was the **challenge** of making something new and useful out of something old and broken.

7   Justin wondered what he should do with them. They were just taking up space in the garage. He remembered that when he was younger, he used to live near a large brick building called the Kilbarchan Home for Boys. It was a place for boys whose parents couldn't care for them for one reason or another.

8   He found "Kilbarchan" in the phone book and called the director, who said the boys would be **thrilled** to get two bicycles. The next day when Justin and his mother unloaded the bikes at the home, two boys raced out to greet them. They leapt aboard the bikes and started tooling around the semicircular driveway, doing wheelies and pirouettes, laughing and shouting.

---

[1] **garage sale:** a sale of used furniture, clothes, toys, etc. that you no longer want, usually held in your garage

[2] **yard sale:** another phrase for garage sale

(continued on next page)

9   The Lebos watched them for a while, then started to climb into their car to go home. The boys cried after them, "Wait a minute! You forgot your bikes!" Justin explained that the bikes were for them to keep. "They were so happy." Justin remembers. "It was like they couldn't believe it. It made me feel good just to see them happy."

10   On the way home, Justin was silent. His mother assumed he was lost in a feeling of **satisfaction**. But he was thinking about what would happen once those bikes got wheeled inside and everybody saw them. How could all those kids decide who got the bikes? Two bikes could cause more trouble than they would solve. Actually they hadn't been that hard to build. It was fun. Maybe he could do more . . .

11   "Mom," Justin said as they turned onto their street, "I've got an idea. I'm going to make a bike for every boy at Kilbarchan for Christmas." Diane Lebo looked at Justin out of the corner of her eye. She had rarely seen him so **determined**.

12   When they got home, Justin called Kilbarchan to find out how many boys lived there. There were twenty-one. It was already June. He had six months to make nineteen bikes. That was almost a bike a week. Justin called the home back to tell them of his plan. "I could tell they didn't think I could do it," Justin remembers. "I knew I could."

13   Justin knew his best chance to build bikes was almost the way General Motors or Ford builds cars: in an assembly line. He figured it would take three or four junkers to produce enough parts to make one good bike. That meant sixty to eighty bikes. Where would he get them?

14   Garage sales seemed to be the only hope. It was June, and there would be garage sales all summer long. But even if he could find that many bikes, how could he ever pay for them? That was hundreds of dollars.

15   He went to his parents with a **proposal**. "When Justin was younger, say five or six," says his mother, "he used to give away some of his allowance[3] to help others in need. His father and I would **donate** a dollar for every dollar Justin donated. So he asked us if it could be like the old days, if we'd match every dollar he put into buying old bikes. We said yes."

16   Justin and his mother spent most of June and July hunting for cheap bikes at garage sales and thrift shops.[4] They would haul the bikes home, and Justin would start stripping them down in the yard.

17   But by the beginning of August, he had **managed** to make only ten bikes. Summer vacation was almost over, and school and homework would soon cut into his time. Garage sales would dry up when it got colder, and Justin was out of money. Still he was determined to find a way.

18   At the end of August, Justin got a break. A neighbor wrote a letter to the local newspaper describing Justin's project, and an editor thought it would make a good story. In her **admiring** article about a boy who was **devoting** his summer to help kids he didn't even know, she said Justin needed bikes and money, and she printed his home phone number.

19   Overnight, everything changed. "There must have been a hundred calls," Justin says. "People would call me up and ask me to come over and

[3] **allowance:** money you are given regularly or for a special reason
[4] **thrift shops:** stores that sell used goods, especially furniture, clothes, and toys, often in order to raise money for a charity

pick up their old bike. Or I'd be working in the garage, and a station wagon would pull up. The driver would leave a couple of bikes by the curb. It just snowballed.[5]"

20   The week before Christmas Justin delivered the last of the twenty-one bikes to Kilbarchan. Once again, the boys poured out of the home and leapt aboard the bikes, tearing around in the snow.

21   And once again, their joy **inspired** Justin. They reminded him how important bikes were to him. Wheels meant freedom. He thought about how much more the freedom to ride must mean to boys like these who had so little freedom in their lives. He decided to keep on building.

22   "First I made eleven bikes for the children in a foster home[6] my mother told me about. Then I made bikes for all the women in a battered women's shelter. Then I made ten little bikes and tricycles for children with AIDS. Then I made twenty-three bikes for the Paterson Housing Coalition."

23   In the four years since he started, Justin Lebo has made between 150 and 200 bikes and given them all away. He has been careful to leave time for his homework, his friends, his coin collection, his new interest in marine biology, and of course, his own bikes.

24   Reporters and interviewers have asked Justin Lebo the same question over and over: "Why do you do it?" The question seems to make him uncomfortable. It's as if they want him to say what a great person he is. Their stories always make him seem like a saint, which he knows he isn't. "Sure it's nice of me to make the bikes," he says, "because I don't have to. But I want to. In part, I do it for myself. I don't think you can ever really do anything to help anybody else if it doesn't make you happy."

25   "Once I overheard a kid who got one of my bikes say, 'A bike is like a book; it opens up a whole new world.' That's how I feel, too. It made me happy to know that kid felt that way. That's why I do it."

---

[5] **snowballed:** got bigger quickly or got harder to control
[6] **foster home:** a home where a child is taken care of for a period of time by someone who is not a parent or legal guardian

MAIN IDEAS

1 Look again at your answers to the questions from the Preview on page 158. How did your answers help you understand the story?

2 Work with a partner. Read the statements and decide which three represent the main ideas of Reading One. Then discuss the reasons for your choices.

1. Justin paid $6.50 for the first bike he fixed up.

2. Justin needed to find a way to get a lot of used bikes.

3. Justin was able to fix up and donate hundreds of bikes because of the support of his parents and community.

4. Justin's hobby was bike racing.

5. Justin is a special boy because he likes to help others.

6. After the newspaper article, people called Justin and offered him their old bikes.

DETAILS

The chart lists some benefits of doing community service. Complete the chart with examples of how Justin Lebo benefited from his experience.

THE BENEFITS OF COMMUNITY SERVICE	EXAMPLES OF JUSTIN LEBO
Encourages people to use their free time constructively	*Justin spent his free time in the summer making bicycles for the children at the Kilbarchan Home for Boys.*
Gives a sense of satisfaction; builds self-esteem	
Opens volunteers' eyes to the great variety of people in need by providing opportunities to meet new and different types of people	
One successful community service experience leads to performing other services	
Volunteers learn they can help solve real social problems and needs	
Helps people to find out who they are, what their interests are, and what they are good at	

MAKE INFERENCES

INFERRING PEOPLE'S REACTIONS

By reading carefully, it is often possible to increase your understanding by inferring how different people in a story react to an event or to a person's decisions.

Look at the example and read the explanation.

In Reading One, paragraph 15, the author writes, "He [Justin] went to his parents with a proposal. 'When Justin was younger, say five or six,' says his mother, 'he used to give away some of his allowance to help others in need. His father and I would donate a dollar for every dollar Justin donated. So he asked us if it could be like the old days, if we'd match every dollar he put into buying old bikes. We said yes.'"

How would you describe the reaction of Justin's parents to his proposal?

    a. excited   **b.** skeptical   **c.** supportive

The correct answer is *c*. His parents agreed to help Justin buy more old bikes. They supported him by agreeing to give him money.

Work with a partner. Think about the people mentioned in Reading One. How do they react to Justin and his ideas? Read the questions and look at the paragraphs indicated. Then choose the best answer.

1. What was the Kilbarchan boys' first reaction when Justin started to leave without taking his bikes? *(paragraph 9)*

    a. confused   **b.** admiring   **c.** appreciative

2. How do you think Justin's mother felt about his idea to build one bike for every boy at Kilbarchan? *(paragraph 11)*

    a. excited   **b.** unsure   **c.** appreciative

3. How would you characterize the Kilbarchan director's reaction to Justin's proposal to build a bike for every boy at Kilbarchan? *(paragraph 12)*

    a. confused   **b.** helpful   **c.** skeptical

4. How did the people who called and left bikes react to the letter in the newspaper? *(paragraph 19)*

    a. stubbornly   **b.** enthusiastically   **c.** resentfully

5. How do you think the kid who Justin overheard felt about getting a bike? *(paragraph 25)*

    a. proud   **b.** surprised   **c.** appreciative

EXPRESS OPINIONS

Work with a partner. Discuss your ideas. Then report your ideas to the class.

1. Justin was able to combine something he loved to do with philanthropic work. Is it very important to love what you are volunteering to do? Why?

2. Who do you think received more from Justin's philanthropic work, Justin or the people that he gave the bikes to? Explain.

3. No one forced Justin to do what he did. Do you believe this makes Justin an exceptional young man? Explain.

GO TO MyEnglishLab TO GIVE YOUR OPINION ABOUT ANOTHER QUESTION.

READING TWO SOME TAKE THE TIME GLADLY PROBLEMS WITH MANDATORY VOLUNTEERING

READ

Many educational organizations in the United States require high school students to devote a certain number of hours outside of the classroom to community service in order to graduate. Supporters of mandatory volunteering believe that the school's role should include both preparing children to be academically successful and helping them to be responsible citizens who are active participants in their communities.

However, not everybody believes that mandatory volunteering is a good idea. Those opposed to the requirement believe that the term "mandatory volunteering" is an oxymoron, a contradiction; they believe that volunteering should be something you do of your own free will. It is not something that is forced on you.

1 Look at the boldfaced words in the two opinions and think about the questions.

1. Which words do you know the meanings of?

2. Can you use any of the words in a sentence?

2 Read the two opinions about mandatory volunteering. As you read, notice the boldfaced vocabulary. Try to guess its meaning from the context.

SOME TAKE THE TIME GLADLY

By Mensah Dean (from the *Washington Times*)

1   Mandatory volunteering made many members of Maryland's high school class of '97 grumble with **indignation**.

2   Future seniors,[1] however, probably won't be as resistant now that the program has been broken in. Some, like John Maloney, already have completed their required hours of approved community service. The Bowie High School sophomore[2] earned his hours in eighth grade[3] by volunteering two nights a week at the Larkin-Chase Nursing and Restorative Center in Bowie.

3   He played shuffleboard, cards, and other games with the senior citizens.[4] He also helped plan parties for them and visited their rooms to keep them company.

4   John, fifteen, is not finished volunteering. Once a week he videotapes animals at the Prince George County animal shelter in Forestville. His footage is shown on the Bowie public access television channel in hopes of finding homes for the animals.

5   "Volunteering is better than just sitting around," says John, "and I like animals; I don't want to see them put to sleep."[5]

6   He's not the only volunteer in his family. His sister, Melissa, an eighth grader, has completed her hours also volunteering at Larkin-Chase.

7   "It is a good idea to have kids go out into the community, but it's frustrating to have to

write essays about the work," she said. "It makes you feel like you're doing it for the requirement and not for yourself."

8   The high school's service learning office, run by Beth Ansley, provides information on organizations seeking volunteers so that students will have an easier time **fulfilling** their hours.

9   "It's ridiculous that people are opposing the requirements," said Amy Rouse, who this summer has worked at the Ronald McDonald House[6] and has helped to rebuild a church in Clinton.

10   "So many people won't do the service unless it's mandatory," Rouse said, "but once they start doing it, they'll really like it and hopefully it will become a part of their lives—like it has become a part of mine."

---

[1] **seniors:** students in the last year of high school, approximately 17–18 years old

[2] **sophomore:** a student in the second year of high school, approximately 15–16 years old

[3] **eighth grade:** The U.S. public school system begins with kindergarten and continues with grades 1–12. A student in eighth grade is approximately 13–14 years old.

[4] **senior citizens:** people over the age of 65

[5] **put to sleep:** give an animal drugs so that it dies without pain

[6] **Ronald McDonald House:** a residence, usually near a hospital, which provides a home and other support services for the families of children who require a lot of time in the hospital because of serious illness

Problems with Mandatory Volunteering

1   I think the school board's plan to implement a mandatory volunteering program is a terrible idea.

2   First of all, let me say that I am already a volunteer and proud of it. In fact, I do volunteer work at my local library as well as tutor elementary school kids at my church's after-school program. I believe that, at least in part, the reason that I enjoy volunteering and am effective at it is that I am not being forced to do it. In addition, I can choose to volunteer with people and organizations that interest me; that is not always the case with mandatory volunteering.

3   I am a new transfer student in this district and am very happy that we currently do not have a mandatory volunteering program here; however, my last school did, and for many students it was not a good experience. Imagine how new students must feel when they are told that to graduate they will have to volunteer hundreds of hours! They are already overwhelmed by schoolwork and so often end up just completing their hours, but not putting in any effort. As a result, the quality of their volunteer work is much worse than the work done by volunteers who actually choose to volunteer. In addition, students who are told they must volunteer may become **resentful** and not want to volunteer in the future. Volunteering becomes a negative experience. On the other hand, many students do already volunteer, and those who choose to do so make a real difference.

4   Another problem is that many students have busy after–school schedules: they have family, work, and athletic responsibilities. For example, many students need to be able to work after school in order to help out their families or to save money for college. Some have to take care of younger siblings or grandparents, and still others use this time to participate in athletics. School starts and ends at set times, and any school-related activity after those times is extracurricular, such as the football team or science club. To participate in these activities is a personal choice, just as volunteering should be. Nothing should be required of a student after school except homework.

5   Finally, the term 'mandatory volunteering' is an **oxymoron**. Volunteering is something you do of your own free will. If it is mandatory, it is not volunteering. For all these reasons, I am totally **opposed** to our school implementing a mandatory volunteering program and suggest that volunteering be left as a personal choice. It should not be made mandatory.

COMPREHENSION

Both writers give reasons to support their opinions in the editorials. Complete the chart with reasons found in the editorials. Share your list with the class.

FOR MANDATORY VOLUNTEERING	AGAINST MANDATORY VOLUNTEERING
1.	1. *Volunteering is a personal choice.*
2.	2.
3.	3.
	4.
	5.
	6.

GO TO MyEnglishLab *FOR MORE VOCABULARY PRACTICE.*

READING SKILL

1 Go back to the two opinions in Reading Two. What words do the authors use to show that the opposing point of view makes no sense? Why do they choose to use these words?

RECOGNIZING PERSUASIVE LANGUAGE

When trying to persuade a reader to agree with their ideas, writers use persuasive language. These words or phrases add structure and depth to writers' ideas. Writers use persuasive language to support their own points of view and also to oppose ideas they are trying to refute. In many cases, persuasive language evokes strong emotions.

Look at this quote from paragraph 9 of "Some Take the Time Gladly": "'It's ridiculous that people are opposing the requirements,' said Amy Rouse, who this summer has worked at the Ronald McDonald House and has helped to rebuild a church in Clinton."

What words does the author use to persuade the reader that his point of view is the only sensible way to think?

He uses a quotation that connects the words *ridiculous* and *opposing* to support his point of view and dismiss those who don't agree with him. The writer could have stated the same idea without evoking such strong emotions. For example, instead of using that quotation, he could have written, "It *doesn't make sense* that people *don't like* the requirements," but that would not be as persuasive. The word *ridiculous* suggests that it is impossible to take people's reactions seriously; they make no sense. With *opposing*, the writer shows that it is not just that people don't like the idea of mandatory volunteering but that they are actively trying to stop it. This choice of words is strong and creates a clear difference in attitudes toward mandatory volunteering.

2 Reread Reading Two and find the persuasive words that describe the opposing point of view. Look in the indicated paragraphs.

SOME TAKE THE TIME GLADLY

Paragraph and number of words or phrases	Persuasive words that evoke negative emotions
1 (2)	
2 (1)	
7 (1)	
9 (2)	*ridiculous* *opposing*

PROBLEMS WITH MANDATORY VOLUNTEERING

Paragraph and number of words or phrases	Persuasive words that evoke negative emotions
1 (1)	
3 (5)	
5 (2)	

3 With a partner, look at the words and phrases you have selected and discuss the questions.

1. How do these words influence your thinking about the topic of mandatory volunteering?

2. Do these words make you agree more or less with the writers' opinions?

3. Which two words from each of the articles were most effective in making you agree with the authors?

GO TO MyEnglishLab FOR MORE SKILL PRACTICE.

STEP 1: Organize

The readings in this unit address four issues relating to volunteering.

- Personal enrichment
- Personal choice
- Time commitment
- Dedication to work

Go back to the indicated paragraphs in the readings and find quotes or statements that relate—either positively or negatively— to one or more of the issues. Underline the passages in the text. Then write the issue(s) next to the correct paragraph number in the chart. Some issues may be used more than once.

JUSTIN LEBO (R1)	
PARAGRAPH	ISSUE
22	Dedication to work
23	
24	

SOME TAKE THE TIME GLADLY (R2)	
PARAGRAPH	ISSUE
2	
5	

PROBLEMS WITH MANDATORY VOLUNTEERING (R2)	
PARAGRAPH	ISSUE
2	
3	
4	

STEP 2: Synthesize

Imagine you are Justin Lebo. Use a separate piece of paper or go to MyEnglishLab and write a letter to one of the two authors of the editorials in Reading Two. Be sure to clearly state your opinion about mandatory volunteering. Use Justin's experience as a volunteer to either disagree with or support the position stated in the editorial and explain why. Use the quotes or statements that you underlined in Step 1.

GO TO MyEnglishLab TO CHECK WHAT YOU LEARNED.

3 FOCUS ON WRITING

VOCABULARY

REVIEW

1 Look at the word forms chart. The vocabulary from the unit is boldfaced.

NOUN	VERB	ADJECTIVE	ADVERB
admiration	admire	**admiring**	admiringly
challenge	challenge	challenging	X
determination	determine	**determined**	X
devotion	**devote**	devoted	devotedly
donation	**donate**	donated	X
fulfillment	fulfill	fulfilled **fulfilling**	X
indignation	X	indignant	indignantly
inspiration	**inspire**	inspired inspirational	inspirationally
management	**manage**	manageable	manageably
opposition	**oppose**	opposite opposing	X
oxymoron	X	oxymoronic	X
passion	X	passionate	passionately
pride	X	proud	**proudly**
proposal	propose	proposed	X
resentment	resent	**resentful**	resentfully
ridicule	ridicule	**ridiculous**	ridiculously
satisfaction	satisfy	satisfied satisfying satisfactory	satisfactorily
thrill	thrill	**thrilled** thrilling	thrillingly

2 Complete the sentences using words from the word form chart in Exercise 1. Pay attention to verb tense and subject-verb agreement.

1. Justin Lebo had to rely on _____ from people in order to complete the
   (donate)
   bicycles for the children at Kilbarchan.

2. Justin felt _____ when he saw how the boys enjoyed the first two
   (inspire)
   bicycles he had made.

3. Many people hope that after experiencing mandatory volunteering, students will

   become _____ about volunteering in general.
   (passion)

4. Justin Lebo met the _____ of making a bike for each boy at Kilbarchan.
   (challenge)

5. When Justin _____ that his parents give a dollar for every dollar he
   (proposal)
   donated, they agreed.

6. Critics worry that students who are forced to volunteer and have a bad experience may

   become _____ and never volunteer again.
   (resent)

7. Although many people support mandatory volunteering, there is still a lot of

   _____ to it.
   (oppose)

8. Justin feels a lot of _____ in the fact that he was able to donate so many
   (proudly)
   bikes.

9. Justin's neighbor _____ his accomplishments.
   (admiring)

10. In many schools, students are not able to graduate without _____ a
    (fulfill)
    volunteering requirement.

11. Mandatory volunteering is an emotionally charged issue. Many critics are

    _____ that volunteering is not left up to the individual.
    (indignation)

EXPAND

A **phrasal verb** consists of a verb and a particle. The combination often has a meaning that is different from the meaning of the separate parts.

Work in a small group. Read the sentences. Circle the best explanation for each underlined phrasal verb.

1. Supporters of mandatory volunteering say volunteering for community service is time better spent than <u>sitting around</u> all day watching television or playing computer games.

   a. doing nothing special or useful

   b. sitting with friends in a circle

   c. not taking part in something

2. Justin Lebo has <u>fixed up</u> between 150 and 200 bikes and has given them all away.

   a. arranged a date for someone

   b. repaired or restored something to working order

   c. bought at a low price

3. Supporters of mandatory volunteering hope that students will <u>keep on</u> volunteering after they have fulfilled their requirement.

   a. hold

   b. consider

   c. continue

4. At first, Justin could not <u>figure out</u> what to do with his two bikes.

   a. satisfy

   b. make a plan for

   c. take part in

5. Justin had so many bikes that he had to <u>clear out</u> his basement and start building them there.

   a. make room on a table

   b. clean an area or place

   c. empty an area or place

6. When the students <u>found out</u> the new graduation requirements, they were indignant and completely opposed to them.

   a. created something

   b. discovered something lost

   c. learned new information about something

7. After the newspaper article was published, many people <u>called</u> Justin <u>up</u> and offered him their old bikes.

   a. discussed a situation

   b. spoke disrespectfully to someone

   c. got in touch with by phone

8. People fear that if students do not do community service, they will <u>end up</u> being uncaring and unsympathetic individuals.

   a. complete a project

   b. be in a situation without planning it

   c. stop something

9. When people donate old clothes to a community center, the center staff will often come to the house and <u>pick up</u> the donations.

   a. start to increase

   b. clean something

   c. collect something

10. Justin was afraid that the garage sales would <u>dry up</u> by the end of the summer.

    a. be dull and uninteresting

    b. slowly come to an end

    c. become useless

CREATE

Imagine you are a reporter interviewing the people below. How would they respond to the questions? Write answers using the words given. Change the word form or tense if necessary. Use a separate piece of paper or go to MyEnglishLab.

1. | ~~devote~~ | ~~determined~~ | ~~keep on~~ | ~~proudly~~ |

REPORTER: Your son Justin is quite remarkable, isn't he?

DIANE LEBO: Yes, he is. After Justin saw the boys having so much fun on their bicycles, he became devoted to the project. He was determined to get every boy on a bicycle, so he kept on working hard. I'm very proud of him.

2. | challenge | inspired | passion | sit around |

REPORTER: After fixing the first bike, did you ever think you would end up repairing and donating over 150 more?

JUSTIN LEBO: _____

_____

_____

_____

3. | donate | end up | manage | proposal |

REPORTER: What did you think when Justin first told you he was planning on building a bicycle for every boy at Kilbarchan?

DIRECTOR OF THE KILBARCHAN SCHOOL: _____

_____

_____

_____

4. | donate | figure out | fulfilling | proudly |

REPORTER: Why do you support mandatory volunteering?

STUDENT SUPPORTING
MANDATORY VOLUNTEERING: _____

_____

_____

_____

5. | find out | indignant | manage | oxymoron |

REPORTER: Why are you opposed to mandatory volunteering?

STUDENT OPPOSING
MANDATORY VOLUNTEERING: _____

_____

_____

_____

GO TO MyEnglishLab *FOR MORE VOCABULARY PRACTICE.*

GRAMMAR

1 Examine the sentences and answer the questions with a partner.

a. **<u>Even though</u>** <u>Justin was not required by his school to volunteer</u>, he chose to work on bikes and donate them.

b. **<u>Despite the fact that</u>** <u>many students initially don't want to volunteer</u>, they learn to love it and continue after the school requirements are fulfilled.

c. It is a good idea to get students to go out into the community **<u>although</u>** <u>it can be frustrating to have to write about it.</u>

1. Each sentence is composed of two clauses.[1] What are the clauses in each sentence?

2. Do the clauses that begin with the concessions *although, even though,* and *despite the fact that* introduce a positive or negative opinion of mandatory volunteering?

3. Do the three sentences have the same punctuation? If not, why not?

4. Which clauses express the writer's main idea: the clauses with the concessions *although, even though,* and *despite the fact that . . .* or the other clauses?

CONCESSIONS

1. Use **concessions** when expressing an opinion, where you need to support your opinion but, at the same time, recognize and describe the opposing opinion. Presenting similarities and differences in contrasting points of view makes your argument stronger.

2. Use these words to concede or acknowledge similarities or differences between two contrasting ideas.

although	even though	despite the fact that
though	in spite of the fact that	

Note that these words do not introduce a complete thought—they introduce **dependent clauses**. A dependent clause cannot stand alone as a sentence. It must be joined to an independent (main) clause.

3. The **main clause** usually describes the point that is more important.

a. Even though Justin was not required by his school to volunteer, he chose to work on bikes and donate them.

<u>Writer's opinion</u>: Justin's school had no requirement for volunteering, but he still wanted to use his time to help others.
<u>Acknowledging the opposite view</u>: You would expect Justin not to volunteer unless he was forced to.

b. It is a good idea to get students to go out into the community **although it can be frustrating to have to write about it**.

---

[1] **clause**: a group of words containing a subject and verb that forms part of a sentence. Clauses can be dependent or independent.

Writer's opinion: There may be problems with assignments relating to mandatory volunteering, but students should still be required to go out into the community. Acknowledging the opposite view: Being forced to write about your volunteering takes away from any benefit you may receive from it.

4. When a sentence begins with a dependent clause, use a comma to separate it from the main clause.

   Even though garage sales had dried up by the end of August, Justin got enough old bikes as the result of a letter to the newspaper.

5. When the sentence begins with an independent clause, do not use a comma.

   Justin got enough old bikes as the result of a letter to the newspaper **even though garage sales had dried up by the end of August**.

2 Combine each pair of sentences using the words in parentheses. Does your new sentence support mandatory volunteering or oppose mandatory volunteering?

1. Supporters of mandatory volunteering say that it is a good way for students to get valuable work experience. Critics say students should be paid if they are doing work. (even though)

   Supporters of mandatory volunteering say it is a good way for students to get valuable experience even though they are not paid.

   (supports mandatory volunteering) / opposes mandatory volunteering

2. Critics of mandatory volunteering maintain that a school should not require a student to do anything after school except homework. Supporters of mandatory volunteering say that volunteering is better than just sitting around watching TV or playing video games. (though)

   _____

   _____

   supports mandatory volunteering / opposes mandatory volunteering

3. Opponents argue that volunteering is a personal choice, and so it shouldn't be mandatory. Supporters note that schools have many required classes that may not be a student's personal choice. (although)

   _____

   _____

   supports mandatory volunteering / opposes mandatory volunteering

(continued on next page)

4. Critics worry that a bad volunteering experience will stop people from volunteering again in the future. Supporters maintain that most student volunteers have successful experiences, and many continue to volunteer later in life. (in spite of the fact that)

_____

_____

supports mandatory volunteering / opposes mandatory volunteering

5. Supporters believe that mandatory volunteering can benefit the community. Critics feel that mandatory volunteers may do a bad job and, therefore, cause more harm than good. (despite the fact that)

_____

_____

supports mandatory volunteering / opposes mandatory volunteering

3 Write sentences expressing your opinion about each educational issue. Use the concession words in the box. Does your sentence support mandatory volunteering (**S**) or oppose mandatory volunteering (**O**)? Write **S** or **O** on the line.

although	even though	though
despite the fact that	in spite of the fact that	

1. busy after-school schedules __S__

   Although many students do have busy after-school schedules, with planning,

   most should be able to find some time to volunteer either after school or

   during free class periods.

2. personal choice _____

_____

_____

_____

3. good to get students out into the community _____

_____

_____

_____

4. volunteer may do a bad job _____

_____

_____

_____

5. builds self-esteem _____

_____

_____

_____

■■■■■■■■■■■   *GO TO* MyEnglishLab *FOR MORE GRAMMAR PRACTICE AND TO CHECK WHAT YOU LEARNED.*

FINAL WRITING TASK

In this unit, you read about the pros and cons of mandatory volunteering. Imagine that your school has proposed a mandatory community service program. Students can choose an organization to volunteer for and are required to give at least five hours of time a month. Students must volunteer after school but will receive academic credit.

You are going to *write a persuasive essay explaining your opinion about the volunteering program*. Use the vocabulary and grammar from the unit.*

PREPARE TO WRITE: Using a T-Chart

A **T-chart** is a prewriting tool that helps you examine two aspects of a topic, such as the pros and cons associated with it. When you want to persuade someone to agree with your point of view, you need to have strong reasons to support your opinion (pros). You also need to acknowledge and address possible arguments against your opinion (cons).

1 Work in a small group. On a separate piece of paper, complete a T-chart like the one below with reasons to support a mandatory community service program (pros) and reasons against it (cons). Share your ideas with the class.

PROS	CONS

---

* For Alternative Writing Topics, see page 187. These topics can be used in place of the writing topic for this unit or as homework. The alternative topics relate to the theme of the unit but may not target the same grammar or rhetorical structures taught in the unit.

2 Use your T-chart to decide if this program should be implemented or not. Write a thesis statement stating your opinion.

WRITE: A Persuasive Essay

In a **persuasive essay**, your goal is to convince the reader to agree with your position. Here are some important points:

1. **State your position in the thesis statement**. The reader must know how you feel at the start of the essay.

2. **Present strong arguments to support your position**.

3. **Present strong support for your arguments**. Provide detailed examples, anecdotes, quotes, and statistics.

4. **Acknowledge the counterarguments presented by the opposing side**. Then refute the counterarguments by showing why they are weak. This will make your argument stronger.

1 Read the persuasive essay and answer the questions with a partner.

Cutting Our Sports Teams Is Not a Healthy Decision

Obesity rates are escalating! Students are more stressed than ever before! These are just a couple of recent news headlines. At the same time, ironically, our school administration has recently proposed eliminating all sports teams, citing a decrease in team participation, low attendance, and overall high cost of maintaining these teams. While cutting team sports from the budget would save money, the immediate and long-term negative results would not be worth the money saved.

First, though it is true that many teams have not had high numbers of participants, this is not a reason to cut *all* teams. A few teams still do have high participation rates and very dedicated players. One solution is to keep one or two high participation sports per season, for example, fall football, winter basketball and swimming, and spring track and baseball.

Second, the school is concerned about poor audience attendance at the games and uses this argument to support the idea that there is a decreasing interest in our teams. Although there may be lower audience numbers than in the past, the students who do go are loyal fans. Moreover, this devoted fan base has helped build a community that promotes school spirit across the campus.

This school spirit affects all students whether or not they attend each game. For example, after last year's baseball finals, more baseball hats were sold in the campus store than ever before even though most of the students wearing the hats had not attended one game! Adam Deering, a student, stated, "Even though I don't go to all of the games, I am still supportive of my school and proud of it. School can be really stressful, and the teams help reduce that stress and give students something else to focus on and bring them together besides academics."

Finally, the administration states that the cost of keeping team sports is just too costly. Though the cost of sports teams may be high, the price paid for cutting the teams in the long term is even higher. Sports teams are a daily reminder of the importance of maintaining a balanced, healthy life style. School sports help promote life-long healthy habits. With this in mind, shouldn't the school be putting more money into sports rather than taking it away?

1. What is the student's main position in regards to cutting school sports?

   _____

2. What are the three main arguments the school uses to support cutting school sports? Complete the left side of the chart.

3. What are the counterarguments the student presents? Complete the right side of the chart.

ARGUMENTS TO CUT SCHOOL SPORTS	COUNTERARGUMENTS

4. Do you think the counterarguments are convincing? Why or why not?

   _____

   _____

5. What examples are used to strengthen the student's argument? Underline them.

2 Start planning your essay by looking at your list of pros and cons in Prepare to Write. Choose three of the strongest arguments you will use to support your position and write them in sections 2–4 in the brace map below. Add details on the lettered lines to support your arguments.

1. Introduction and Thesis Statement:

2.

a. _____

b. _____

c. _____

3.

a. _____

b. _____

c. _____

4.

a. _____

b. _____

c. _____

5. Conclusion

3 Look at the arguments in support of your position in your brace map. Write them in the left column. What are the possible counterarguments? Write them in the middle column. Why are those counterarguments weak? Write the reasons in the right column. You will acknowledge the counterarguments in your essay using a concession clause and then refute them.

ARGUMENTS FOR / AGAINST COMMUNITY SERVICE PROGRAMS	COUNTERARGUMENTS	REFUTATION (REASONS WHY THE COUNTERARGUMENT IS WEAK)

4 Now write the first draft of your persuasive essay. Use the information in Prepare to Write and your brace map to plan your essay. Include an introductory and a concluding paragraph. When writing the body, be sure to acknowledge the counterarguments by using a concession clause. Be sure to use vocabulary and grammar from the unit.

REVISE: Writing Introductions and Conclusions

The Introduction

The **introduction** to an essay can have several functions. It states the thesis, or controlling idea, and gives the reader an idea of what will be discussed. It can also provide background information on the topic. However, one of the most important functions is to engage the reader's interest and make the reader want to continue reading. Here are three common techniques used in introductions:

1. State why the topic is important.

2. Ask a provocative question.

3. Tell a relevant story or anecdote.

1 Work with a partner. Read the three introductions. Underline the thesis statements. Then label each introduction with the letter of the technique used.

Introduction 1   Technique: _____

Society today is obsessed with commercialism. People think only about making money and buying more and more possessions. Many college students choose their majors by deciding which careers will pay the most money. Young people today are not learning enough about the nonfinancial rewards in life. They are not learning about the joy and fulfillment of helping others. This is a very serious problem with education today. It is important to support the proposal for a mandatory community service program so that young people will learn the value of giving to others.

Introduction 2   Technique: _____

When I was in high school, I was required to take part in a community service project. At first, I really didn't want to do it. I thought it would be boring and a waste of time. The school let us choose our project, and I decided to work at an animal shelter. I like animals, and I thought the work wouldn't be too difficult. I worked all semester helping the veterinarian take care of sick and abandoned animals. I was surprised to find that by the end of the semester, I really liked my community service job. In fact, it was my favorite part of the week, and I signed up to work another semester. So I am a perfect illustration of the benefits of mandatory community service programs in school. This is why I support a program of mandatory community service in our university.

Introduction 3   Technique: _____

We all want to live in a better world, don't we? Poor children do not get enough to eat. The school system is not educating our kids. The environment is getting more and more polluted. What would happen if we all did something to solve the problems around us? Well, we can do something, and we should. A mandatory community service program in our school will give students a valuable experience and also help solve important problems in our community.

2 Look at the introduction of your essay. Make sure you have a thesis statement and use one of the three techniques for writing an effective introduction.

The Conclusion

The **conclusion** of an essay should bring the ideas of the essay to a close. Most commonly, the conclusion restates the thesis of the essay and offers the writer's final thoughts on the topic. Here are three common techniques used in conclusions:

1. Tell a relevant story or anecdote.

2. Ask a final question that the reader can think about.

3. Make a prediction about the future.

3 Work with a partner. Read the three conclusions. Underline the sentences that restate the thesis of the essay. Label the conclusion with the letter of the technique used.

Conclusion 1   Technique: _____

I urge everyone to support the mandatory community service program in our university. It has many benefits for both students and the community, including teaching students new skills, building bridges between students and community members, and exposing students to new experiences. I believe that if students try volunteering, many of them will discover that community service can be an enjoyable and rewarding experience.

Conclusion 2   Technique: _____

As you can see, community service benefits everyone. I know my life will never be the same after my experience in the veterinary clinic. Before I did my service, I wasn't sure what I wanted to do for a career. This experience has broadened my future and helped shape my goals. Now I know for certain that I want to do something in the animal sciences. Without this experience, I'm not sure I would have known what I wanted to do. Isn't this called a win-win situation?

Conclusion 3   Technique: _____

On a final note, I'd like to share a personal experience. Last year I started tutoring an elementary school student whose parents don't speak English. At first, he was resentful that he had to stay after school and do more schoolwork. Truthfully, it was also hard for me knowing he did

(continued on next page)

not want to be there. But as the year progressed, I got to know him and the kind of books he liked to read. He began to look forward to our weekly sessions and was eager to see what books I had brought for him. Now we are not just reading friends, but we are real friends. I know I have made a difference in his life, and he has certainly made a difference in mine. If I hadn't been required to do community service, I know I would not have had this experience. And I would not have discovered what a difference I can make.

4 Look at the conclusion of your essay. Make sure you have restated the thesis and have included your final thoughts by using one of the three conclusion techniques.

▪▪▪ *GO TO* MyEnglishLab *FOR MORE SKILL PRACTICE.*

EDIT: Writing the Final Draft

Go to MyEnglishLab and write the final draft of your essay. Carefully edit it for grammatical and mechanical errors, such as spelling, capitalization, and punctuation. Make sure you use some of the grammar and vocabulary from the unit. Use the checklist to help you write your final draft. Then submit your essay to your teacher.

FINAL DRAFT CHECKLIST

❏ Does the essay have an introduction, three body paragraphs, and a conclusion?

❏ Does the introduction include a thesis statement? Does it engage the interest of the reader?

❏ Does each body paragraph have a topic sentence? Do all the topic sentences support the thesis statement?

❏ Do the body paragraphs present your arguments for or against mandatory volunteering? Do you acknowledge and then refute possible counterarguments?

❏ Did you use concessions to introduce the counterargument?

❏ Does the conclusion restate the thesis and offer final thoughts?

❏ Have you used the vocabulary from the unit?

UNIT PROJECT

What are ways that people are incorporating philanthropy into their lives in your area? Research a community center or project. Follow these steps:

STEP 1: As a class, brainstorm a list of community centers or community work in your area, or list community centers you have heard about. Discuss the services these centers offer, such as serving food, offering shelter, meeting medical or educational needs, helping repair homes, and cleaning up the neighborhood.

STEP 2: Work in a small group. Research a community center or project. Then, individually or in groups, go to a center or project headquarters and gather information to organize your ideas on a separate piece of paper. You may also take photos and collect brochures. If there is no center or project near you, go to the library or use the Internet to find information about activities in another area.

- Name of center or project
- History: When was it started? Who started it? Why?
- Type of people helped

- Types of services offered
- Type of people who work there. Are there volunteers? How many?
- Funding: How are activities paid for? Where does the funding come from?

STEP 3: Prepare a PowerPoint™ presentation or a poster with photos and present your findings to the class.

ALTERNATIVE WRITING TOPICS

Write an essay about one of the topics. Use the vocabulary and grammar from the unit.

1. Imagine you are responsible for setting up a community service program in your city. What kind of program would you start? Who would it serve? Would there be volunteers? Who would they be? What would you hope to accomplish? Be specific.

2. Read John Bunyan's quotation about philanthropy.

   "He who bestows[1] his goods upon the poor,
   Shall have as much again, and ten times more."
   —John Bunyan, *Pilgrim's Progress,* Part Two, Section VII

   What is Bunyan trying to say? There are many different ways to "[bestow your] goods upon the poor." What are some ways, and why do people perform these acts?

   ---
   [1] **bestows:** gives someone something important

GO TO MyEnglishLab *TO WRITE ABOUT ONE OF THE ALTERNATIVE TOPICS, WATCH A VIDEO ABOUT A LOCAL TEEN MAKING A DIFFERENCE, AND TAKE THE UNIT 6 ACHIEVEMENT TEST.*

THE EMPTY
Classroom

1 FOCUS ON THE TOPIC

1. Look at the unit title and the photograph. Fewer students are studying in the classroom. Where are they studying?

2. A new model of online distance learning, called a Massive Online Open Course or MOOC,[1] is becoming increasingly popular. What do you think the benefits and the challenges of this type of model are?

3. What would happen if online distance learning were the future of education?

---

[1] **MOOC:** online courses designed to have open access that are offered by many universities as well as private organizations. They are typically tuition-free because they do not offer academic credit.

GO TO MyEnglishLab *TO CHECK WHAT YOU KNOW.*

READING ONE   TEACHING TO THE WORLD FROM CENTRAL NEW JERSEY

VOCABULARY

1 Read the timeline of the history of distance education. Try to understand the boldfaced words from the context.

Distance Education Timeline	
1728	Caleb Phillips, of Boston, challenges the **assumption** that education must take place in a classroom. He offers a correspondence course in shorthand.[2] He communicates with students using the mail.
1840	Because of a newly established affordable postage rate, the **issue** of cost is eliminated from distance education. Sir Isaac Pittman from London is able to successfully market his shorthand correspondence course, which **enhances** the existing method of shorthand.
1858	Distance education takes a **crucial** step forward as University of London becomes the first university in the world to offer distance-learning degrees.
1873	Anna Ticknor **analyzes** the existing educational opportunities for women and decides to create the *Society to Encourage Study at Home*, which offers correspondence courses to more than 10,000 women over the next two decades.
1885	William Rainey Harper, future president of the University of Chicago, predicts, in **anticipation** of the direction distance education is moving, "the day is coming when the work done by correspondence will be greater in amount than that done in the classrooms of our academies and colleges."
1906	University of Wisconsin, in a **subsequent** advance, records lectures and sends them to students on phonograph records.
1920s	Schools experiment with course delivery **via** radio broadcasts.
1930s	Television is first used as a method of course delivery.
1950s	College credit courses are offered via television. Television instruction in **collaboration** with correspondence study is used.
1989	Options for course delivery **significantly** change as a result of the World Wide Web, which allows online document sharing.
1995	First course delivered over the Internet is taught at Penn State University.

---

[2] **shorthand:** a fast method of writing using special signs or shorter forms to represent letters, words, and phrases

2000s	Distance education courses are delivered using **virtual** classrooms—multimedia resources, video conferencing, webcams etc. . . .
2008	The term MOOC is first used.
2012	The **diversity** of the student body grows as students from around the world enroll in MOOC courses. More than 150,000 students sign up for one MOOC course, "Introduction to Artificial Intelligence."

2 Write the words from the box next to their definitions.

analyze	collaboration	enhance	subsequent
~~anticipation~~	crucial	issue	via
assumption	diversity	significantly	virtual

1. ____anticipation____ the act of expecting something to happen

2. _____ a range of different people or things; variety

3. _____ extremely important

4. _____ a subject or problem that people discuss

5. _____ made, done, seen etc. on the Internet or on a computer, rather than in the real world

6. _____ something that you think is true although you have no proof

7. _____ the act of working together to make or produce something

8. _____ to examine or think about something carefully in order to understand it

9. _____ noticeably or importantly

10. _____ by way of or through

11. _____ coming after or following something else

12. _____ to make something better

GO TO MyEnglishLab FOR MORE VOCABULARY PRACTICE.

You are going to read an article about a Princeton University professor's experience teaching 40,000 students from 113 countries.

Read the first paragraph of "Teaching to the World from Central New Jersey." Then work with a partner to answer the questions.

1. What challenges do you think Professor Duneier will face teaching so many students?

2. What do you predict will be the positive impact of having students from 113 countries in the course?

3. What do you predict will be some of the problems resulting from having students from so many different countries in the course?

Keep your discussion in mind as you read the rest of the article.

TEACHING TO THE WORLD FROM CENTRAL NEW JERSEY
By Mitchell Duneier

1   A few months ago, just as the campus of Princeton University had grown nearly silent after commencement, 40,000 students from  113 countries arrived here via the Internet to take a free course in introductory sociology. The noncredit Princeton offering came about through a collaboration between Coursera, a new venture in online learning, and 16 universities, including my own.

2   When my class was announced last spring, I was both excited and nervous. Unlike computer science and other subjects in which the answers are pretty much the same around the globe, sociology can be very different depending on the country that you come from. As letters and e-mail messages began arriving in **anticipation** of my course, I wondered how I, an American professor, could relate my subject to people I didn't know from so many different societies.

3   Would my lectures become yet another example of American ethnocentrism[3] and imperialism as I presented my sociological concepts like so many measuring sticks for the experiences of others around the world? Was it really possible, I asked myself, to provide quality education to tens of thousands of students in more than 100 countries at the same time? And in a way that would respond to the **diversity** of viewpoints represented from six continents?

4   My concerns grew deeper as I sat before the cold eye of the camera to record my first lecture. With nobody to ask me a question, or give me bored looks, or laugh at my jokes, I had no clues as to how the students might be responding. Staring into this void, it was hard for me to imagine that anyone was listening. Can we even call these "lectures" when there is no audience within the speaker's view? Aren't those interpersonal cues—those knowing nods and furrowed brows—that go

[3] **ethnocentrism:** based on the idea that your own race, nation, group, etc. is better than any other; used in order to show disapproval

from the audience to the professor as **crucial** to the definition of a lecture as the cues that go from the lecturer to the audience?

5   My opening discussion of C. Wright Mills's classic 1959 book, *The Sociological Imagination*, was a close reading of the text, in which I reviewed a key chapter line by line. I asked students to follow along in their own copies, as I do in the lecture hall. When I give this lecture on the Princeton campus, I usually receive a few penetrating questions. In this case, however, within a few hours of posting the online version, the course forums came alive with hundreds of comments and questions. Several days later there were thousands.

6   Although it was impossible for me to read even a fraction of the pages of students' comments as they engaged with one another, the software allowed me to take note of those that generated the most discussion. I was quickly able to see the **issues** that were most meaningful to my students.

7   In addition to the course lectures, I arranged live exchanges **via** a video chat room, in which six to eight students from around the world—some selected from the online class, others volunteers here at Princeton—participated with me in a seminar-style discussion of the readings while thousands of their online classmates listened in to the live stream or to recordings later. During these weekly sessions, I found that I was able to direct the discussion to issues that had been raised in the online postings.

8   Along with two Princeton students, our online seminar included university students from Nepal, Siberia, Iran, and Nigeria, a travel agent from Georgia, a civil servant from Singapore, and a fireman from Philadelphia. Their comments often revealed precisely how American sociology's **assumptions** about social life need to be **analyzed** and reconstructed in light of experiences elsewhere.

9   With so much volume, my audience became as visible to me as the students in a traditional lecture hall. This happened as I got to know them by sampling their comments on the forums and in the live, seminar-style discussions. As I developed a sense for them as people, I could imagine their nods and, increasingly, their critical questions. Within three weeks I had received more feedback on my sociological ideas than I had in a career of teaching, which **significantly** influenced each of my **subsequent** lectures and seminars.

10   Before the class began, I had played down this kind of teaching as inevitably a pale reflection of on-campus learning, both in terms of student-faculty interaction and the residential-college experience. Yet as I got to know some of my students, I came to feel that the difference was not of the sort I had imagined. For most of them, the choice was not between an online course and a traditional university. It was, as one student put it, "a choice between online class versus no class."

11   Nor had I imagined the **virtual** and real-time continuous interaction among the students. There were spontaneous and continuing in-person study groups in coffee shops in Katmandu and in pubs in London. Many people developed dialogues after following one another's posts on various subjects, while others got to know those with a common particular interest, such as racial differences in IQ, the prisoner abuses that took place at Abu Ghraib, or ethnocentrism— all topics covered in the lectures.

12   As one of hundreds who posted in the past few days wrote, "It has been an incredible experience for me, one that has not only taught me sociology, but the ways in which other cultures think, feel, and respond. I have many new 'friends' via this class. . . ." Another wrote, "It started as intellectual activity but

(continued on next page)

it's ending in an indescribable emotional relationship with all my classmates."

13   This is my cue. As I prepare to re-enter the lecture hall at Princeton this September and go back online in February, I am asking myself how I can translate the benefits of online technology to **enhance** the dialogue with and among my on-campus students, and between them and my online students around the globe. I had begun worrying about how I could bring the New Jersey campus experience to them; I ended by thinking about how to bring the world back to the classroom in Princeton.

Mitchell Duneier is a professor of sociology at Princeton University.

MAIN IDEAS

1 Look again at the Preview on page 192. How did your discussion help you understand the article?

2 Reading One discusses professor Duneier's feelings and concerns before, during, and after his MOOC. Circle the sentence that best answers the question. Share your answers with a partner.

1. **Before:** What was Professor Duneier's biggest concern about teaching the online course?

   a. No one would laugh at his jokes or be able to make eye contact with him.

   b. It might not be possible to provide quality education to students from more than 100 countries.

   c. Students wouldn't do the reading or participate in the forums because the course was free.

2. **During:** How did student participation affect Professor Duneier's feelings about his new course?

   a. Professor Duneier was overwhelmed by the number of student comments and so wasn't sure what issues were important to the students.

   b. Professor Duneier didn't know when students had a problem understanding him because of the lack of interpersonal cues.

   c. Student feedback influenced the direction Professor Duneier took in subsequent video chats.

3. **After:** What was the most important conclusion that Professor Duneier drew about online teaching after teaching this course?

    a. There were many benefits to online teaching that he would like to incorporate into his on-campus classes.

    b. It was a pale reflection of on-campus learning.

    c. For some students, the choice was an online class or no class at all.

DETAILS

Read each statement. Decide if it is **T** (true) or **F** (false) according to the reading. Write the number of the paragraph that supports your answer. If the statement is false, change it to make it true. Discuss your answers with a partner.

_T_ **1.** Professor Duneier realized that teaching sociology to students from many different societies would not be as easy as teaching them computer science.
    paragraph: _2_

_____ **2.** Before the first class even had ended, it was obvious from the number of comments and questions that students were interested.
    paragraph: _____

_____ **3.** The fact that Professor Duneier recorded his lectures in an empty classroom made it easy because no one would interrupt or distract him.
    paragraph: _____

_____ **4.** Although it was impossible to answer all the student comments and questions, he did answer the majority of them.
    paragraph: _____

_____ **5.** All the participants in the online seminar were Princeton students.
    paragraph: _____

_____ **6.** Because the course was delivered over the Internet, Professor Duneier felt disconnected from his students.
    paragraph: _____

_____ **7.** Students in the class did not remain anonymous to each other.
    paragraph: _____

_____ **8.** Professor Duneier's next online course will be in September.
    paragraph: _____

MAKE INFERENCES

INFERRING DEGREE OF CONCERN

Writers sometimes suggest their level of concern about something without stating it directly.

Look at the example and read the explanation.

In the text, Professor Duneier expresses several worries and concerns about the new course he will be teaching online.

How concerned is Professor Duneier that he is able to relate his sociology course to people he doesn't know from so many different societies?

(*paragraph 2*)

Where would you place his concern on the continuum?

Not very concerned	Somewhat concerned	Concerned	Very concerned

Answer: Somewhat concerned

- In the last sentence of paragraph 2, Professor Duneier uses the word "wonder" as he considers his new student population. This word does not express very much worry; he is asking himself questions.

- In the first sentence of paragraph 2, he says he is both "excited" and "nervous." These words express both positive and negative feelings.

After reading the text closely, we can infer that Professor Duneier is "somewhat concerned" about how he will be able to relate his course to this new student population. The language he uses suggests a concern but also an interest or excitement about his new endeavor.

For each concern or worry expressed by Professor Duneier in the reading, decide how concerned he is. Write an **X** in the column that best corresponds to his degree of concern. Refer to the paragraphs in parentheses.

HOW CONCERNED IS PROFESSOR DUNEIER THAT . . .	NOT VERY CONCERNED	SOMEWHAT CONCERNED	CONCERNED	VERY CONCERNED
1. his course will be perceived as ethnocentric and imperialistic? (*paragraph 3*)				
2. he will be able to deliver quality education? (*paragraph 3*)				
3. he will be able to respond to the diversity of his recorded lectures? (*paragraph 4*)				
4. he will not be able to see his audience during comments and questions? (*paragraph 4*)				

HOW CONCERNED IS PROFESSOR DUNEIER THAT . . .	NOT VERY CONCERNED	SOMEWHAT CONCERNED	CONCERNED	VERY CONCERNED
5. he would be able to respond to his students' questions, comments, and discussions? *(paragraphs 5, 6, 7)*				
6. he would be able to direct the discussion? *(paragraph 7)*				
7. he would develop a sense of his students as people? *(paragraph 9)*				
8. there would be student-faculty interaction? *(paragraph 10)*				
9. he would be able to take his online experience back to the classroom in Princeton? *(paragraph 13)*				

EXPRESS OPINIONS

Discuss the questions in a small group. Then share your ideas with the class.

1. Do you think it is possible to teach all subjects as MOOCs, or are there some subjects that must be taught face-to-face in a classroom or with a smaller enrollment? Explain.

2. Would you enjoy and be successful in a MOOC? Why or why not? Be specific.

3. Do you think distance learning is the future of education? Do you think we will still have classrooms as we know them in 50 or 100 years?

■■■■■■■■■■■■■■■■■■■■■■ *GO TO MyEnglishLab TO GIVE YOUR OPINION ABOUT ANOTHER QUESTION.*

READ

1 Look at the boldfaced words in the reading and think about the questions.

1. Which words do you know the meanings of?

2. Can you use any of the words in a sentence?

This story was written by Isaac Asimov in 1951. It addresses the question of distance learning using a computer. At that time, the idea of this type of learning was science fiction, and having a home computer was unimaginable. Most people did not even own a television set at the time!

2 Read the story, *The Fun They Had*. As you read, notice the boldfaced vocabulary. Try to guess its meaning from the context.

THE FUN THEY HAD
By Isaac Asimov
(from *Earth Is Room Enough*)

1   Margie even wrote about it that night in her diary. On the page headed May 17, 2157, she wrote, "Today Tommy found a real book!"

2   It was a very old book. Margie's grandfather once said that when he was a little boy, his grandfather told him that there was a time when all stories were printed on paper.

3   They turned the pages, which were yellow and crinkly,[1] and it was awfully funny to read words that stood still instead of moving the way that they were supposed to—on a screen, you know. And then, when they had turned back to the page before, it had the same words on it that it had had when they read it the first time.

4   "Gee," said Tommy, "what a waste. When you're through with the book, you just throw it away, I guess. Our television screen must have had a million books on it, and it's good for plenty more. I wouldn't throw it away."

5   "Same with mine," said Margie. She was eleven and hadn't seen as many books as Tommy had. He was thirteen.

6   She said, "Where did you find it?"

7   "In my house." He pointed without looking, because he was busy reading. "In the attic."

8   "What's it about?"

9   "School."

10 Margie was scornful.[2] "School? What's there to write about school? I hate school."

---

[1] **crinkly:** having many folds or wrinkles; dried out
[2] **scornful:** critical of someone or something that you think is not good

11   Margie had always hated school, but now she hated it more than ever. The mechanical teacher[3] had been giving her test after test in geography, and she had been doing worse and worse until her mother had shaken her head sorrowfully and sent for the County Inspector.

12   He was a round little man with a red face and a whole box of tools with dials and wires. He smiled at Margie and gave her an apple, then took the teacher apart. Margie hoped he wouldn't know how to put it together again, but he knew how all right, and after an hour or so, there it was again, large and square and ugly, with a big screen on which all the lessons were shown and the questions were asked. That wasn't so bad. The part Margie hated most was the slot[4] where she had to put homework and test papers. She always had to write them out in a punch code[5] they made her learn when she was six years old, and the mechanical teacher calculated the mark[6] in no time.

13   The Inspector had smiled after he was finished and patted Margie's head. He said to her mother, "It's not the little girl's fault, Mrs. Jones. I think the geography **sector**[7] was geared a little too quick. Those things happen sometimes. I've slowed it up to a ten-year level. Actually, the **overall** pattern of her progress is quite satisfactory." And he patted Margie's head again.

14   Margie was **disappointed**. She had been hoping they would take the teacher away altogether. They had once taken Tommy's teacher away for nearly a month because the history sector had blanked out[8] completely.

15   So she said to Tommy, "Why would anyone write about school?"

16   Tommy looked at her with very superior eyes. "Because it's not our kind of school, stupid. This is the old kind of school that they had hundreds and hundreds of years ago." He added loftily, pronouncing the word very carefully, "Centuries ago."

17   Margie was hurt. "Well, I don't know what kind of school they had all that time ago." She read the book over his shoulder for a while, then said, "Anyway, they had a teacher."

18   "Sure they had a teacher, but it wasn't a regular teacher. It was a man."

19   "A man? How could a man be a teacher?"

20   "Well, he just told the boys and girls things and gave them homework and asked them questions."

21   "A man isn't smart enough."

22   "Sure he is. My father knows as much as my teacher."

23   "He can't. A man can't know as much as a teacher."

---

[3] **mechanical teacher:** a computer (in this story)

[4] **slot:** an opening for a paper

[5] **punch code:** a pattern of holes put on a card that was used in past times for putting information in a computer

[6] **mark:** a number score or letter grade

[7] **sector:** an area

[8] **blanked out:** been erased

(continued on next page)

24   "He knows almost as much, I betcha."[9]

25   Margie wasn't prepared to **dispute** that. She said, "I wouldn't want a strange man in my house to teach me."

26   Tommy screamed with laughter. "You don't know much, Margie. The teachers didn't live in the house. They had a special building and all the kids went there."

27   "And all the kids learned the same thing?"

28   "Sure, if they were the same age."

29   "But my mother says a teacher has to be **adjusted** to fit the mind of each boy and girl it teaches and that each kid has to be taught differently."

30   "Just the same, they didn't do it that way then. If you don't like it, you don't have to read the book."

31   "I didn't say I didn't like it," Margie said quickly. She wanted to read about those funny schools.

32   They weren't even half-finished when Margie's mother called, "Margie! School!"

33   Margie looked up. "Not yet, Mama."

34   "Now!" said Mrs. Jones. "And it's probably time for Tommy, too."

35   Margie said to Tommy, "Can I read the book some more with you after school?"

36   "Maybe," he said nonchalantly.[10] He walked away whistling, the dusty old book tucked beneath his arm.

37   Margie went into the schoolroom. It was right next to her bedroom, and the mechanical teacher was on and waiting for her. It was always on at the same time every day except Saturday and Sunday, because her mother said little girls learned better if they learned at regular hours.

38   The screen was lit up, and it said: "Today's arithmetic lesson is on the addition of proper fractions. Please insert yesterday's homework in the proper slot."

39   Margie did so with a sigh. She was thinking about the old schools they had when her grandfather's grandfather was a little boy. All the kids from the whole neighborhood came, laughing and shouting in the schoolyard, sitting together in the schoolroom, going home together at the end of the day. They learned the same things, so they could help one another on the homework and talk about it.

40   And the teachers were people . . .

41   The mechanical teacher was flashing on the screen: "When we add the fractions $1/2$ and $1/4$—"

42   Margie was thinking about how the kids must have loved it in the old days. She was thinking of the fun they had.

---

[9] ***I betcha***: "I'll bet you"; "I'm sure"
[10] **nonchalantly**: calmly, in an informal way

COMPREHENSION

Discuss the questions in a small group. Then share your ideas with the class.

1. What does Tommy discover in his attic, and why is it such an important discovery?

2. What does Margie think about the discovery?

3. How does Margie feel about the "old days"?

4. How do you think the writer feels about the future of books?

■■■■■■■■■■■■■■■■■■■■■■■■■■■■■■ GO TO MyEnglishLab FOR MORE VOCABULARY PRACTICE.

READING SKILL

1 In Reading Two, paragraph 13, the author writes, "The Inspector had smiled after he was finished and patted Margie's head. He said to her mother, 'It's not the little girl's fault, Mrs. Jones. I think the geography sector was geared a little too quick.'"

Who is speaking in the quoted section of the excerpt (underlined)? How do you know?

RECOGNIZING THE SPEAKER IN DIRECT SPEECH

Authors often include direct speech (quoted dialogue) in their writing. This can be confusing for readers, especially if more than two people are conversing. As a reader, you can use clues such as pronoun referents or the back and forth order of conversations to understand exactly who is speaking. You can also use background knowledge of a character's opinions or ideas. If you misinterpret who is speaking, it can be hard to understand the story.

Look at the example and read the explanations.

Read the paragraphs from *The Fun They Had* and complete the exercise.

4 "Gee," said Tommy, "what a waste. When you're through with the book, you just throw it away, I guess. Our television screen must have had a million books on it, and it's good for plenty more. I wouldn't throw it away."

5 "Same with mine," said Margie. She was eleven and hadn't seen as many books as Tommy had. He was thirteen.

6 She said, "Where did you find it?"

7 "In my house." He pointed without looking, because he was busy reading. "In the attic."

8 "What's it about?"

9 "School."

Identify the person who is speaking in each paragraph and explain how you know.

Paragraphs 4–5: Tommy, Margie; the authors state the names of the speakers.

Paragraphs 6–7: Margie, Tommy; the authors use pronoun referents—*she* for Margie, *he* for Tommy.

Paragraphs 8–9: Margie, Tommy; the reader must rely on the back and forth order of most conversations to identify the speakers.

2 Go back to Reading Two, *The Fun They Had*. Reread paragraphs 15–42. Work with a partner to underline or highlight what each speaker says (Margie, Tommy, Margie's mother, the mechanical teacher). Write the speaker's name in the margin or use a different color highlight for each speaker. Be prepared to explain how you know.

GO TO MyEnglishLab FOR MORE SKILL PRACTICE.

CONNECT THE READINGS

STEP 1: Organize

Reading One (R1) and Reading Two (R2) describe different models of education. Complete the chart comparing the readings.

	TEACHING TO THE WORLD (R1)	THE FUN THEY HAD (R2)
1. Is there a teacher? If yes, describe the teacher.		
2. Where does the "school" take place?		
3. When does "class" take place?		
4. Are students exposed to a variety of academic opinions?		
5. What options are there for students who don't understand or who need more support?		
6. When and where do students socialize with friends or classmates?		
7. What do the students and/or teacher think about the learning experience?		

STEP 2: Synthesize

Choose one of the scenarios. For number 1, write a response from Margie. For number 2, write a response from Professor Duneier. Use the information from Step 1. Write on a separate piece of paper.

1. **From a MOOC student to Margie:** "You are really lucky that you learn via technology. Before I took this MOOC course, I had always wanted to have the flexibility that an online course allows. I also enjoy the international perspective offered by my cyber-classmates; now I am so happy. You must be, too."

2. **From Tommy to Professor Duneier:** "Margie and I hate learning at home without other students. We don't understand why your students would choose to take online courses. Wouldn't they have more fun and friends in a school? Also, wouldn't they learn more?"

GO TO My*English*Lab *TO CHECK WHAT YOU LEARNED.*

3 FOCUS ON WRITING

VOCABULARY

REVIEW

Read the prompt and the forum response posted by one of Professor Duneier's MOOC students. Complete her response using the words above each paragraph.

Now that the course has finished, please write about your experience taking a MOOC. Include information about your past online learning experience, your expectations, the problems and benefits of taking a MOOC, and the overall experience.

assumption   via   anticipation   crucial

When I heard about Professor Duneier's Sociology MOOC, I was excited but also a bit anxious because I had never taken a completely online course before. In _____

1.

of the class, I e-mailed Professor Duneier with many of my questions. He graciously replied, but for him, too, this was going to be a new experience. Knowing this actually helped me to relax a little. One _____ I had about distance learning was that

2.

self-motivation and self-discipline would play a _____ role in my success. I

3.

knew it would be easy to fall behind because the classes were not going to be at a set time. This turned out to be true. I also knew that learning _____ the Internet

4.

might also pose other problems.

(continued on next page)

The Empty Classroom   203

virtual   adjust   collaboration   diversity

I would have to _____ to a completely different method of interacting with
5.
my teacher and classmates. For example, it seemed to me that _____ between
6.
students would be more difficult and, therefore, less common than in a traditional
classroom. This actually didn't turn out to be the case. I was able to have _____
7.
interactions with as many students as I wanted or had time for. In addition, because the
class included students from more than 100 countries, I was exposed to a
_____ of viewpoints.
8.

issue   significantly   sector   enhanced

Being exposed to so many different opinions actually _____ learning.
9.
In fact, I think I learned _____ more from my online classmates than I would
10.
have from classmates in a small traditional classroom setting. I chose to take this class
instead of a traditional class at my university, but this was not the case for a
_____ of the student population. For these students, the _____ was
11.   12.
not whether to take an online course or a traditional course; their only option was an
online course.

dispute   overall   analyze   disappointed

Now that the course is over, I have been able to _____ my MOOC experience.
13.
I cannot _____ that there are many drawbacks to taking a completely online
14.
course. However, I can truthfully say that I was not _____ with the class, the
15.
method of course delivery, or the amount that I learned. Despite some minor problems,
the _____ experience by far surpassed my expectations. I look forward to
16.
taking another MOOC in the future.

—Jacqui

EXPAND

Complete the chart with the forms of the words from the readings. If you need help, use a dictionary. (Note: An **X** indicates there is no form in that category.)

NOUN	VERB	ADJECTIVE	ADVERB
adjustment adjustability	adjust	(well) adjusted adjustable	X
	analyze		X
anticipation			X
assumption			X
collaboration			
X	X	crucial	
	disappoint		
	dispute		X
diversity			
	enhance		X
issue		X	X
sector	X	X	X
			significantly
X	X	subsequent	
X	X	virtual	

CREATE

Imagine you are a reporter interviewing the students and the professor from Reading One and Reading Two. How would they respond to the questions? Write answers using the words in the boxes. Change the word form or tense if necessary.

> ~~adjustment~~   ~~crucial~~   ~~subsequent~~   ~~via~~

1. **REPORTER:** How difficult was it for you to adjust to this new format of course delivery?

   MOOC STUDENT: _The adjustment was not too difficult once I realized that self-discipline and self-motivation were crucial to my success. Because a "normal" class is at set times, it makes it easier to stay on track. However, learning via the Internet allows you the option of "going to class" whenever you want, in the early morning or late at night. A MOOC student needs to learn to control this freedom. In any subsequent MOOC that I take, this knowledge will help me avoid some of the problems I faced in this course._

(continued on next page)

anticipation	assume	disappointment	issue

2. **REPORTER:** This is the first MOOC that you were involved in. What were your expectations before you took the course, and how did it turn out to be different from what you expected?

MOOC STUDENT: _____

_____

_____

collaboration	diversity	significantly	virtual

3. **REPORTER:** Were you able to feel a connection to your classmates and teacher, or did you feel isolated?

MOOC STUDENT: _____

_____

_____

analyze	overall	sector	subsequent

4. **REPORTER:** This was the first MOOC that you have taught. How do you think it went, and what will you do differently in the next MOOC you teach?

PROFESSOR DUNEIER: _____

_____

_____

collaborate	dispute	enhance	significantly

5. **REPORTER:** What do you think about the schools of the twenty-first century compared to your school?

TOMMY: _____

_____

_____

GO TO MyEnglishLab FOR MORE VOCABULARY PRACTICE.

GRAMMAR

1 Examine the pairs of sentences and answer the questions with a partner.

Direct Speech	Indirect Speech
• One student said, "It was a choice between online class versus no class."	• A student said it had been a choice between online class versus no class.
• Professor Duneier told his students, "Sociological concepts may change from country to country."	• Professor Duneier told his students that sociolgical concepts might change from country to country.
• Professor Duneier commented, "I am excited about teaching this course. I think it will be really interesting."	• Professor Duneier commented that he was excited about teaching that course. He thought it would be really interesting.

1. What are the differences in punctuation between direct and indirect speech?

2. What other differences are there between direct and indirect speech? Which words are different? How do they change?

DIRECT AND INDIRECT SPEECH

Speech (and writing) can be reported in two ways:

Direct speech (also called *quoted speech*) reports the speaker's exact words.
Indirect speech (also called *reported speech*) reports what the speaker said without using the exact words.

Punctuation

For direct speech, put quotation marks before and after the words being quoted. Use a comma to separate the words in quotation marks from the reporting verbs such as *say, tell,* and *report*.

For indirect speech, there is no special punctuation.

Verb Tense Changes

For indirect speech, when the reporting verb is in the past tense (**said, told, reported**), the verbs inside the quotation marks change.

DIRECT SPEECH		INDIRECT SPEECH
Margie said, "I **do** my homework at night."		Margie said she **did** her homework at night.
do / does	→	**did**
(simple present)		(simple past)
am / is / are doing	→	**was / were doing**
(present progressive)		(past progressive)
did	→	**had done**
(simple past)		(past perfect)

(continued on next page)

DIRECT SPEECH		INDIRECT SPEECH
was / were doing	→	**had been doing**
(past progressive)		(past perfect progressive)
has / have done	→	**had done**
(present perfect)		(past perfect)
will	→	**would**
(modal)		(past modal)
can	→	**could**
(modal)		(past modal)
may	→	**might**
(modal)		(past modal)

Time and Location Word Changes

For indirect speech, time and location words may change to keep the speaker's original meaning.

DIRECT SPEECH		INDIRECT SPEECH
Tommy said, "I don't have to study **now**."		Tommy said he didn't have to study **at that time**.
now	→	**then / at that time**
tomorrow	→	**the next (following) day**
ago	→	**before / earlier**
here	→	**there**
this	→	**that**

Pronoun and Possessive Changes

For indirect speech, pronouns and possessives change to keep the speaker's original meaning.

DIRECT SPEECH	INDIRECT SPEECH
Professor Duneier said, "**I** . . ."	Professor Duneier said **he** . . .
Professor Duneier said, "**My** students . . ."	Professor Duneier said **his** students . . .

2 Read the first sentence in each item. It is indirect speech. Then circle the speaker's exact words.

1. The MOOC student said that he learned more in Professor Duneier's MOOC than he did in a traditional class.

   a. "I have learned more in Professor Duneier's MOOC than I have in a traditional class."

   b. "I had learned more in Professor Duneier's MOOC than I did in a traditional class."

   c. "I learn more in Professor Duneier's MOOC than I do in a traditional class."

2. A Nigerian student reported that he had never participated in a MOOC.

   a. "I have never participated in a MOOC."

   b. "I never participate in a MOOC."

   c. "I may never participate in a MOOC."

3. A Princeton student noted that in order to get the most out of the MOOC experience, she had to organize in-person study groups.

   a. "In order to get the most out of the MOOC experience, I will have to organize in-person study groups."

   b. "In order to get the most out of the MOOC experience, I have to organize in-person study groups."

   c. "In order to get the most out of the MOOC experience, I have had to organize in-person study groups."

4. The sociology department chairperson told us that Professor Duneier would teach two MOOCs the next year.

   a. "Professor Duneier teaches two MOOCs next year."

   b. "Professor Duneier taught two MOOCs last year."

   c. "Professor Duneier will teach two MOOCs next year."

5. Tommy argued that he didn't think that a man could know as much as a teacher.

   a. "I didn't think that a man could know as much as a teacher."

   b. "I don't think that a man can know as much as a teacher."

   c. "I don't think that a man could have known as much as a teacher."

(continued on next page)

6. Margie admitted that they hadn't had time to think about the book.

    a. "We didn't have time to think about the book."

    b. "We don't have time to think about the book."

    c. "We may not have time to think about the book."

7. Professor Duneier explained that many of his colleagues were teaching MOOCs, too.

    a. "Many of my colleagues were teaching MOOCs, too."

    b. "Many of his colleagues are teaching MOOCs, too."

    c. "Many of my colleagues are teaching MOOCs, too."

3 Write the direct speech statements in indirect speech. Remember to keep the speaker's original meaning.

1. Tommy said, "My father knows as much as my teacher."

    <u>Tommy said that his father knew as much as his teacher.</u>

2. The inspector told Margie's mother, "I think the geography sector was a little too quick."

    _____

3. He added, "I've slowed it up to a ten-year level."

    _____

4. Tommy said, "This is the old kind of school that they had hundreds and hundreds of years ago."

    _____

5. Margie told Tommy, "My mother says a teacher has to be adjusted to fit the mind of each boy and girl it teaches."

    _____

6. Tommy told Margie, "You can read the book with me again tomorrow."

    _____

■■■■■■■■■■■■■■■ **GO TO** MyEnglishLab **FOR MORE GRAMMAR PRACTICE AND TO CHECK WHAT YOU LEARNED.**

FINAL WRITING TASK

In this unit, you read about how Professor Duneier and his students feel about their educational experience as a result of the MOOC. You also read about how Tommy and Margie feel about their educational experience in the year 2157.

Now you are going to *write a comparison-and-contrast essay describing two different educational experiences you have participated in.* You can write about two different classes that you have taken, two different teachers that you have had, two different schools you have attended, etc. . . . Use the vocabulary and grammar from the unit.*

PREPARE TO WRITE: Charting

Charting is a prewriting activity that helps you organize information before you write. It is especially useful when you are comparing and contrasting, because you can easily make sure that you included similar information for both things that you are going to write about.

1 Think of different schools that you have attended, different classes you have taken, or different teachers that you have had. Write some notes about how they were the same and how they were different. Then discuss with a partner.

_____

_____

_____

_____

_____

_____

_____

_____

_____

_____

---

* For Alternative Writing Topics, see page 223. These topics can be used in place of the writing topic for this unit or as homework. The alternative topics relate to the theme of the unit but may not target the same grammar or rhetorical structures taught in the unit.

2 Look at the chart. The writer has described her experience taking a course in a traditional school and taking a MOOC course.

POINTS TO COMPARE / CONTRAST	MOOC	TRADITIONAL SCHOOL CLASS
Where the class takes place	*Wherever there is an Internet connection*	*In a classroom in a school*
When the class takes place	*Sometimes at specific times, but generally whenever the student wants*	*At set times*
Mode of student-teacher communication	*Via Internet videos, e-mail, online forums, live-stream seminar-style discussions etc.*	*Listening and taking notes, face-to-face talking, writing papers, e-mail*
Mode of student-student communication	*Forums, in-person study groups (rare)*	*Face-to-face talking, texting, e-mail, in-person study groups*
Ability to communicate nonverbally (nods, eye contact, intonation . . .)	*Only for professor and videoed students in seminars, but not for the majority of students*	*For students and professors*
Class size and makeup	*100,000 + students from 100 + countries*	*Generally 25–30, although some large lecture classes could be for a hundred or more students; Students are predominantly from one country.*
Socializing with classmates	*Yes, through virtual and real-time communication via forums* *In-person study groups (rare)*	*Yes, before, between, and after classes; in clubs, sports teams, in-person study groups etc.*

3 Brainstorm a list of areas to compare for your essay. Make a chart like the one above. Complete it with details about the two different educational experiences that you are comparing.

WRITE: A Comparison-and-Contrast Essay

A **comparison-and-contrast essay** explains the similarities and differences between two topics (ideas, people, or things).

Here are some important points:

1. **Have an introduction**. Include relevant background information about the two topics being compared and contrasted.

2. **Include a thesis statement**. Make sure it indicates the purpose for comparing and contrasting.

3. **Support your thesis throughout the essay**. Make sure your examples and details relate directly to the thesis.

4. **Include all points of comparison and contrast**. All points need to be discussed for each topic.

5. **Add specific details and examples**. Make sure they illustrate the similarities and differences.

6. **Have a conclusion**. Summarize the main ideas of the essay and include any final thoughts.

There are two common ways to organize a comparison-and-contrast essay. With **point-by-point organization**, you write about the similarities and differences of different aspects of each of the two topics you are comparing. With **block organization**, you first write a paragraph only about all aspects of the first topic and then another paragraph only about all aspects of the second topic. Note that in the block method, you usually compare the same aspects of each topic, but in separate paragraphs. It is also possible to put all similarities in one paragraph and all differences in another. This is another type of block organization.

1 Look at the outlines of an essay comparing and contrasting MOOCs and a traditional classroom experience. One outline is using point-by-point organization and the other block organization. Are the differences between them clear? Discuss with a partner.

POINT-BY-POINT ORGANIZATION

I. **Where and when the class takes place**

   A. Wherever there is an Internet connection; sometimes at set times, but generally when the student wants

   B. In a classroom in a school; at set times

II. **Student-teacher communication**

   A. Via Internet videos, e-mail, online forums, live-stream seminar-style discussions, etc.

   B. Face-to-face talking and listening, writing papers, e-mail

III. **Class size and makeup**

   A. Up to 100,000 or more students from 100 or more countries

   B. Generally 25–30, but possibly more than a hundred; students are usually predominantly from one country.

(continued on next page)

BLOCK ORGANIZATION

I. MOOC

    A. Location—Wherever there is an Internet connection

    B. Time—Sometimes at set times, but generally when the student wants

    C. Student-teacher communication—Via Internet videos, e-mail, online forums, live-stream seminar-style discussions, etc.

    D. Class size—Up to 100,000 or more students

    E. Class makeup—Students from 100 or more countries

II. Traditional School Class

    A. Location—In a classroom in a school

    B. Time—At set times

    C. Student-teacher communication—Face-to-face talking and listening, writing papers, e-mail

    D. Class size—Generally 25–30, but possibly more than a hundred

    E. Class makeup—Students are usually predominantly from one country.

2 Read the essay excerpts. How are they organized? How do you know? Circle *Point-by-Point* or *Block*. Discuss your answers with a partner.

1. I am taking five courses this semester. I am happy with all my teachers, but my English and history teachers are definitely my favorites. They are both extremely enthusiastic and knowledgeable about their subjects. In fact, my English teacher, Mr. Dadio, has recently received an award for his teaching. My history teacher, Ms. Mantell, has written history textbooks that are being used by many school systems. They both have a good sense of humor. Mr. Dadio likes to joke with the students, which helps us relax. Ms. Mantell is witty, and her comments also help reduce the stress many students feel because of our school's demanding curriculum. Both teachers insist that we work hard, and we do. The type of work that they give is different. Mr. Dadio expects us to read complete novels in only a couple of days, and he grades us on our essays comparing the characters or plots. Ms. Mantell expects us to read a chapter every two classes, and, instead of grading us on papers, she gives us tests that are usually short answer or multiple-choice questions. Despite their differences, they are both excellent teachers.

    (Point-by-Point / Block)

2. My old school in Lima was very small. There were only about 75 students, and we all knew each other well. The teachers knew every student by name. My school was only for boys; girls went to another school. In Lima, we spoke only Spanish at school. Students had to wear uniforms. We had very little technology in Lima. There were only a couple of computers in the whole school, and students rarely got to use them.

   In New York, my school is gigantic. There are over 1,400 students. The immense halls are filled with unfamiliar faces, male and female. Here we mostly speak English but sometimes Spanish. Uniforms are not required in New York, and students wear all different kinds of clothes. In New York, every student is given a laptop at the beginning of ninth grade, and assignments are posted on class websites. I often e-mail my homework and questions to teachers. I like school in New York, but sometimes I miss the intimacy of my old school.

   (Point-by-Point / Block)

3. Two English courses that many students take in college are Creative Writing and English Literature. Both of these courses involve a lot of reading and writing. The types of reading assignments given are different in each course. In a literature course, students read entire books by famous authors. The books often deal with a central topic or a certain time in history. The reading assignments for a Creative Writing class are usually much shorter. They are often excerpts or news articles chosen to elicit an opinion from the student.

   The types of writing assignments are also different. The writing assignments in a literature class are directly related to the books being read. They may involve analyzing structure and symbolism and comparing and contrasting different books or authors. In a creative writing class, the assignments are more general. Students may be given a broad topic but are expected to find their own personal way of approaching the writing. Journals and other types of reflection pieces may also be required.

   (Point-by-Point / Block)

3 Look at your chart from Prepare to Write, Exercise 3. Make outlines for your essay using both types of organization. Then share your outlines with a partner. In what ways are the two types of organization different? Which outline was easier to read and which was easier to write? Discuss which of your outlines you think works better and why.

4 Now write the first draft of your comparison-and-contrast essay. Use the outline you have chosen and the information from Prepare to Write to plan your essay. Include relevant information about the two educational experiences you are comparing. Include a thesis statement that indicates how these experiences are similar and different. Be sure to add specific details and examples to illustrate the similarities and differences. In your conclusion, summarize the main ideas in the essay and include any final thoughts about your experience. Be sure to use vocabulary and grammar from the unit.

REVISE: Using Subordinators and Transitions

Certain words act as signals to introduce points of comparison or contrast.

1 Examine the paragraph and answer the questions with a partner.

I am quite happy with all my courses this semester, but I have two favorites, Intermediate Algebra and Biology I, and they are very different. First is the amount of time we spend in class. Algebra has two one-hour classes a week **while** biology has three one-hour classes plus a lab section that sometimes takes more than two hours. The teachers are very different, too. The biology teacher is young and somewhat inexperienced, but she has a lot of enthusiasm and current knowledge. **In contrast**, my algebra teacher has over 30 years of teaching experience and knows how to relate to all types of learners. In addition, he is available every day after class for extra help **whereas** my biology teacher can never help us right after class because she has another class then. However, she does have office hours before class two days a week and will answer e-mail questions very quickly. My algebra teacher expects students to do all homework and reading before class **in the same way** the biology teacher does; if you don't, you won't be successful in the class. Since I love both of these classes, this is not a problem for me.

1. Look at the boldfaced words. Which words introduce ideas that are similar? Which words introduce ideas that are different?

2. Four topics are compared and contrasted in this paragraph. What are they?

COMPARISONS AND CONTRASTS

Comparisons point out ideas that are similar. **Contrasts** point out ideas that are different.

Subordinators

Subordinators are used to compare or contrast the ideas in two clauses. They join the independent clause to the dependent clause being compared or contrasted. Examples of subordinators include *while, whereas, just as, as.* These words introduce dependent clauses, not complete thoughts. The independent clause usually describes the point that is being emphasized or is more important.

COMPARISON SUBORDINATORS INCLUDE:	CONTRAST SUBORDINATORS INCLUDE:
just as	whereas
as	while

Transitions

Transitions show the connection between two independent clauses (two sentences).

COMPARISON TRANSITIONS INCLUDE:	CONTRAST TRANSITIONS INCLUDE:
similarly	in contrast
in the same way	on the other hand
likewise	however

- Two independent clauses can be combined in one sentence by using a semicolon (;) and a comma (,):

    I love my biology class; **however**, I don't like all the memorization it requires.

- The two independent clauses can also be written as separate sentences:

    Our grade in algebra is based entirely on three tests and a final exam. **However**, our biology grade is based on tests, a final exam, lab reports, and a research paper.

- Two independent clauses can also be combined as a simple sentence using the phrase *in the same way*.

    The biology teacher expects a lot of hard work from her students *in the same way* the algebra teacher does.

2 Combine the pairs of sentences to make comparisons and contrasts.

1. likewise

- A MOOC student receives his or her assignments via the Internet.

- Tommy and Margie's computer is their teacher, and it tells them what to do and study.

    MOOC students are taught and submit papers via the Internet; likewise, Tommy and Margie also are taught via the computer.

(continued on next page)

2. in the same way

- Professor Duneier enjoyed the new course delivery method of a MOOC.

- The MOOC students were excited about the use of educational technology in their sociology course.

_____

_____

3. similarly

- Margie thought a man couldn't know enough to be a teacher.

- Professor Duneier was worried he wouldn't be able to effectively teach students from so many different countries.

_____

_____

4. on the other hand

- Margie wanted to go to a traditional school like in the old days.

- Many students today are tired of traditional school and want to incorporate distance learning in their education.

_____

_____

5. in contrast

- Many of Professor Duneier's MOOC students chose his course instead of a traditional sociology course.

- For others, the choice was his MOOC or no sociology course at all.

_____

_____

6. while

- _The Fun They Had_ describes the future as it was imagined in 1951.

- "Teaching the World from Central New Jersey" describes a present that may seem futuristic to some people.

_____

_____

3 Work with a partner. Read the paragraphs. Decide where the writer is comparing and where he or she is contrasting. Add transitions or subordinators of comparison or contrast to each paragraph to make the writer's meaning clear. Discuss which type of organization requires more transitions and subordinators.

1.   I am taking five courses this semester. I am happy with all my teachers.

_____, my English and history teachers are definitely my favorites. They are

both extremely enthusiastic and knowledgeable about their subjects. For example, my English

teacher, Mr. Dadio, has recently received an award for his teaching. _____,

my history teacher, Ms. Mantell, also clearly knows her subject. In fact, she has written history

textbooks that are being used by many school systems. They both have a good sense of humor.

Mr. Dadio likes to joke with the students, which helps us relax. _____,

Ms. Mantell's witty comments also help reduce the stress many students feel because of

our school's demanding curriculum. Both teachers insist that we work hard, and we do.

_____, the type of work that they give is different. Mr. Dadio expects us to

read complete novels in only a couple of days, and he grades us on our essays comparing the

characters or plots. _____, Ms. Mantell expects us to read a chapter every two

classes, and, instead of grading us on papers, she gives us tests that are usually short answer or

multiple-choice questions. Despite their differences, they are both excellent teachers.

2.   Each new level of education brings new challenges and demands to students. Moving from

high school into college can be especially difficult because of the freedom students experience

in college along with a new set of expectations.

   In high school, students usually live at home, and their parents take care of all their physical

needs such as food and housing. Students do not usually have to shop for their food, take time

to pay bills, or even do their own laundry. Parents are also there to help with and make sure

that the student's homework is done. During the school day, students rarely have free time. They

go directly from one class to the other. Teachers are always around to tell the students what to

(continued on next page)

do. Finally, the work itself is not so challenging. Students can often complete their homework and reading in a short time.

_____, in college, students often live away from home in dorms or apartments. They may be responsible for shopping, paying bills, and laundry. They also may have to cook their own meals. Their parents are not around to help with homework or even to check that it has been done. _____ to students in high school, students in college may have a lot of free time between classes, but must discipline themselves to use this time productively for homework and other assignments. Most important, college requires a higher level of thinking and a lot more work than high school.

3.   My old school in Lima was very small. _____, my school In New York is gigantic. There were only about 75 students in my Lima school, and we all knew each other well. The teachers knew every student by name. _____, in New York there are over 1,400 students, and the immense halls are filled with unfamiliar faces, male and female.

_____, my school in Lima was only for boys; girls went to another school. In Lima, we spoke only Spanish at school _____ here we mostly speak English but sometimes Spanish. The teachers in Lima were very good and always were able to answer any question that we had. _____, in New York the teachers are also excellent. Use of technology is another difference between the two schools. We had very little technology in Lima. There were only a couple of computers in the whole school, and students rarely got to use them. _____, in New York, every student is given a laptop at the beginning of ninth grade, and assignments are posted on class websites. In fact, I often e-mail my homework and questions to teachers. I like school in New York, but sometimes I miss the intimacy of my old school.

4 Look at your first draft. Add comparison-and-contrast transitions and/or subordinators as needed.

GO TO MyEnglishLab FOR MORE SKILL PRACTICE.

EDIT: Writing the Final Draft

Go to MyEnglishLab and write the final draft of your essay. Carefully edit it for grammatical and mechanical errors, such as spelling, capitalization, and punctuation. Make sure you use some of the vocabulary and grammar from the unit. Use the checklist to help you write your final draft. Then submit your essay to your teacher.

FINAL DRAFT CHECKLIST

❏ Does the essay have an introduction which includes relevant background information about the two educational experiences?

❏ Does the essay have a thesis statement that indicates how these experiences are similar and different?

❏ Does your essay clearly follow a point-by-point or block organization?

❏ Does the essay use effective subordinators and transitions to show comparison and contrast?

❏ Does the essay include specific details and examples to illustrate the similarities and differences?

❏ Does the essay have a conclusion summarizing the main ideas of the essay?

❏ Does the essay use reported speech?

❏ Have you used vocabulary from the unit?

UNIT PROJECT

Distance education has changed substantially since it was first used in 1728. Many different models have been used over the last three centuries. You are going to work in a small group and choose a model of distance learning. The model you choose can be from the past and does not have to be used currently. You will write a report about the model based on your research. Follow these steps:

STEP 1: Research a current or past model of distance learning. Go to the library or use the Internet to do your research.

STEP 2: Prepare a list of questions you would like to find answers to as you research distance learning. Divide your questions among the members of your group and conduct your research. Some possible questions could include:

- How long has this model of distance learning been in existence?
- Where and how did it originate?
- How is the course delivered? What technology is necessary?
- Do/Did students have to be in "class" at a specific time?
- Where does/did student learning take place?
- How do/did students and teachers interact?
- Can/Could students interact with other students? If so, how?
- Where are/were the students from?
- Who is/was allowed to take the course? Do/Did you have to be a high school graduate or enrolled in college?
- What is/was the cost of the course?
- Do/Did students receive credit for the course?

STEP 3: Share your research with your group. Combine your information and write a report using this outline.

> **Part I: Introduction**
> - A brief introduction to your topic (distance learning)
> - An explanation of what information you were looking for (your original questions)
> - An explanation of where and how you found your information
>
> **Part II: Results**
> - The information you collected and the answers to your questions
>
> **Part III: Conclusions**
> - Final conclusions and opinions about distance learning

STEP 4: Present your report to the class.

ALTERNATIVE WRITING TOPICS

Write about one of the topics. Use the vocabulary and grammar from the unit.

1. Different subjects require different teaching methods. Do you think any subject could be effectively taught as a MOOC, or are certain subjects more easily adapted to the MOOC format? Explain.

2. How do you envision education in the future? Do you think the traditional classroom with one teacher, 20–25 students, and a chalkboard is a thing of the past? What role do you think technology will play in education in the future? What effects will these changes have on the student?

GO TO MyEnglishLab TO WRITE ABOUT ONE OF THE ALTERNATIVE TOPICS, WATCH A VIDEO ABOUT A HOLIDAY FROM HOMEWORK, AND TAKE THE UNIT 7 ACHIEVEMENT TEST.

MANAGING YOUR Smartphone

1 FOCUS ON THE TOPIC

1. In addition to making calls, what are cell phones used for?

2. *Nomophobia* is the fear of being without your mobile phone. *Phantom vibration syndrome* is an associated problem in which people think they feel or hear their phone vibrate and check it expecting to find a message or a call—but the phone did not vibrate. Do you think you suffer from nomophobia and/or have you experienced phantom vibration syndrome? If so, explain.

3. Do you think you would be able to happily "survive" a week without your phone? What would be hardest about not having a phone for a week?

GO TO MyEnglishLab TO CHECK WHAT YOU KNOW.

VOCABULARY

Reading One is an article about smartphone dependency. Read the letter a woman wrote to a newspaper advice columnist about her husband's smartphone usage. Circle the letter of the definition that best defines each boldfaced word or phrase.

1. **a.** aversion
   b. strong need
   c. understanding

2. **a.** normal
   b. boring
   c. uncontrollable

3. **a.** fix
   b. make something happen
   c. stop

4. **a.** strong desire
   b. message
   c. distraction

5. **a.** awake
   b. aware
   c. unclear

6. **a.** taking money from a bank
   b. bad feelings when you stop doing something
   c. learning

7. **a.** decision
   b. reliance
   c. technology

8. **a.** inability to work normally
   b. disease
   c. mood

9. **a.** worry
   b. relaxation
   c. experience

10. **a.** benefit from
    b. learn to use better
    c. gradually stop doing

ASK HELPFUL HANNAH

Dear Helpful Hannah,

I've got a problem with my husband, Sam. He bought a smartphone a couple of months ago, and he took it on our recent ski vacation to Colorado. It was a great trip except for one problem. He has a constant **(1) urge** to check for text messages; he checks his phone every five minutes! He's **(2) compulsive** about it. He can't stop checking even at inappropriate times like when we are eating in a restaurant and I am talking to him! It is almost as if any small amount of boredom can **(3) trigger** a need for him to check his phone even when he knows he shouldn't. The **(4) temptation** to see who is contacting him is just too great. When I ask him to please put down the phone and stop ignoring me, he says, "In a minute," but still checks to see if there is an important text or if someone has posted something new on Facebook. I don't think he is even **(5) conscious** that he is being rude! If we go somewhere and I ask him to leave the phone at home, he suffers from **(6) withdrawal** symptoms. I just keep thinking that maybe this **(7) dependency** on his smartphone has become more than an everyday problem.

I recently read an article about "nomophobia." It's a real illness people can suffer from: the fear of being without your phone! I am worried that Sam may be suffering from this **(8) dysfunction**. Why? Because he experiences a great deal of **(9) anxiety** if he doesn't have his phone with him, even for a short time. It is so bad that he sometimes brings it into the bathroom with him.

While we were in Colorado, we talked a little about his "problem," and he agreed to try to slowly **(10) wean** himself **away from** the phone. But, so far, I don't think the amount of time he spends using his phone each day is

11. a. increasing
   b. decreasing
   c. finishing

12. a. tools or machines
   b. plans
   c. methods

really **(11) diminishing**. He's got to do something, or I am going to throw his phone away while he is sleeping!

Who would have thought that little **(12) devices** like these could be such a blessing and yet such a curse!

Sick and Tired Sadie

GO TO MyEnglishLab FOR MORE VOCABULARY PRACTICE.

PREVIEW

You are going to read an article about smartphone addiction. Read the questions and discuss your answers with a partner.

1. What behaviors have you noticed about people and their smartphones?

2. Why do people enjoy their smartphones so much?

3. Are there any negative consequences of owning a smartphone? Explain.

Keep your ideas in mind as you read Davis's article.

Addicted to Your Smartphone?

Here's What to Do. Why smartphones hook us in, plus tips on reclaiming your time and concentration

By Susan Davis

1   I'll admit it: I check my smartphone compulsively. And the more I use it, the more often the **urge** to look at it hits me.

2   In the orthodontist's office. Walking my kids to school. In meetings. Even while making breakfast. Sometimes it is in my hand before I even know what I'm searching for. Sometimes I tap the screen absentmindedly—looking at my e-mail, a local blogger, my calendar, and Twitter.

3   I'm not the only one struggling with this very modern compulsion. According to a 2012 survey by the Pew Research Center, 46% of all American adults now own a smartphone—up a whopping 25% from 2011.

4   And smartphone use can get very heavy. In a study of 1,600 managers and professionals, Leslie Perlow, PhD, the Konosuke Matsushita professor of leadership at the Harvard Business School, found that:

- 70% said they check their smartphone within an hour of getting up.
- 56% check their phone within an hour of going to sleep.

(continued on next page)

- 48% check over the weekend, including on Friday and Saturday nights.

- 51% check continuously during vacation.

- 44% said they would experience "a great deal of **anxiety**" if they lost their phone and couldn't replace it for a week.

5   "The amount of time that people are spending with the new technology, the apparent preoccupation, raises the question 'why?'" says Peter DeLisi, academic dean of the information technology leadership program at Santa Clara University in California. "When you start seeing that people have to text when they're driving, even though they clearly know that they're endangering their lives and the lives of others, we really have to ask what is so compelling about this new medium?"

Hook or Habit?

6   Whether smartphones really "hook" users into **dependency** remains unclear.

7   But "we already know that the Internet and certain forms of computer use are addictive," says David Greenfield, PhD, a West Hartford, Conn., psychologist and author of *Virtual Addiction: Help for Netheads, Cyber Freaks, and Those Who Love Them*.

8   "And while we're not seeing actual smartphone addictions now," Greenfield says, "the potential is certainly there."

9   A true addiction entails a growing tolerance to a substance (think drugs or alcohol) so you need more to get "high," uncomfortable symptoms during **withdrawal**, and a harmful impact on your life, Greenfield says.

10   Computer technologies can be addictive, he says, because they're "psychoactive." That is, they alter mood and often **trigger** enjoyable feelings.

11   E-mail, in particular, gives us satisfaction due to what psychologists call "variable ratio reinforcement." That is, we never know when we'll get a satisfying e-mail, so we keep checking, over and over again. "It's like slot machines," Greenfield says. "We're seeking that pleasurable hit."

12   Smartphones, of course, allow us to seek rewards (including videos, Twitter feeds, and news updates, in addition to e-mail) anytime and anywhere. Is such behavior unhealthy?

13   "That really depends on whether it's disrupting your work or family life," Greenfield says.

14   Such a disruption could be small—like ignoring your friend over lunch to post a Facebook status about how much you're enjoying lunch with your friend.

15   Or it could be big—like tuning out a distressed spouse or colleagues in a meeting to check e-mail, or feeling increasingly stressed by the fact that everyone else seems to be on call 24/7, so perhaps we should be, too.

16   Other researchers are seeing clear signs of **dysfunction**, if not an "addiction."

17   According to a 2011 study published in the journal *Personal and Ubiquitous Computing*, people aren't addicted to smartphones themselves as much as they are addicted to "checking habits" that develop with phone use—including repeatedly (and very quickly) checking for news updates, e-mails, or social media connections.

18   That study found that certain environmental triggers—like being bored or listening to a lecture—trigger the habits. And while the average user checks his or her smartphone 35 times a day—for about 30 seconds each time, when the information rewards are greater (e.g., having contact info linked to the contact's whereabouts), users check even *more* often.

The Interrupted Life

19   Besides creating a compulsion, smartphones pose other dangers to our mental life, says Nicholas Carr, author of *The Shallows: What the Internet Is Doing to Our Brains*.

20   "The smartphone, through its small size, ease of use, proliferation of free or cheap apps, and constant connectivity, changes our relationship with computers in a way that goes well beyond what we experienced with laptops," he says. That's because people keep their smartphones near them "from the moment they wake up until the moment they go to bed," and throughout that time the **devices** provide an almost continuous stream of messages and alerts as well as easy access to a myriad[1] of compelling information sources.

21   "By design," he says, "it's an environment of almost constant interruptions and distractions. The smartphone, more than any other gadget,[2] steals from us the opportunity to maintain our attention, to engage in contemplation and reflection, or even to be alone with our thoughts."

22   Carr, who writes extensively in *The Shallows* about the way that computer technology in general may be **diminishing** our ability to concentrate and think deeply, does not have a smartphone.

23   "One thing my research made clear is that human beings have a deep, primitive desire to know everything that's going on around them," he says.

24   "That instinct probably helped us survive when we were cavemen and cavewomen. I'm sure one of the main reasons people tend to be so **compulsive** in their use of smartphones is that they can't stand the idea that there may be a new bit of information out there that they haven't seen. I know that I'm not strong enough to resist that **temptation**, so I've decided to shun[3] the device altogether."

(continued on next page)

---

[1] **myriad:** a very large number of something
[2] **gadget:** a small tool or machine that makes a particular job easier
[3] **shun:** to deliberately avoid someone or something

Managing Your Smartphone Use

25   Can't give up your phone altogether? Experts suggest these steps to control your usage:

- **Be conscious** of the situations and emotions that make you want to check your phone. Is it boredom? Loneliness? Anxiety? Maybe something else would soothe you.

- **Be strong** when your phone beeps or rings. You don't always have to answer it. In fact, you can avoid temptation by turning off the alert signals.

- **Be disciplined** about not using your device in certain situations (such as when you're with children, driving, or in a meeting) or at certain hours (for instance, between 9 P.M. and 7 A.M.). "You'll be surprised and pleased to rediscover the pleasures of being in control of your attention," Carr says.

26   One group of business people at The Boston Group, a consulting firm, discovered just that when they participated in an experiment run by Perlow.

27   As described in her book, *Sleeping with Your Smartphone*, the group found that taking regular "predictable time off" (PTO) from their PDAs resulted in increased efficiency and collaboration, heightened job satisfaction, and better work-life balance.

28   Four years after her initial experiment, Perlow reports, 86% of the consulting staff in the firm's Northeast offices—including Boston, New York, and Washington, D.C.—were on teams engaged in similar PTO experiments.

29   To manage my own smartphone well, more smartly, I **weaned** myself **away from** it.

30   I started by not checking it for 15 minutes at a time, then 30, then 60 (unless I was dealing with an urgent situation).

31   I decided to avoid using the web browser on the smartphone unless I truly needed information (such as an address or phone number).

32   And I swore off using social media on it entirely. I also made a firm commitment to not text, e-mail, or surf the web on my smartphone while driving.

33   The result? Even after a few days of this self-discipline, I found that I was concentrating better, more aware of my surroundings, and more relaxed—and I was more aware of when I was looking for something specific, as opposed to just looking for some kind of connection.

MAIN IDEAS

1 Look again at your ideas from the Preview on page 227. How did your answers to the questions help you understand the article?

2 Reading One is divided into four sections. Write one or two sentences that summarize each part of the article. Use your own words.

Part I: (*paragraphs 1–5*)
What are the signs of compulsive use of smartphones?

_____

_____

Part II: Hook or Habit? (*paragraphs 6–18*)
Is smartphone usage an addiction? Explain.

_____

_____

Part III: The Interrupted Life (*paragraphs 19–24*)
Explain how smartphones are a problem for our mental life.

_____

_____

Part IV: Managing Your Smartphone Use (*paragraphs 25–33*)
How can you control your usage?

_____

_____

DETAILS

Circle the best answer according to the reading.

1. People text while they are driving even though they know

   a. they might get a ticket.

   b. it is difficult to text and drive at the same time.

   c. they are putting their lives in danger.

(continued on next page)

2. Computer technologies can be considered addictive because

   a. they can change your mood and cause enjoyable feelings.

   b. they cause you to suffer withdrawal symptoms if you are not able to use them.

   c. they interfere with concentrating on more important activities.

3. Dr. Greenfield says that

   a. smartphone addiction is a reality because 44% of managers and professionals now experience anxiety about losing their smartphone.

   b. smartphone addiction is possible, but he hasn't seen it yet.

   c. there are currently many smartphone addicts.

4. Smartphone usage can be considered unhealthy if

   a. it is caused by "variable ratio reinforcement."

   b. you use it to work on the weekends.

   c. it disrupts your work or family life.

5. According to the journal *Personal and Ubiquitous Computing*, people aren't addicted to smartphones themselves, but rather to

   a. checking habits.

   b. social media.

   c. using them while listening to lectures.

6. According to the journal *Personal and Ubiquitous Computing*, checking habits include checking for all of the following except

   a. e-mails.

   b. GPS directions.

   c. news updates.

7. Nicholas Carr believes our relationship with smartphones is different from our relationship with computers, even laptops, for all the following reasons except that

   a. apps are free or cheap.

   b. we constantly have them with us.

   c. we can use them to access social media.

8. Carr believes that humans have a deep primitive desire to know everything that is going on around them. This instinct is/was especially helpful when

   a. checking social media.

   b. trying to survive in primitive situations.

   c. getting news updates.

9. In order to control smartphone use, experts suggest

   a. not always answering your phone and even turning it off.

   b. using your phone when you are with children, but not in a meeting.

   c. feeling anxious or bored when your phone doesn't ring.

10. Taking predictable time off (PTO) caused all of the following effects <u>except</u>

   a. more collaboration.

   b. getting a new job

   c. improved work-life balance.

MAKE INFERENCES

APPEAL TO AUTHORITY

To help make their ideas more believable, authors often refer to experts who support their point of view. Experts add importance and validity to the author's position. The author may quote an expert directly or either paraphrase or summarize the expert's ideas. Statistics can also help support an author's point of view.

Look at the example and read the explanation.

In Reading One, Susan Davis uses statistics and quotations from many experts that support her ideas about smartphones.

Look at paragraphs 2 and 3. In paragraph 3, she includes statistics (underlined) from a survey done by the Pew Research Center and from a study done by Leslie Perlow, PhD. Why does Davis do this? What is the idea that she is trying to support?

2 "In the orthodontist's office. Walking my kids to school. In meetings. Even while making breakfast. Sometimes it is in my hand before I even know what I'm searching for. Sometimes I tap the screen absent mindedly—looking at my e-mail, a local blogger, my calendar, and Twitter.

3 I'm not the only one struggling with this very modern compulsion. <u>According to a 2012 survey by the Pew Research Center, 46% of all American adults now own a smartphone—up a whopping 25% from 2011</u>."

Davis shows us that excessive use of smartphones goes beyond her personal experience.

The statistics strengthen Davis's argument. She begins writing her opinion with a personal anecdote about her own compulsive smartphone habits. She then shares the survey information in order to show us that she is not alone and that many other professionals are struggling with this behavior.

For each quote from an expert, provide two kinds of information: the opinion of the author that the quote supports, and how the quote strengthens the author's argument.

1. David Greenfield, PhD *(paragraphs 12–13)*:

   "Smartphones, of course, allow us to seek rewards (including videos, Twitter feeds, and news updates, in addition to e-mail) anytime and anywhere. Is such behavior unhealthy?

   'That really depends on whether it's disrupting your work or family life,' Greenfield says."

   Author's opinion that the underlined part of the quote supports: _____

   _____

   How the quote strengthens the author's argument: _____

   _____

2. The journal, *Personal and Ubiquitous Computing (paragraph 17)*:

   "According to a 2011 study published in the journal *Personal and Ubiquitous Computing,* people aren't addicted to smartphones themselves as much as they are addicted to 'checking habits' that develop with phone use—including repeatedly (and very quickly) checking for news updates, e-mails, or social media connections."

   Author's opinion that the quote supports: _____

   _____

   How the quote strengthens the author's argument: _____

   _____

3. Nicholas Carr *(paragraph 21)*:

   "By design," he says, "it's an environment of almost constant interruptions and distractions. The smartphone, more than any other gadget, steals from us the opportunity to maintain our attention, to engage in contemplation and reflection, or even to be alone with our thoughts."

   Author's opinion that the quote supports: _____

   _____

   How the quote strengthens the author's argument: _____

   _____

4. Leslie Perlow, PhD *(paragraphs 27–28)*:

"As described in her book, *Sleeping with Your Smartphone*, the (experiment) group found that taking regular 'predictable time off' (PTO) from their PDAs resulted in increased efficiency and collaboration, heightened job satisfaction, and better work-life balance.

Four years after her initial experiment, Perlow reports, 86% of the consulting staff in the firm's Northeast offices—including Boston, New York, and Washington, D.C.—were on teams engaged in similar PTO experiments."

Author's opinion that the quote supports: _____

_____

How the quote strengthens the author's argument: _____

_____

EXPRESS OPINIONS

Work with a partner. Discuss your ideas about the questions. Then report your ideas to the class.

1. Which examples in the article describe your own behaviors? Do you think you have an addiction to smartphones or some other technology?

2. Go back to paragraph 25, page 230. Reread the advice for managing smartphone use. Are you likely to take this advice? Why or why not? Do you have any ideas of your own for managing smartphone use?

■■■■■■■■■■■■■■■■■■■ *GO TO* MyEnglishLab *TO GIVE YOUR OPINION ABOUT ANOTHER QUESTION.*

READD

1 Look at the boldfaced words in the reading and think about the questions.

  1. Which words or phrases do you know the meanings of?

  2. Can you use any of the words or phrases in a sentence?

2 Read the article about a technology-free vacation. As you read, notice the boldfaced vocabulary. Try to guess its meaning from the context.

Unplugging Wired Kids: A Vacation from Technology and Social Media
The Momoir Project

1   It's day one of our vacation on Cortes, a remote island in the BC wilderness[1] and my son is **literally** lying on the couch of our rustic[2] A-frame moaning, "iPhone. iPhone. iPhone." In front of him is a wall of windows facing a glistening ocean and coming in from the open deck doors—a warm, beautiful breeze. Clearly, he sees and feels none of it. He's too deep in his electronics withdrawal.

2   Back at home in Vancouver, after five minutes of listening to this kind of groveling, I'd normally **relent**. Instead of screaming "Shut up," I'd hand it over in defeat. He'd win.

3   Not here. We came here to get away from it all—our lives, technology, the constant pull of e-mail, Facebook, video games, and the never-ending ping of the iPhone.

4   Before we left, I told my 10-year-old son the rules: We were all going electronic-free for a week. There could be a few movies on the odd[3] night, but no TV, no video games, no e-mail. And here we are on day one and already, he can't stand it.

5   My 6-year-old daughter and my husband are doing just fine. They are outside on the deck carving pieces of driftwood and singing. Meanwhile, my son is inside blinded to the opportunities in front of him, complaining that he doesn't like the beach.

---

[1] **wilderness:** a large natural area of land that has never been farmed or built on
[2] **rustic:** simple and old-fashioned in a way that is attractive and typical of the countryside
[3] **odd:** different from what is expected

6   Confounded, I walk outside to let him suffer. I walk down the grassy pathway to the beach. It's so stunning, I can barely manage to read on my blanket. I just want to stare out at the islands and the glistening ocean. The eagles soar overhead. The seals pop their heads out of the water, and there isn't another soul in sight. My son can do whatever he wants. But he's not going to ruin the quiet and beauty of this trip for me.

7   Day 2. We spend the entire morning, and part of the afternoon, digging for clams and oysters and swimming in the lagoon. My son is one with his shovel, looking for the smallest clams and filling buckets with shellfish and other sea treasures. When we get back to our cabin, I give my son his book, put him in the shade on a lovely garden swing and it's almost dinner when he looks up.

8   The next few days pass in a blur of sun and sand. My husband **ensures** we do something every day to get out of the cabin and explore. One day, we all spend an afternoon swimming at the freshwater lake. Another day, my husband takes my son on a three-hour hike around the headland.

9   On day 6, he's lying beside me on the beach watching the sunset. We are wrapped together in a blanket and as I watch him play with the sand in his hands, the grains slipping through his fingers, I realize how much time has slowed down for both of us. It's exactly what I wanted. Finally, after just a few days, we are able to sit quietly without **twitching**, without thinking about screens, without the constant interruptions of phone calls and e-mail. Two hours pass, and, in that time, he happily throws rocks into the water, listens to a man play guitar down the beach, plays Frisbee in the grassy field behind us.

10   He's too young to see it, but it's clear to me. A week away from our dependence on electronics and we've slowed right down. We are breathing deeper and, literally, noticing the grains of sand. Life is good. If only we could live on vacation.

11   How do you handle the **influx** of technology in your house? How do your kids handle it? Do you ever feel the need for a vacation from technology?

COMPREHENSION

Work with a partner. Complete each statement according to the reading.

1. At the beginning of the vacation, the author's son couldn't enjoy himself because _____

   _____.

2. This vacation was unusual because _____

   _____.

3. One way the husband helped break the dependence on electronics was _____

   _____.

4. The result of a week away from electronics was _____

   _____.

■■■■■■■■■■■■■■■■■■■■■■■■■■■■■■■■■■■■■ GO TO MyEnglishLab FOR MORE VOCABULARY PRACTICE.

READING SKILL

1 Go back to Reading Two. In the last sentence of paragraph 7, underline the pronouns "we," "I," and "he." What person does each pronoun refer to?

IDENTIFYING REFERENTS FOR THE PRONOUN *IT*

Pronouns usually clearly refer to a previously mentioned person or thing. In this passage from paragraph 5, "My 6-year-old daughter and my husband are doing just fine. **They** are outside on the deck carving pieces of driftwood and singing," *they* clearly refers to "my daughter and my husband."

The referent for the pronoun *it* is sometimes not as clear. *It* may refer to an idea, not a concrete person or thing.

In paragraph 1 the author writes:

"In front of him is a wall of windows facing a glistening ocean and coming in from the open deck doors—a warm, beautiful breeze. Clearly, he sees and feels none of **it**."

What does "it" refer to?

"It" = the beautiful environment: the glistening ocean and the beautiful weather.

At times, pronouns can also refer to information that follows the pronoun. In paragraph 3, the author writes:

"We came here to get away from **it** all—our lives, technology, the constant pull of e-mail, Facebook, video games, and the never-ending ping of the iPhone."

What does "it" refer to in this passage?

"It" = their everyday lives including all aspects of technology: e-mail, Facebook, video games, and iPhones.

2 Read the excerpts from Reading Two. Explain in your own words what the boldfaced pronouns refer to.

1. "We were all going electronic-free for a week. There could be a few movies on the odd night, but no TV, no video games, no e-mail. And here we are on day one and already, he can't stand **it**." *(paragraph 4)*

   Explanation: _____

   _____

2. "I realize how much time has slowed down for both of us. **It**'s exactly what I wanted." *(paragraph 9)*

   Explanation: _____

   _____

3. "He's too young to see **it**, but **it**'s clear to me. A week away from our dependence on electronics and we've slowed right down." *(paragraph 10)*

   Explanation: _____

   _____

GO TO MyEnglishLab *FOR MORE SKILL PRACTICE.*

STEP 1: Organize

Reading One (R1) and Reading Two (R2) both address the problems caused by our growing dependence on smartphones and other electronic devices. They suggest some specific problems associated with this dependence. In R1, along with her personal experiences, Susan Davis also includes the opinions of experts regarding dependency issues. In R2, the writer uses her son as an example of some problems that overreliance on smartphones and other electronic devices *may* cause. Both readings also offer solutions for how to manage smartphone dependency.

Complete the graphic organizer by categorizing the items as either problems or solutions. According to the readings, each problem has specific solutions.

- ~~Slowly diminish use~~
- Make commitment not to use phone in certain situations
- ~~No texting and driving~~
- Self-discipline

- ~~Turn off alerts~~
- Use at inappropriate times
- Anxiety if lost or unavailable
- Predictable time off
- Avoid using web browsers

- Constant availability
- Make specific times smartphone-free
- ~~Continuous checking~~
- Wean yourself away

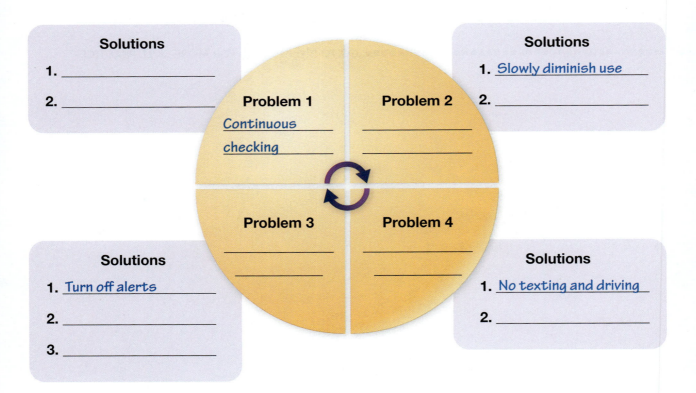

Solutions

1. _____
2. _____

Problem 1
Continuous
checking

Problem 2
_____
_____

Solutions

1. _Slowly diminish use_____
2. _____

Problem 3
_____
_____

Problem 4
_____
_____

Solutions

1. _Turn off alerts_____
2. _____
3. _____

Solutions

1. _No texting and driving__
2. _____

STEP 2: Synthesize

Go back to pages 226–227 and reread the letter that Sick and Tired Sadie wrote describing her husband's smartphone dependency. Using information from Step 1, work with a partner to complete the advice columnist's response to Sadie explaining how she can help her husband manage his dependency.

Dear Sick and Tired Sadie,

    I applaud you for recognizing that your husband has a problem. You are definitely doing the right thing by trying to help him manage his smartphone dependency. It is not going to be easy for either of you, but there are definite strategies you can employ to make the smartphone a blessing again, and not a curse.

    First of all, you need to help him to stop compulsively checking his smartphone. Tell

him to _____

_____

    There are also things he can do to alleviate the anxiety he feels when he doesn't have

his phone nearby. For example, _____

_____

    If one of his problems is that information is constantly available to him, I suggest ____

_____

_____

    Finally, to help him stop using the phone at inappropriate times, you could tell him to

_____

_____

    If your husband is able to implement these strategies, he (and you) will see a big change. He will feel more relaxed and more aware of his surroundings. His relationship with friends, family, and co-workers may also improve. I hope this advice helps, and I wish you and your husband good luck overcoming this problem.

Helpful Hannah

■■■■■■■■■■■■■■■■■■■■■■■■■■■■■■■■■■■■ GO TO MyEnglishLab TO CHECK WHAT YOU LEARNED.

VOCABULARY

REVIEW

Complete the sentences with the words in the boxes.

diminish	relent	trigger	wean away from

1. For some people, boredom often can _____ the need to check their smartphone to see if they have any new e-mail or news updates.

2. Asking employees to make an effort to _____ the amount of time they spend on their smartphones is one strategy that businesses are employing.

3. Although it is difficult, these employees report that they have been able to slowly _____ themselves _____ their smartphones.

4. Despite the fact that I did not believe my son needed a smartphone, his constant begging for one caused me to _____ and buy him one.

anxiety	dependency	devices	twitching	urge

5. Some students report that sitting in class can trigger a(n) _____ to check their smartphones for news updates and e-mail.

6. In the past, people kept connected through their PC or laptop, but today there are many new _____, such as tablets, mini-laptops, and smartphones, that allow people to stay connected at all times.

7. Many professionals say they would experience "a great deal of _____" if they lost their smartphone and couldn't replace it for a week.

8. Scientists disagree on whether smartphone _____ can really be considered an addiction.

9. Some signs of heavy smartphone usage can be mental—loss of concentration, inability to focus on your surroundings—and others can be physical, such as _____ and headaches from eye strain.

compulsive	conscious	dysfunction	influx	literally	temptation

10. Although extreme smartphone usage may not actually be an addiction, there are signs, such as focusing on your phone at inappropriate times, that it may be a(n) _____.

11. In order to cut down on your smartphone dependency, you need to be able to resist the _____ to constantly check it for updates and e-mail.

12. You might not be _____ of it, but your constant checking behavior is not allowing you to concentrate on your work.

13. In the case of an emergency, your smartphone can _____ save your life.

14. _____ use of electronic devices can lead to physical ailments such as tendonitis, carpal tunnel syndrome, and eye strain.

15. The constant _____ of new information is one of the reasons that people compulsively check their phones.

EXPAND

Look at the boldfaced words and phrases in the following sentences. They have similar meanings but different degrees of intensity. In each sentence one of the words has a "stronger" meaning. Circle the word or phrase with the stronger meaning.

1. Many people feel the **urge / compulsion** to check their smartphones up to 35 times a day.

2. When I misplace my phone, I **search / look** for it until I find it.

3. His smartphone usage could be considered a(n) **addiction / dependency**.

4. For some people, being in class can **cause / trigger** a need to check their phone for news updates.

5. Because my wife is constantly checking her smartphone, I feel as if she is **ignoring me / tuning me out**.

6. Last night during dinner, my brother was **repeatedly / frequently** checking his email on his phone.

7. As a result of her continuous phone checking at the beach, I feel like my sister was **blinded to / not aware of** the beauty of our surroundings.

8. After I expressed my concerns to her, she made a **commitment / decision** to wean herself away from her phone.

(continued on next page)

9. The smartphone, more than any other gadget, **steals / takes** from us the opportunity to maintain our attention, to engage in **thought / contemplation** and reflection.

10. I **dislike / can't stand** when people interrupt a conversation to answer their smartphone.

11. If you know you are not strong enough to resist the temptation of constantly checking your e-mail, you should probably **shun / avoid** people who constantly text you.

CREATE

Imagine you are the person answering each question. How would you respond? On a separate piece of paper, write answers using the words given. Change the word form or tense if necessary.

1. **compulsion, influx, trigger, urge**
   To a manager or professional surveyed by Leslie Perlow, PhD (Reading One)
   Why are you constantly checking your smartphone from the moment you wake up until you go to bed, even when you are on vacation?

2. **commitment, conscious, diminishing, wean away from**
   To Susan Davis, author of Addicted to Your Smartphone? *(Reading One)*
   How are you able to manage your smartphone usage, and what effect did it have on your life?

3. **dependency, dysfunction, temptation, withdrawal**
   To David Greenfield PhD, author of Virtual Addiction: Help for Netheads, Cyber Freaks, and Those Who Love Them *(Reading One)*
   Why don't you consider extreme smartphone usage a true addiction?

4. **anxiety, contemplation, dependency, diminishing, ensure**
   To a businessman or businesswoman who participated in the Predictable Time Off (PTO) *experiment run by Dr. Perlow (Reading One)*
   What was the effect on your business and on your life of taking predictable time off (PTO)?

5. **can't stand, device, relent, repeatedly, twitching**
   To the ten-year-old boy who went electronic-free for a week (Reading Two)
   At the start of the week, what did you think of your mother's idea of going without electronics? How did the way you feel change as the week progressed?

GO TO MyEnglishLab FOR MORE VOCABULARY PRACTICE.

GRAMMAR

1 Examine these three sentences and answer the questions with a partner.

    a. <u>When we get back to our cabin</u>, I give my son his book.

    b. <u>You should turn off smartphone alert signals to avoid temptation</u>.

    c. <u>If you can't give up your phone altogether</u>, what should you do?

1. What is the verb in the underlined section of each sentence?

2. What is the difference between *get* and *get back*?

3. What is the difference between *turn* and *turn off*?

4. What is the difference between *give* and *give up*?

PHRASAL VERBS

1. A **phrasal verb** consists of a verb and a particle (an adverb or preposition). The combination often has a meaning that is different from the meaning of the separate parts. Phrasal verbs are often used in everyday communication.

2. Phrasal verbs (also called two-part or two-word verbs) combine a verb with a **particle**.

Verb	+	Particle	=	Meaning
go	+	back	=	return
tune	+	out	=	ignore
get	+	up	=	stand

3. Some phrasal verbs (also called three-part or three-word verbs) combine with a **preposition**.

Phrasal Verb	+	Preposition	=	Meaning
come up	+	with	=	imagine or invent
think back	+	on	=	remember
wean away	+	from	=	stop (gradually)
look up	+	to	=	admire someone

4. Some phrasal verbs are **transitive**. They take a direct object. Many (two-word) transitive phrasal verbs are **separable**. This means the verb and the particle can be separated by the direct object.

She	**tuned**	**out**	her husband.
	[verb]	[particle]	[object]

She	**tuned**	her husband	**out**.
	[verb]	[object]	[particle]

(continued on next page)

5. However, when the direct object is a pronoun, it must go between the verb and the particle.

She **picked** it **up**.
    [verb] [object] [particle]

NOT

She **picked** up **it**.
    [verb] [particle] [object]

---

6. Some phrasal verbs are **intransitive**. They do not take a direct object. Intransitive phrasal verbs are always **inseparable**. This means that the verb and particle are never separated.

I liked our vacation on Cortes Island. I want to **go** **back** next year.
      [verb] [particle]

---

7. The words in a phrasal verb are usually common, but their meanings change when the words are used together. Therefore, it can be difficult to guess the meaning of the verb from its individual parts.

call off	=	cancel
get together with	=	meet

---

8. Some phrasal verbs have more than one meaning.

She **took off** her jacket.	=	She **removed** her jacket.
She **took off** for work at 7:00 A.M.	=	She **departed** for work.
She **took** a day **off** from using her smartphone.	=	She **didn't** use her smartphone for a day.

---

9. Some verbs are combined with different particles or prepositions. Each combination creates a phrasal verb with a different meaning.

She **turned down** the volume on the phone.	=	She **lowered** the volume on the phone.
She **turned on** the phone.	=	She **started** the phone.
Smartphone technology has **turned up** in many new devices.	=	Smartphone technology has **appeared** in many new devices.
It **turned out** that the PTO method worked very well.	=	It **resulted** that the PTO method worked very well.
His smartphone use **turned into** a problem.	=	His smartphone use **became** a problem.
Using his smartphone, he **turned in** his application online.	=	Using his smartphone, he **submitted** his application online.

2 Work in a small group. Complete the sentences with the word or phrase from the box that has the same meaning as the underlined phrasal verb.

become popular	examine	~~ignore~~	persuade

1. Because my brothers are constantly checking their phones, they often <u>tune</u> me <u>out</u> when I am speaking to them. __*ignore*__

2. The writer of *Unplugging Wired Kids* (Reading Two) had to <u>talk</u> her family <u>into</u> not using electronics for a week. _____

3. You should <u>check out</u> this new grammar app I downloaded to my smartphone.

   _____

4. Smartphones are starting to <u>catch on</u> all over the world. _____

conduct	discard	like	postpone

5. The Pew Research Center plans to <u>carry out</u> a new smartphone survey next year.

   _____

6. Although I know I should take an electronic-free week soon, I am going to <u>put</u> it <u>off</u> until next month. _____

7. Don't <u>throw</u> your phone <u>away</u> just because you are using it too much. Instead, be disciplined in your usage. _____

8. Although, at first, Americans were only moderately interested in smartphone technology, now they are starting to <u>take to</u> it. _____

(continued on next page)

9. Sometimes I think we need to <u>get back</u> to the old days before smartphones were

   invented. _____

10. I want to <u>come up with</u> new ways to entertain myself, so I am not so reliant on my

    smartphone. _____

11. We ought to actually <u>get together with</u> friends instead of just texting and e-mailing

    them. _____

12. I just received a text from Mr. Martin. He says he thinks they are going to <u>call off</u> the

    3:00 meeting. _____

13. Try using the predictable time off strategy, so your smartphone dependency doesn't <u>turn</u>

    <u>into</u> a problem. _____

14. Don't forget to <u>turn off</u> your phone when you are in class or in a meeting.

    _____

15. I'm going to <u>turn on</u> the computer to see if there are any news updates.

    _____

16. Although a few years ago they weren't so popular, smartphones are beginning to <u>turn up</u>

    all over the world. _____

3 Complete the paragraph with phrasal verbs from Exercise 2 on pages 247–248 and the grammar box on pages 245–246 in place of the verbs in parentheses. Be sure to use the correct verb tense.

When I _____ my first year in college, it is difficult for me to understand
      1. (remember)

how addicted I was to online gaming. At the time, I didn't know it would _____
                                                      2. (become)

such an enormous problem. I started online gaming in high school, and, in fact, I didn't

_____ it immediately. Slowly, the amount of time I spent online increased,
    3. (like)

and gaming became my number one priority. I would _____ excuses not
                                          4. (invent)

to go to social and sports events. I would say I was sick or had too much homework when,

in fact, I was gaming. When I did _____ friends, all I could think about
                                5. (meet)

was _____ to my computer. As soon as I got home, I would immediately
      6. (returning)

_____ my computer and stay up all night playing with my cyber-friends.
    7. (start)

Reality finally hit. I was not _____ assignments and was missing class
                      8. (submitting)

because I couldn't wake up in the morning. My parents realized I had a problem and told

me I was _____ my life _____. Eventually, they were
           9. (discarding)

able to _____ me _____ seeing an addiction therapist. I
      10. (persuade)

_____ myself _____ my dependency, but it wasn't easy. One
  11. (slowly stopped)

thing that helped was that my friends did not abandon me. I am lucky that, because of my

therapist, family, and friends, everything _____ all right, and now I am doing
                             12. (resulted)

well in school.

■■■■■■■■■■ **GO TO** MyEnglishLab **FOR MORE GRAMMAR PRACTICE AND TO CHECK WHAT YOU LEARNED.**

FINAL WRITING TASK

In this unit, you read about the negative consequences of smartphone dependency as well as the positive consequences of managing smartphone use.

You are going to **write a cause-and-effect essay focusing on the effects that another technology used today has had on its users and on society**, such as Tablets (iPad®, Galaxy®), e-readers (Kindle®, Nook®), MP3 players, and GPS. Use the vocabulary and grammar from the unit.*

PREPARE TO WRITE: Using a Flowchart

A **flowchart** shows how a series of actions, events, or parts of a system are related. Look at the flowchart showing the effects of smartphones. Which effects are positive? Which are negative? Some of the effects cause another effect and in some cases a further effect, like a chain.

1 In your opinion, are these effects positive, negative, or both? In a corner of each box, mark them as (+), (−), or (+ −). Then discuss with a partner. Did you agree with your partner?

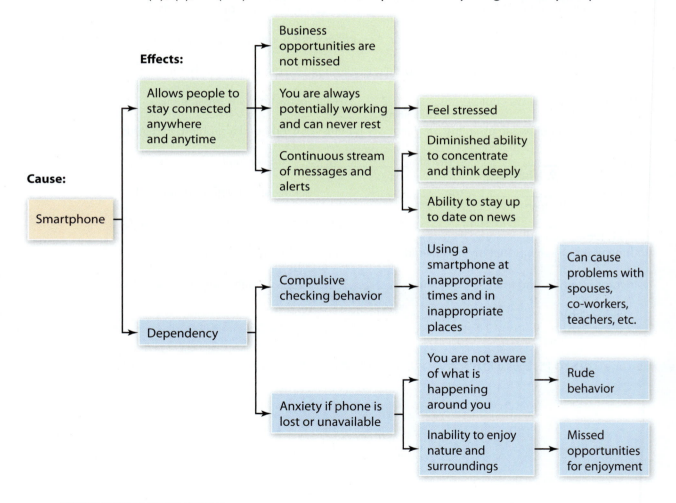

---

* For Alternative Writing Topics, see page 259. These topics can be used in place of the writing topic for this unit or as homework. The alternative topics relate to the theme of the unit but may not target the same grammar or rhetorical structures taught in the unit.

2 Create a flowchart of the effects of a technology you would like to discuss in your essay. Mark the effects as positive, negative, or both.

WRITE: A Cause and Effect Essay

A **cause-and-effect essay** discusses the causes (reasons) for something, the effects (results), or both causes and effects. Your essay will focus primarily on the effects a particular technology has had on the user and society, not the causes leading up to its creation.

1 Read the excerpt from Reading One. Then complete the cause-and-effect chart.

People keep their smartphones near them "from the moment they wake up until the moment they go to bed," and throughout that time the devices provide an almost continuous stream of messages and alerts as well as easy access to a myriad of compelling information sources.

"By design," [Carr] says, "it's an environment of almost constant interruptions and distractions. The smartphone, more than any other gadget, steals from us the opportunity to maintain our attention, to engage in contemplation and reflection, or even to be alone with our thoughts." Carr, who writes extensively in *The Shallows* about the way that computer technology, in general, may be diminishing our ability to concentrate and think deeply, does not have a smartphone.

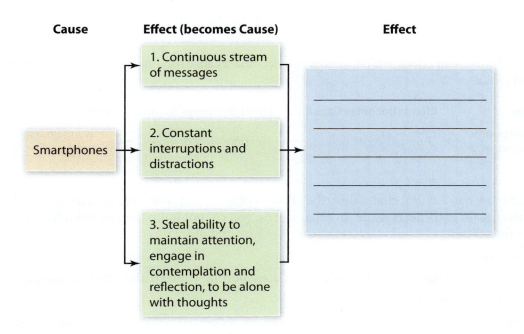

Cause	Effect (becomes Cause)	Effect
Smartphones	1. Continuous stream of messages	
	2. Constant interruptions and distractions	
	3. Steal ability to maintain attention, engage in contemplation and reflection, to be alone with thoughts	

There are many ways to organize causes and effects and show how they are related. A cause may have only one effect, multiple effects, or cause a chain of effects.

A **simple** cause and effect:

One cause with **multiple effects**:

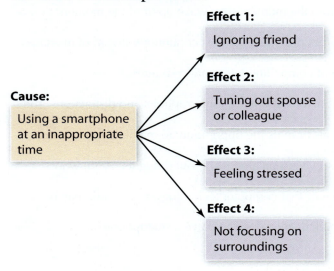

A cause leads to an effect, which in turn can become a cause for a new effect. This is called a **causal chain**.

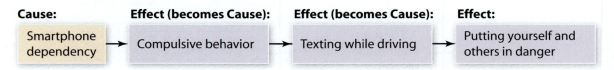

If your essay has a causal chain, describe all steps of the chain so the reader can fully understand how the causes and effects relate. In other words, you cannot jump directly from the initial cause to the final effect.

> Incorrect example
> Because of smartphone dependency, you are putting yourself and others in danger.

> Correct example
> Smartphone dependency may lead to compulsive behavior. This behavior may include using your smartphone at inappropriate times. For example, some people feel compelled to text all the time, even when driving. This behavior may put you and others in danger.

2 Answer the questions with a partner.

1. Look at the flowchart from Prepare to Write, Exercise 1, on page 250. What are some examples of multiple effects of the technology that you chose?

2. What is an example of a causal chain?

3. Look at your flowchart from Prepare to Write, Exercise 2, on page 251. Are there examples of multiple effects and causal chains? Look at your partner's flowchart. Can you find examples of multiple effects and causal chains?

3 Use an outline to organize your cause-and-effect essay. Look at the outline of paragraphs 1–8 in Reading Two. Note that the author sometimes introduces a cause first and then writes about the effect. At other times, the author starts with the effect and then states the cause. In addition, a cause can have multiple effects.

CAUSE	I. Writer wants her family to enjoy an electronic-free vacation.
EFFECT	
	A. They go to a remote island in the wilderness of British Columbia, Canada.
CAUSE	
EFFECT	1. Writer's son is suffering iPhone withdrawal.
CAUSE	a. Son cannot enjoy the beauty of their surroundings.
EFFECT	2. Husband and daughter are doing fine because they have found things to do that don't rely on electronics.
CAUSE	a. They are suffering no withdrawal symptoms.
EFFECT (BECOMES CAUSE)	3. Time passes
	a. Son seems to have forgotten about iPhone.
MULTIPLE EFFECTS (1–3)	1. He spends an enjoyable day at the beach.
	2. He reads in the garden.
	3. He stays active swimming and hiking.

4 Complete the cause-and-effect outline for the Managing Your Smartphone Use section in Reading One (paragraphs 25–33). Use the information in the box.

Increased collaboration	More aware of surroundings	Slowly diminished time between checking	More relaxed
Stopped using phone for social media	Took Predictable Time Off	Stopped using phone for texting and e-mailing while driving	Better work—life balance

| CAUSE

EFFECT (BECOMES CAUSE)
MULTIPLE EFFECTS (1–3)

MULTIPLE CAUSES (A–D)

MULTIPLE EFFECTS (A–D) | **I.** The Boston Group participated in an experiment run by Leslie Perlow, PhD.

  A. _____
    1. Increased efficiency
    2. _____
    3. _____

II. Writer's plan to manage own smartphone use by using multiple strategies
  A. _____
  B. Stopped using phone for web browsing
  C. _____
  D. _____
    1. Overall effects
      a. Concentrating better
      a. _____
      b. _____
      c. More focused use of smartphone |

5 Make an outline about the effects the technology you have chosen has had on its users and on society. Think about how you will organize and order the causes and effects from your flowchart. Make sure to include background information, a thesis, and a conclusion. Your conclusion could be a prediction, a solution, or a summary of key points. Share your outline with a partner and suggest changes, if necessary.

6 Now write the first draft of your cause-and-effect essay. Use the information in Prepare to Write, your flowchart, and your outline to plan your essay. Be sure to use grammar and vocabulary from the unit.

REVISE: Signal Words: Subordinators, Prepositional Phrases, and Transitions

Certain words act as signals in sentences to show cause-and-effect relationships. Sentences in cause-and-effect essays have two clauses. The **cause clause** explains why something happened. The **effect clause** explains the result of what happened.

Cause: Because more and more people have smartphones today,

Effect: people have more and more interruptions in their lives.

SUBORDINATORS, PREPOSITIONAL PHRASES, AND TRANSITIONS

Subordinators, prepositional phrases, and transitions show the relationship between the two clauses.

Introducing the Cause		Introducing the Effect
SUBORDINATORS	PREPOSITIONAL PHRASES	TRANSITIONS
since	due to (the fact that)	as a result
because	due to + (noun)	consequently
as	as a consequence of + (noun)	so
	as a result of + (noun)	for this reason
	because of (the fact that)	therefore
	because of + (noun)	thus
		as a consequence

Stating Causes with Subordinators and Prepositional Phrases

- The **cause clause** is introduced by *because, since, as*. When the cause is at the beginning of the sentence, use a comma (,).

  Because you can receive a continuous stream of messages and alerts on a smartphone, you are able to stay up-to-date on news anytime and anyplace.

- When the cause is at the end of the sentence, do not use a comma.

  You are able to stay up-to-date on news anytime and anyplace **because you can receive a continuous stream of messages and alerts on a smartphone.**

Stating Effects with Transitions

- The **effect** is introduced by words such as *consequently, as a result, for this reason, therefore,* and *thus*. Cause and effect can be combined into one sentence by using a semicolon (;) and a comma (,).

  You can receive a continuous stream of messages and alerts on a smartphone; **consequently, you are able to stay up-to-date on news anytime and anyplace.**

- They can also be two separate sentences.

  You can receive a continuous stream of messages and alerts on a smartphone. **As a result, you are able to stay up-to-date on news anytime and anyplace.**

- Be careful. A sentence with *so* uses only a comma.

  You can receive a continuous stream of messages and alerts on a smartphone, **so you are able to stay up-to-date on news anytime and anyplace.**

1 Complete the paragraph based on the outline in Write, Exercise 3, page 253. Use appropriate subordinators and transitions.

The writer of the *Unplugging* article wanted her family to enjoy an electronic-free vacation;

_____, she took them to a remote island in the wilderness of British Columbia. On the

first day of the vacation, her son couldn't enjoy the beauty of their surroundings _____

he was suffering from acute iPhone withdrawal. On the other hand, her husband and daughter

were doing fine. They had found things to do that didn't rely on electronics, _____

they suffered no withdrawal symptoms. As time passed, her son forgot about his iPhone.

_____, he was able to have a good time at the beach and enjoy reading. He was also

able to have fun hiking and swimming _____ he was no longer thinking only about

his iPhone.

2 Write **C** (cause) or **E** (effect) for each set of sentences. Then combine the sentences two ways. Use commas and semicolons correctly.

1. __C__ Employees at usemyphone.com started taking predictable time off.

   __E__ There was increased efficiency and collaboration among employees at usemyphone.com.

   (as a result) _Employees at usemyphone.com started taking predictable time off; as a result, there was increased efficiency and collaboration among employees._

   (because) _Because employees at usemyphone.com started taking predictable time off, there was increased efficiency and collaboration among employees._

2. _____ It is easy to stay in contact with people even when they are not at home.
   _____ Many people have smartphones.

   (since) _____

   _____

   (therefore) _____

   _____

3. _____ People cannot concentrate or think deeply.

_____ Smartphones create an environment of constant interruptions and distractions.

(consequently) _____

_____

(due to the fact that) _____

_____

4. _____ There are approximately 40,000 medical apps available today for smartphones and tablets.

_____ It is like having a health expert at your fingertips.

(as a result) _____

_____

(thus) _____

_____

5. _____ Smartphone apps can remotely turn on and off the heat in your home when you are out.

_____ Homeowners can save money and help to cut down on the use of fossil fuels.

(because) _____

_____

(so) _____

_____

6. _____ The number of hardcover and paperback books being sold has declined.

_____ Many people use tablets and e-readers for most of their reading.

(for this reason) _____

_____

(because of the fact that) _____

_____

3 Look at your first draft. Add cause-and-effect signal words as needed.

■■ *GO TO* MyEnglishLab *FOR MORE SKILL PRACTICE.*

EDIT: Writing the Final Draft

Go to MyEnglishLab and write the final draft of your essay. Carefully edit it for grammatical and mechanical errors, such as spelling, capitalization, and punctuation. Make sure you use some of the grammar and vocabulary from the unit. Use the checklist to help you write your final draft. Then submit your essay to your teacher.

FINAL DRAFT CHECKLIST

❏ Does the essay have a clear topic and controlling idea?

❏ Does the essay follow your outline?

❏ Does the essay have effective support and details or examples?

❏ Does the essay have appropriate cause-and-effect sentences?

❏ Does the essay have an effective or thought-provoking conclusion?

❏ Did you use phrasal verbs correctly?

❏ Have you used vocabulary from the unit?

UNIT PROJECT

Work with a partner to conduct a survey about the evolution of technological devices and then research them. Prepare a presentation for the class. Follow these steps:

STEP 1: Create a survey in which you ask participants about their observations concerning the evolution of (choose one) personal computers, laptops, tablets, or cell phones.

Here are a few questions you might ask. Add some of your own.

1. How long have you owned a _____?

2. What changes have taken place with this device?

3. Has the cost changed? How?

4. Has the size changed? How?

5. Have the features changed? How?

6. What do you think are the most significant technological advances for this device?

7. What technological advances of this device have affected you most?

8. Do you feel the need to keep buying the latest model of the device? Explain.

STEP 2: On the Internet, research the electronic devices the survey participants talk about. For example, if they discuss personal computers, find out what the earliest personal/desktop computers looked like and were capable of doing. Be sure to include information about cost, size, features, availability, etc.

STEP 3: Using the information you learned from the survey participants and what you learned from your Internet research, create a PowerPoint™ presentation for the class.

ALTERNATIVE WRITING TOPICS

Write an essay about one of the topics. Use the vocabulary and grammar from the unit.

1. Try to go smartphone-free (or do without another electronic device) for at least two days. Write about your experience. Did you suffer any withdrawal symptoms? What was hard about the experiment? Were there any benefits to being tech-free? Explain.

2. Computer technologies have both advantages and disadvantages for their users and for society in general. What do you think are the three biggest advantages and the three biggest disadvantages? Explain.

GO TO MyEnglishLab *TO WRITE ABOUT ONE OF THE ALTERNATIVE TOPICS, WATCH A VIDEO ABOUT DISCONNECTING FROM WORK EMAIL AFTER HOURS, AND TAKE THE UNIT 8 ACHIEVEMENT TEST.*

GRAMMAR BOOK REFERENCES

NorthStar: Reading and Writing Level 4, Fourth Edition	Focus on Grammar Level 4, Fourth Edition	Azar's Understanding and Using English Grammar, Fourth Edition
Unit 1 Modals and Semi-Modals	**Unit 15** Modals and Similar Expressions: Review **Unit 16** Advisability in the Past **Unit 17** Speculations and Conclusions about the Past	**Chapter 11** The Passive: 11-1, 11-2, 11-3
Unit 2 Gerunds and Infinitives	**Unit 9** Gerunds and Infinitives: Review and Expansion	**Chapter 14** Gerunds and Infinitives, Part 1 **Chapter 15** Gerunds and Infinitives, Part 2
Unit 3 Past Unreal Conditionals	**Unit 24** Past Unreal Conditionals	**Chapter 20** Conditional Sentences and Wishes: 20-1, 20-4
Unit 4 Identifying Adjective Clauses	**Unit 13** Adjective Clauses with Subject Relative Pronouns **Unit 14** Adjective Clauses with Object Relative Pronouns or *When* and *Where*	**Chapter 13** Adjective Clauses
Unit 5 Contrasting the Simple Past, Present Perfect, and Present Perfect Continuous	**Unit 3** Simple Past, Present Perfect, and Present Perfect Progressive	**Chapter 1** Overview of Verb Tenses 1-1, 1-3, 1-4, 1-5 **Chapter 2** Present and Past; Simple and Progressive: 2-7, 2-8 **Chapter 3** Perfect and Perfect Progressive Tenses: 3-1, 3-4

NorthStar: Reading and Writing Level 4, Fourth Edition	Focus on Grammar Level 4, Fourth Edition	Azar's Understanding and Using English Grammar, Fourth Edition
Unit 6 Concessions	See *Focus on Grammar 5, Fourth Edition*, Unit 19: Adverb Clauses	**Chapter 19** Connectives that Express Cause and Effect, Contrast, and Condition: 19-6
Unit 7 Direct and Indirect Speech	**Unit 25** Direct and Indirect Speech	**Chapter 12** Noun Clauses: 12-6, 12-7
Unit 8 Phrasal Verbs	**Unit 11** Phrasal Verbs: Review **Unit 12** Phrasal Verbs: Separable and Inseparable	**Appendix** Unit E: Preposition Combinations See also Appendix B-1: Phrasal Verbs in Azar's *Fundamentals of English Grammar, Fourth Edition*

UNIT WORD LIST

The Unit Word List is a summary of key vocabulary from the Student Book. Words followed by an asterisk (*) are on the Academic Word List.

UNIT 1

anxious	image*
assimilate	interaction*
benefit*	persistence*
compensate*	predictable*
disabled	retain*
emerging*	savant
estimate*	sum*
expertise*	transforms*
flexible*	

UNIT 2

abandonment*	misery
accountable	poverty
defeated	self-reliance
dilapidated	shame
gives up	sordid
hopelessness	struggle
laborious	tormented
meager	yearned for

UNIT 3

advocate*	interaction*
alternative*	interpreting*
aspects*	linked*
consensus*	potential*
consulted*	reliable*
conventional*	revolutionized*
elicit	risk factor*
environment*	skeptical
impact*	

UNIT 4

achieve*	discern
acquired*	obvious*
apparently*	perception*
approach*	sensory
behavior	trait
category*	unconscious
cognition	unique*
confront	viable
controversy*	

UNIT 5

awesome
chilly
disparate
emphatic*
fond of
immeasurably
impetuous
inevitably*
insufferable

loveless
presumptuous
punctually
radically*
tolerable
ultimately*
utterly
vigorous
worrisome

UNIT 6

admiring
challenge*
determined
devote*
donate
fulfilling
indignation
inspired
manage

opposed
oxymoron
passion
proposal
proudly
resentful
satisfaction
thrilled

UNIT 7

adjusted*
analyzes*
anticipation*
assumption*
collaboration
crucial*
disappointed
dispute
diversity*

enhances*
issue*
overall*
sector*
significantly*
subsequent*
via*
virtual*

UNIT 8

anxiety
compulsive
conscious
dependency
devices*
diminishing*
dysfunction
ensures*
influx

literally
relent
temptation
trigger*
twitching
urge
wean away from
withdrawal

THE PHONETIC ALPHABET

Consonant Symbols				
/b/	be		/t/	to
/d/	do		/v/	van
/f/	father		/w/	will
/g/	get		/y/	yes
/h/	he		/z/	zoo, busy
/k/	keep, can		/θ/	thanks
/l/	let		/ð/	then
/m/	may		/ʃ/	she
/n/	no		/ʒ/	vision, Asia
/p/	pen		/tʃ/	child
/r/	rain		/dʒ/	join
/s/	so, circle		/ŋ/	long

Vowel Symbols				
/ɑ/	far, hot		/iy/	we, mean, feet
/ɛ/	met, said		/ey/	day, late, rain
/ɔ/	tall, bought		/ow/	go, low, coat
/ə/	son, under		/uw/	too, blue
/æ/	cat		/ay/	time, buy
/ɪ/	ship		/aw/	house, now
/ʊ/	good, could, put		/oy/	boy, coin